By the same author

CONTACT

DRIVE

Drive

Marie S. Newberry

Colonel Charles R. Codman

DRIVE

by
Colonel Charles R. Codman

With Illustrations

An Atlantic Monthly Press Book
Boston • Little, Brown and Company • *Toronto*

LIBRARY OF CONGRESS CATALOG CARD NO. 57-6445

SECOND PRINTING

ATLANTIC—LITTLE, BROWN BOOKS
ARE PUBLISHED BY
LITTLE, BROWN AND COMPANY
IN ASSOCIATION WITH
THE ATLANTIC MONTHLY PRESS

Published simultaneously in Canada
by Little, Brown & Company (Canada) Limited

PRINTED IN THE UNITED STATES OF AMERICA

To my son
First Lieutenant Charles R. Codman, Jr.

Author's Note

THIS book is compiled from letters written to my wife during thirty-three months of service (1942–1945) in the European theater of operations during World War II.

At the end of the North African campaign, I was appointed A.D.C. to General George S. Patton, Jr., serving from then on as his senior aide-de-camp until after V–E Day and his return to the United States. While General Patton is naturally the central and dominating figure of this journal, the latter is in no sense an attempt at either biography or military analysis. It is simply an account describing such day-to-day personal experiences in wartime Africa and Europe as I felt might interest or amuse my wife.

To the original letters I have added the names of places, individuals, and units which at the time of writing would have been disallowed by the censor. Certain passages of a personal nature have been omitted.

For their friendly assistance and editorial advice I wish to thank the following: Edward Weeks of the *Atlantic Monthly;* Lieutenant General Hobart R. Gay; Bernard S. Carter; John P. Marquand; Archibald S. Alexander; William A. Parker; Edward P. Creed; General Marie Jean Piatte; Frances and Charles P. Curtis.

CHARLES R. CODMAN

Boston, July 1956

Introduction

by
John P. Marquand

BY a happy combination of circumstances, Lieutenant Colonel Charles Codman and I happened to meet overseas in the summer of 1943 at the Hotel Aletti in Algiers. The General officers' mess was located in that crumbling caravansary, and experience showed why General officers avoided it when possible. In spite of the salt and atabrine tablets served free of charge, the old *salle à manger* was a dismal place with wrapping paper for napkins and truncated beer bottles for glasses. I can still remember the Colonel's expression of restrained enthusiasm when we examined the Hotel Aletti's menu. It was not a suitable place for my friend and Harvard classmate who had, between two world wars, become a professional consultant on wines and also an authority on cooking. Colonel Codman was aide-de-camp to General George S. Patton, Jr. I had arrived in North Africa from Washington accompanying Brigadier General James S. Simmons on a rather obscure intelligence mission.

I had learned on my first visit to Allied Force Headquarters that Colonel Codman was with General Patton in Sicily and thus it was a pleasant surprise when he called at the Hotel Aletti. He had just arrived from Sicily in General Patton's C-47 plane to do a series of confidential errands. The moment I saw Charles Codman I remember that two thoughts crossed my mind. The first was that his uniform, which was A, fitted him like a West Pointer's, although his face was not conventional Army. His wings, battle ribbons, and Croix de Guerre with Palm indicated his distinguished career in World War I, but he

looked too young for a Retread. In spite of a congenital disinclination
for exercise, deplored by his more athletic friends, he was obviously
standing up to his second war much better than a lot of his more strenuous contemporaries. In fact, it did not appear to have worn him down
at all. My second thought was that in spite of the bizarre background of
wartime Algiers, Charley Codman was just the same as always,
amused, diverted, but basically unworried by the extraneous. The war
had not changed him and already he had seen a lot of war since he had
climbed down the cargo nets at the North African landing. A reassuring naturalness that he always displayed anywhere is perhaps what all
of his friends remember best about him, and it is also a trait which
everyone will observe between the lines of his book.

The Colonel said that General Patton had entrusted him with several
commissions on which he must start working immediately and he was
in great need of a car and driver. I was happy to tell him that my General had gone off to Casablanca for three days leaving me his car and
that if I was not in the way I would be glad to go with him on his
errands. We saw a number of strange places in Algiers and several interesting natives before we were finished and we also had a considerable opportunity to talk about Marrakech and El Glaoui (the Colonel
knew Morocco very well), about early negotiations with the French
Army, and about the late Admiral Darlan and General Giraud. The
Colonel had seen them all, but his main preoccupation was his present
job with General Patton. It was not easy being the General's aide, nor
safe, either, because the General was always up front during combat
and was exhilarated when exposed to fire. In the Sicilian campaign the
situation was so fluid that on several occasions the General and his
party appeared to have got out ahead of everything. One occasion in
particular Charley remembered very distinctly. They had stopped before a Sicilian hill town which no one was wholly certain was occupied. Consequently the General suggested that Colonel Codman go
over and find out.

"It was an unpleasant experience," Charley said, "walking up that
hill, but it turned out that the people there were glad to see me."

Of course, he added, he had been through a good deal of that sort of thing when he was a pilot in the First World War, but it still was unpleasant.

General Patton was a very exceptional man, he said, and when you began to know him, you began to forget the pearl-handled pistols and the white helmet and the Bond Street riding breeches — and to perceive that his eccentricities of dress and speech were based on sound showmanship. Right now, in spite of Sicily's summer heat, every soldier in the Seventh Army was dressed in woolens. Each of them kept his sleeves rolled down by the General's orders and carried a filled canteen on his web belt. The idea was that the Seventh Army should be ready at any moment for an amphibious operation. You might conclude that the order was farfetched, but it also made Seventh Army personnel different from other boys and in the end they were proud of the difference.

I saw many individuals of the Seventh Army myself a week later in Palermo. It was very warm indeed there and they were still in woolens with their sleeves rolled down. Being in civilian clothes, I was able to ask them frankly how they liked it. They did not like it, but I did not speak to a single soldier who had a thing to say against the General. He had projected himself everywhere and he had created morale, which, as they used to say back at Plattsburg, was a main essential of leadership.

As many of Charles Codman's pages deal with General Patton, I am tempted to add a few of my own recollections. If it had not been for Charley, I doubt whether I would have met the General, who was enmeshed at the time with several acute problems, although the Sicilian campaign was over. Charley met us at the airstrip when General Simmons and I arrived at Palermo. Although I had not been in Palermo for a good many years, its streets and crowds looked exactly as I had seen them last. In fact, the citizens appeared surprisingly cheerful and secure, reminding one that Sicily was accustomed to invasions. The bombed water front displayed the usual picture of twisted half-sunken vessels, but most of the docks were already operable.

"Excuse me," Charley said, "but look at those two British sailors fighting."

Sure enough, two British ratings in the comfortable tropical shorts of His Majesty's Navy had come to blows. Civilians walking by only glanced at them, without stopping.

"They're rather clumsy at it, aren't they?" I said.

"Yes," Charley answered, "but their intentions are quite serious."

It was one of those small things characteristic of war, a unit in a long series of episodes without an end or beginning. Headquarters of the Seventh Army was in a building on the hill above the harbor. Charley led General Simmons and me into General Patton's office and there was time to observe a huge rosewood desk and a set of silk upholstered chairs, time also to wonder who had originally owned this elaborate furniture, before the General entered. His appearance was up to advanced billing — pistols, helmet, gloves, boots, riding breeches, everything. He tossed his helmet and gloves on a sort of love seat and shook hands. He was taller and much more impressive than I thought he would be. In fact, he did not need pearl-handled pistols to frame his personality. I remember thinking that his hands were unusually artistic and sensitive for those of a combat General. One always knows instinctively and at once whether or not a man has exceptional talents, and there was no doubt General Patton was head and shoulders above any sort of mediocrity. He reminded me, as I told Charley later, who agreed with me, quite a little of Sinclair Lewis. The eyes and facial expressions were the same and so was the lilt to the voice. The General was sorry he was in a hurry, but his car was outside waiting. He was giving a dinner for the Generals and staff of the Seventh Army at his quarters in the royal palace that night and he asked us to join the party.

"It's quite a palace, as those things go," he said. "The chapel has been bombed, but they have a priest there for my personal convenience — I haven't had time to visit him yet."

He laughed and started for the door, but paused to ask me how I thought Charley was looking. I said I thought he was looking fine, and he asked me the same question again that evening. There was no doubt that he was very fond of Charley and it was easy to see that he was greatly pleased that he had selected him.

Illustrations

(All halftone illustrations, except the frontispiece, appear between pages 164 and 165.)

MAPS

Drive

Foreword

(France — Spring, 1940)

THE spring months usually found my wife and me touring the vineyards and cellars of France, but in 1940 war conditions necessitated a reversal of our normal procedure and by prearrangement the various vineyard proprietors were to meet us in Paris.

On May 9 we dined at Ciro's with the Jacques Bollingers,* who were leaving the next morning for their place in Ay. The restaurant was crowded, the atmosphere thick with cigarette smoke and the scent of rich sauces and well-dressed women. The hum of conversation, laughter, music, dancing. No restrictions on the quantity or quality of food. Outside the street lamps were dimmed to a blue glow, but within all was light and merriment. Somewhere, far away, two armies faced one another from behind impregnable walls. Meanwhile, life in the capital went on as usual. Dorothy Thompson was in town. The Duff Coopers had just gone back to London. Chevalier was at the Casino. As always, there were rumors. Daladier and the Marquise de Crussol were soon to be replaced by Reynaud.

"La porte à côté," as Jacques put it, was about to slam on *"la sardine qui s'est crue sole."* Weygand was returning from Syria to take over from Gamelin, and there was talk of an up-and-coming young colonel called Charles de Gaulle.

At midnight we stepped through the curtained glass doors into the dark, silent street. Bright stars shone from the patches of clear sky between high banks of clouds.

---

* The famous winegrower and merchant of champagnes.

"A perfect night for an air raid," my wife said.

Jacques looked up at the sky.

"You can smell Germans from a long distance away," he said.

"Yes, I believe I can," she replied.

At dawn the siren sounded. By the second wail we were up and dressing, so quickly does one's mind readjust to past experience. In the lobby the night concierge was stretching and rubbing his eyes. We went out into the street. Chimney pots and the trees of the Champs Élysées black against a gray sky. The crackle of antiaircraft guns. People in doorways and on the sidewalk. Men in dressing gowns and slippers, smoking cigarettes. Women in every stage of dress and undress, some of them exercising lap dogs. Bored little girls in curl papers.

Someone said, "There they are," and pointed directly overhead. Eyes turned upward and voices hushed. In the silence the drone of engines plainly audible. Then, we saw them. Five dark birds flying close formation. Clusters of air bursts, pink in the morning sun, surrounded them. A prayer that at least one burst might find its target, but with slow, deliberate progress the marauders passed safely out of sight. A little later the all-clear sounded.

The sun rose higher and warmer, glinting on the glass roof of the Petit Palais. Pigeons strutted complacently about under the *marronniers*. Waiters in shirt sleeves arranging the iron tables and chairs of the sidewalk café. A fat woman in a moth-eaten sweater taking down the shutters of her news kiosk. Children on roller skates. A boy in a black sateen apron rode by on a bicycle, carrying a basket filled with long loaves of bread. He was whistling. Paris, fresh and immaculate under the blue sky, prepared for a new day.

The day was the fateful tenth of May, 1940. At nine o'clock the French Ministry of Information telephoned to announce that the German Army had struck through Holland, Belgium, and Luxembourg. The "phony war" came to a sudden end. The Western world reeled under the impact of "the first shock" — in Mr. Churchill's words — "of the most merciless of all wars of which record has been kept." It took time to sink in. Perhaps that is why it seemed such a long day.

For the tenth of May, 1940, was a long day — a day of extra editions, black headlines, and hourly radio announcements, each less reassuring than the last. For my wife and myself in our hotel room near the Rond Point it was a working day. The first of our visiting vineyard friends to arrive was Monsieur Louis Latour of Beaune. Punctual to the dot, he arrived at 10 A.M. with a small black bag fitted with neat rows of phials, each containing a specimen of his 1937's — Corton, Chambertin, Meursault. Pouilly and other assorted Burgundies. Glasses were set up, evaluations made, prices discussed, provisional reserves duly set aside. In the next room a radio droned interminable meaningless phrases and from the street below rose the raucous voices of news vendors hawking calamity.

Around noon a nonbusiness acquaintance dropped in to impart a particularly pessimistic news flash. The array of goblets appeared to shock him.

"The world is crashing around our ears," he exclaimed, "and this is the way you spend your morning?"

Monsieur Latour was packing his little black bag. Snapping it shut, he gave a slight shrug.

"One must continue to work," he said.

Other visitors, from Chablis, Alsace, Anjou, the Côtes du Rhône. By the end of the day we had toured, by proxy, most of the famous wine regions of France.

Most, but not all. Two — perhaps the most important two — remained. Champagne and Bordeaux. So after much wangling we managed a few days later to catch a ride to Épernay with a French liaison officer. Already half deserted, this important champagne center, with its empty streets and shell-scarred buildings, presented the appearance of World War I. From the cornice of a hotel on the main square a crashed German plane hung crazily.

"Could you take us over to Ay?" we asked our French friend.

"Why Ay?" he asked.

"To see a very old friend, Jacques Bollinger."

His face lit up. "Why, I've known him all my life," he said. "But I thought he was in Paris."

"No, he is mayor of Ay and he is still there."

"The Germans are now within three or four miles of Ay," he said, "but if the bridge isn't down we ought to be able to make it."

We did. It was after dark when we rang the familiar doorbell of the Bollinger house. Jacques himself answered it and after an exclamation of surprise led us into the sitting room. His wife, Lily, was by the fireplace, in which a bundle of charred papers was still burning. We transacted our business and by nine o'clock were ready to leave.

"Why don't you come back to Paris with us?" my wife asked Lily.

"No," she said, "Jacques is the mayor of Ay and our place is here."

As a nightcap and a gesture to World War I, in which Jacques was a combat pilot, he brought up from his cellar a bottle of his great 1915 vintage.

"*À bientôt*," he toasted.

It was not to be. He did not survive the war, but I can see him now by the fireplace, burning his papers as his father had done before him in 1914, and as his grandfather had done before him in 1870. Burning their papers and sticking to their jobs.

Back in Paris, as we went about our small routine affairs, each day the radio ground out its grist of ominous news. "The Germans are on the Albert Canal." Sedan and the Ardennes. The collapse of Corap's Ninth Army. The voice of Reynaud, shaking with cold anger. "On the order of its King, without warning to its French and British comrades, the Belgian Army has suddenly and unconditionally capitulated. This is an event without precedent in history." Next day, Duff Cooper. "This is no time for recriminations. Even if the Allies lost this battle, we shall not have lost the war."

Dunkirk. General Alexander the last man off the beach. Above and over all the reverberating nouns of England's new Prime Minister. "I have nothing to offer but blood, toil, tears and sweat."

At long last the embassy told us we had better get going. My old friend Bunny Carter,* obliged to remain in Paris to move his bank to Bordeaux, gave us his plane reservations for New York and on June 7 we squeezed ourselves — quite literally — into the Sud-Express for Bordeaux. A long trip and a sad one. At the Bordeaux station, amidst scenes of indescribable confusion, we finally, by a miracle, connected with our old friend Francis de Luze, who had come to meet us and take us out to his house for the night. Until a late hour we discussed matters of common interest — including the great clarets and sauternes of 1937. Next day he saw us off at the station on our last leg to Lisbon and the Clipper home.

In the quiet hall of Lisbon's Avize Hotel the radio murmured in desultory fashion. "We interrupt this program . . ." Someone turned up the volume. *Squawk, splutter, squawk.* Normal now. A familiar voice. "The hand that held the dagger . . ."

As our Pan American Clipper winged its way westward over a glittering sea, Mussolini's troops moved into Nice and Corsica and the vanguard of the German Army marched down the Champs Élysées.

* Bernard Carter, director of the Morgan Bank in Paris.

CHAPTER I

Torch

(April–November, 1942)

SHORTLY after Pearl Harbor and the United States' entry into World War II, the Army Air Force let it be known that it would recommission a certain number of ex-combat pilots of World War I. Those accepted were known as Retreads. I was a Retread — for about a quarter of an hour.

On April 22, 1942, I reported to the old Munitions Building in Washington, D.C. Having sworn me in, the A-2 colonel in charge looked doubtful.

"We don't seem to have your complete file here," he said. "Whom were you supposed to report to?"

"Colonel Curtis, A-2."

"I see," he said. "Unfortunately Colonel Curtis is week-ending in Iceland."

"That was last week." Another colonel spoke up from across the room. "Ted left here yesterday for Cairo."

An Infantry colonel came up carrying a sheaf of papers.

"Hi, Bob," the A-2 colonel said. "What can we do for you today?"

The Infantry colonel sank his voice to a whisper.

"I see." The A-2 colonel cleared his throat. "Well, it just so happens, Bob, that I've got exactly the man you're looking for." Then to me, "You're certainly in luck, Major. Colonel Harding here, of G-2, has the perfect job for you."

"What is it?"

"Look, Major," the A-2 colonel said, "it would be wiser not to ask

8

questions. Just take my word for it and run along with the Colonel here. We'll have your orders out right away. You won't be sorry."

As things turned out, he was right.

Behind the sentry-guarded door of a room on the third floor of the same Munitions Building the staff of Western Task Force sweated out the stifling Washington summer of the fateful year of 1942. Partitioned off at one end were the offices of the Chief of Staff and the General. Out in the open bull-pen the staff sections, about whom swirled a never-ending stream of Navy opposite numbers, meteorologists, Air liaison officers, North African consuls, French tugboat captains, and Arab interpreters, struggled with the joint and several problems posed by the first amphibious landings to be launched eastward across the Atlantic Ocean.

Late on the sweltering afternoon prior to our departure, Colonel Percy Black, Assistant Chief of Staff G-2, stopped before the Prisoner Interrogation Section desk, or rather table, shared by Bunny Carter* and myself. Onto the table the Colonel dropped several pounds of fifth-carbon typescript.

"The treaties," he said.

"The treaties?"

"With the French Protectorate of Morocco," he said. "State just got around to sending them over. Three of them. Which one will be applied depends on the circumstances."

The Colonel started to move off.

"Translate them into French," he said. "Six copies of each. And have them on my desk by midnight."

"Yes, sir."

Treaty A: a nice friendly treaty predicated on the French receiving us with open arms.

Treaty B: stern but fair — based on the eventuality of a slight token resistance.

Treaty C: the surrender terms to be imposed on the French forces in the event of an all-out fight. This one was tough.

---

* Major Bernard Carter, G-2, the author's oldest friend, who was with him at Groton and Harvard and during the First World War.

By the time Bunny and I had translated them into understandable if not precisely Quai d'Orsay French and had laid the eighteen copies on the Colonel's desk it was another day — October 23, 1942.

Dawn was breaking over the capital. Having said good-by to our wives, Bunny and I threw our gear into a taxi and buzzed off over the bridge to Fort Myer on our way to the waiting convoy. Twenty-four hours later we were at sea on the first lap of our second world war.

This is a combined operation and until we land, a Navy show. The Navy's mission — to transport the thirty-five thousand troops and two hundred fifty tanks composing the all-American Western Task Force, together with ammunition and supplies, four thousand nautical miles from Norfolk, Virginia, and to land them in Higgins boats on three sets of beaches situated on the Atlantic coast of French Morocco at H hour of D day, 4 A.M., November 8, 1942. Said mission to be synchronized with the Anglo-American task force scheduled to leave England, pass through the Straits of Gibraltar into the Mediterranean to make simultaneous landings in Algeria some five hundred miles away. The purpose — to deny French North Africa to the Axis powers and to open the Mediterranean and a second front. The name — Operation Torch, as of then the largest overseas expeditionary force in history.

But in the opinion of the Pentagon not nearly large enough. A boy sent to do a man's job. In spite of the 1940 debacle in France, the French, it was argued, still have a pretty good African Army, sixty thousand troops in Morocco alone, and, in control of coast defenses, an aggressive Navy embittered by Dakar and Mers-el-Kebir. If loyalty to their soldier's oath to Marshal Pétain and a deeply ingrained sense of obedience to the chain of command inspire them to resist, if the *Luftwaffe* moves in fast, if Franco's Spain and the heavily garrisoned strip of Spanish Morocco which runs along the Mediterranean shore from Tangier, opposite Gibraltar, almost to the Algerian border intervene, if seven or eight million Arabs and Berbers take exception to the infidel Anglo-Saxon presence in their midst, will it, asked the Pentagon, be possible to maintain and supply a beachhead across four thousand miles of open sea? If all goes well and the landing craft *do* manage to find the beaches in the dark, what about the surf? According to the hydrographic boys, small-boat landing conditions around Casablanca during the autumn are no better than a one-to-five shot.

Of the Twelve Apostles of the General Staff, at least one who came down to see us off made it plain that he thought our chances of making it stick were less than fifty-fifty. He was very nice about it, of course, wished us luck and hoped to see us soon.

Aboard the SS *Ancon*

November 3, 1942. Over miles of glittering sea a brave sight. Thirty transports and cargo vessels, their screen of forty to fifty destroyers milling about like polo ponies. The cruisers *Augusta, Cleveland,* and *Brooklyn* — compact, businesslike — and in the dim distance the reassuring presence of the big battle-wagons, *Texas, New York,* and, last but not least, the newly commissioned *Massachusetts.* On the converted Esso oil tankers' decks, clusters of Army P-40's, straining at their leashes, and from the *Ranger's* flight deck, Navy dive bombers and Wildcat fighters roaring and zooming over the convoy.

Well, it won't be long now.

"Attention."

Over the loud-speaker system Major Gardner, Commander of Troops aboard the *Ancon,* will read a message from the Commanding General.

"Soldiers:

"We are now on our way to force a landing on the coast of northwest Africa. We are to be congratulated because we have been chosen as the units of the United States Army to take part in this great American effort.

"Our mission is threefold. First, to capture a beachhead, second, to capture the city of Casablanca, third, to move against the German wherever he may be and destroy him. . . .

"We may be opposed by a limited number of Germans. It is not known whether the French African Army will contest our landing. . . . When the great day of battle comes, remember your training and remember above all that speed and vigor of attack are the sure roads to success. . . . During the first days and nights after you get ashore you must work unceasingly, regardless of sleep, regardless of food. A pint of sweat will save a gallon of blood.

"The eyes of the world are watching us. . . . God is with us. . . . We will surely win.

Signed: G. S. Patton, Jr.

Major General, U.S.A., Commanding"

From all accounts General Patton must be quite a man. Have never seen him close to. To date just an awesome presence beyond that partition in the Munitions Building. At times when it got noisy in the bull pen the partition would vibrate as to a short burst of machine-gun fire.

"Tell 'em to stop that goddam racket. I can't hear myself think."

Out would come Colonel Hap Gay, Chief of Staff.*

"The General wants QUIET."

That would do it.

And now the General is aboard Admiral Hewitt's flagship, the heavy cruiser *Augusta,* enjoying relative quiet, plenty of time to think, and plenty to think about. And in the cavern headquarters inside the Rock of Gibraltar, so, presumably, has the Commander of Operation Torch, Lieutenant General Dwight D. Eisenhower. Even our small G-2 detachment aboard the *Ancon,* headed by Colonel John Ratay, has things on its collective mind, and the same, no doubt, with Bunny on the *Dickman,* and Percy Black, also on the *Augusta.*

November 7, 1942. Midnight. The stars are out, but it's dark as hell on deck. The *Ancon's* engines are down to a slow throb. According to the timetable we should be easing into the transport area preparatory to going over the side. Elements of the 3d Division are lining up at their deck stations adjacent to the disembarkation nets. All very orderly. They seem to know where to go and what to do. They are going over the side now. The technique seems to be to step up on a stanchion and back-climb over the rail. Weighted down with sixty-five pounds of equipment exclusive of steel helmet and Tommy gun, it is something of

* Colonel (later Lieutenant General) Hobart R. Gay.

a trick. A landing net is a mean piece of equipment. With the outward roll of the ship it swings clear. That is fine. You can get your hands and feet into the rungs. The inboard roll is something else again. The net flattens hard against the ship's side, reducing finger and toe holds to next to nothing.

"O.K., Major," said the Navy rating, "heave your right leg over and wait for the outboard roll."

Right leg over. Right foot feeling for a rung. No rung. Inboard roll. Bad luck. Bad timing. Tommy gun fouled with the rail. Oversize steel helmet banging the bridge of the nose. Field glasses slipping down around the knees. Remember your training. What training? The morning constitutional from the Mayflower Hotel to the Munitions Building?

Come on, snap out of it and get going. There's a rung. Down three. Wait. Down four. Wait. Down five. Below, dim upturned faces. The Higgins boat. Another ten feet to go. The Higgins boat falls away like a stone. Back she comes, smashing and banging against the *Ancon's* steel plates.

"Jump, Major," somebody yells. I jump. A long drop into the receptive arms of a couple of G.I.'s.

From the darkness far above, "O.K., Number Four, cast off."

As we chugged away from the black hull of the *Ancon,* Major Al Morse of our G-2 detachment looked at his wrist watch — 5:42. It was still dark, and as the Higgins boat gathered speed, sheets of salt spray lashed at its occupants. After a while one got used to the lurching. At least there wasn't room to fall down. Like a bunch of tightly wrapped asparagus our ship's company swayed back and forth in unison. The tempo of your neighbor's Tommy gun poking you in the back of the neck took on the same insistent rhythm as the refrain "Will the French resist?"

Ashore our agents have contacted many of the key figures of the French North African setup. In Algiers the underground is reported to have made encouraging headway, but in Morocco General Noguès, supreme ruler of the French Military Protectorate, remains an enigma. In the showdown, what will he do?

A predawn purple was creeping over the water when we got the answer. Two blinding orange flashes, almost instantaneous. Two shattering thunderclaps. The next ten or fifteen minutes made very little sense. Purple, red, and yellow tracers. Coming, going, crisscrossing. Concussions that seemed to lift the Higgins boat clear out of the water. Half a mile to starboard something long and black and spouting orange flames veered off in a wide skidding turn, the fanlike wake spreading, creamy.

"The *Brooklyn*," someone volunteered.

"Sounds like Treaty C," Al Morse said.

A naval engagement is a queer thing. Suddenly all hell breaks loose and as suddenly it's all over. As to who was doing what to whom and who paid, none of us had the slightest idea, but it seemed no reasonable time or place to be out in a small open boat.

The abrupt hush had a provisional quality as the sun, struggling through brownish haze, gradually revealed a sight long expected, yet unreal. First, the slow fade-in of the shore line. Pointing at us like a crooked finger, the Cap with its cluster of oil-storage tanks. But wait a minute — why are they a dirty rust-streaked yellow? In the Munitions Building mock-up we had lived with for so many weeks they were a nice bright aluminum. Somebody slipped up on that one. Well, never mind. Inside the Cap, the white villas and beach-front buildings are clearly visible now. Yes, that's more like it. That's Fedala, all right. The Casino, its terrace, its sea wall, and to the left the bathhouses, all just where they should be. Back of them the resort hotel where the German Armistice Commission is billeted. Where is the church? Sure enough, there it is. Further to the left of the Casino beach — Red Beach to us — the long run of sand surmounted by low bluff and open field — Red Beach Two, and the stand of scrub pine programed for divisional C.P. (command post).

The sun is doing better now, and the expanse of sparkling water, backdropped by the neat villas of Fedala, presents a curiously gala appearance. Regatta day. Scores of small craft chugging leisurely towards the yacht-club landing. Only no pennants and no reception committee. No parasols on the Casino terrace. Very empty and quiet. Too quiet.

Fifty yards to our right another Higgins boat seems to be racing us. In the bow a familiar figure scanning the town through his field glasses. Colonel Ratay. We are in quite close now. From the boats ahead, steel helmets and infantry packs are splashing ashore. They avoid the town, jogging across the sand strip towards the low embankment. Those water-logged packs are heavy. One man trips and falls full length on his face. With a convulsive movement he rolls over on his back, arms outstretched, and lies still.

Colonel Ratay's boat has nosed ahead of us. It is practically in. No, it has hit a runnel of sand. Everyone piles out. Six feet of water. A couple of the boys are taking a real ducking. Our boat is in. Nice landing. Only three feet of water and a short wade ashore. The boat retracts and pulls away. So long. Good luck.

Some distance away Colonel Ratay is splashing in with a large bundle under each arm. Not bundles. They are the boys who took the ducking. Lucky for them he happened to be around.

Our copassengers of the 3d Division were making for the embankment. Al and I took the same direction. The man lying on his back stared fixedly up at the sun. Two flies buzzed about his helmet. The rifleman ahead of us stopped, bent down, examined the dog tag, removed the slicker from his own pack, drew it over the waxen face. Strewn with equipment abandoned by the predawn assault wave, the beach had an unhealthy quality. It seemed much broader than on the bull-pen model. One felt naked. One wanted to get off it.

Whee-ee-ee, ZING!

Throughout World War I, the *départ* crack of the French *soixante-quinze* was an enjoyable sound — friendly, reassuring. The *arrivée* was something else again. It still is, particularly on an African beach before breakfast. There goes another one. Come on, this is getting ridiculous.

A steel helmet well heated by the subtropical sun, a slippery Tommy gun, a saturated uniform, trench coat, and full infantry pack are not conducive to speed, but it didn't take us long to scramble up the dune to the crest tufted with coarse grass. Beyond and behind its comforting protection stretched a wide field. It presented a curious appearance. Standing and sitting in small groups, the French officers and coal-black enlisted men of the Fedala garrison. Their rifles were stacked in neat array and most of them were smoking *jaunes.*

"What outfit is this?" we asked a French captain.

"One Hundred Second Company of the Sixth R.T.S." (*Régiment de Tirailleurs Sénégalais.*) "We came over to your side right after H hour," he said pleasantly.

"Is the whole garrison here?"

"No, some of them have gone back to the barracks." He pointed to a row of low wooden buildings at the edge of the town.

"Fedala is yours," said the French captain.

"In that case, what is all the shooting for?"

"Doubtless the Marine battery of seventy-fives out on the end of Cap Fedala. It's a pity, but you know how it is —" he shrugged — "our Navy has always had less comprehension than the Army."

Two small Arab boys loped up. Smiling eyes, extended palms, they had not yet acquired the cigarette, chewing-gum refrain. It was still early.

The French captain shooed them away. He was most cooperative, but he didn't really know anything. The landing, he said, had been a complete surprise. Besides the Senegalese garrison, the only French troops in the town itself were three or four Renault tanks in charge of a Lieutenant Lefèvre, whose heart, it seemed, was in the right place. He had, the captain said, greeted our first assault wave as it landed and had delayed the giving of the alarm by at least an hour. Yes, General Noguès — the Resident General in French Morocco — had given the order to resist, and undoubtedly reserves would be arriving from Rabat and Meknes. Meantime the French Navy, in charge of all coastal defenses, are going all out.

"It is fantastic, but there it is," the French captain said.

"And the German Armistice Commission?" Colonel Ratay asked.

"The Fedala contingent, fifteen of them, have been quartered at the hotel for some months. *Assez correctes, mais de sales types au fond.*"

The Colonel picked up his Tommy gun.

"Let's go take a look at the town," he said.

Our wet trench coats steamed in the hot sun. Peeling them off, we handed them to a Senegalese who was sitting by a stack of rifles. "Hold on to these till we get back." At the time it seemed sensible.

In V formation with Tommy guns at the ready the Colonel, Al, and I advanced to the edge of town. Not far from the Senegalese barracks, a palm-bordered road emerged into the field, and there, having no place to go, ended. A shiny blue and white sign — Boulevard Moulay Ismael. Residential evidently. Next, villas of white stucco, each with its neat little garden and bright-hued shutters tightly closed. At the first intersection we turned left, Avenue Gallieni. More villas. Untenanted? Maybe just very quiet tenants. Another intersection. A wider street paralleling the Boulevard Moulay Ismael. The sign read Rue de Fès. A right turn should get us into the center of the town. Another fifty yards and the Rue de Fès debouched into a small *rond-point*. To the right a driveway flanked by two porters' lodges. A large sign — Hotel Miramar. Shell fire had crumbled both lodges and littered the well-kept driveway with plaster and palm branches. Inside the grounds the palms were larger and more luxuriant — except for the two which had been split as if by lightning.

The hotel itself, a white stucco affair with green tiled roof, appeared at first glance to be undamaged. The kind of place from which one would expect a couple of uniformed doormen and a flock of chasseurs to swoop forth and relieve you of your luggage. Not this morning. We mounted the entrance steps leading past the broad bougainvillaea-covered veranda, and entered through wide-open doors a high-ceilinged lobby in which our footsteps echoed even more hollowly than in the streets of the phantom town. Empty. Very empty.

No one at the reception desk, or in the dining room, or in the smoking room. In the bar a radio was spluttering softly. I turned the knob. "*Allô, Maroc. Allô, Maroc. Le Président des États-Unis, Monsieur Franklin Roosevelt, s'est addressé cette nuit au peuple français.*"

The familiar voice of Lieutenant Fernand Auberjonois of our Psychological Warfare Section broadcasting from the *Texas*. His perfect Geneva French was coming over fine.

"I repeat the integral text of Monsieur Roosevelt's message: 'My friends, my friends who suffer night and day under the crushing Nazi yoke, I speak to you as one who in 1918 was in France with your Army and Navy. . . . All my life I have held a deep friendship for the people of France. I know your farms, your villages, your cities. I know your soldiers, your professors, your workers. . . . We arrive among you with the sole objective of crushing your enemies. We assure you that once the menace of Germany and Italy has been removed we shall quit your territories. I appeal to your realism, to your self-interest, to French national ideals. Do not, I pray you, oppose this great design. Lend us your help wherever you can, my friends, and we shall see again that glorious day when liberty and peace once more reign over the world. *Vive la France Éternelle!'*

"You are listening to a broadcast of the American Forces, Moroccan Sector. . . . *Allô, Maroc. Allô, Maroc. Le Président des États-Unis, Monsieur Franklin Roosevelt, s'est addressé cette nuit . . ."*

I snapped it off.

"Let's take a look around," the Colonel said.

Down the entrance steps again and around the building. What appeared to be the kitchen wing had been hit. The whole end caved in. As we passed a basement window something within moved. The Colonel with a catlike thrust jabbed the muzzle of his Tommy gun through the pane.

"Come up out of there!" he shouted.

Two frightened faces — a man and a woman.

"If you will be so kind as to go around to the other side," the man said in French, "I will let you in."

As we got to the basement door, the man was opening it and we burst in. Catching sight of our small Stars-and-Stripes armbands, his eyes grew round.

"Americans?" he stuttered, unbelieving.

"Naturally."

He couldn't take it in. "We heard it was an Axis invasion," he said. "Germans and Italians."

"Who are you, and who are these people?" the Colonel asked, pointing to the woman and an elderly man who had wandered uncertainly in.

"I am the manager of the Hotel Miramar," he said. "Rougeron is the name. Madame and Monsieur here are trusted employees of long standing."

Turning to his dazed assistants, he clapped his hands sharply. "But what are you waiting for? A bottle of champagne for these gentlemen. And faster than that."

Glasses, bottles, the popping of corks, and amidst the debris of the Miramar's kitchen we clinked foaming goblets to the long life of America and France, and the confusion of the Axis powers. It was all very cozy.

"And now about the German Armistice Commission," the Colonel said.

"Ah, yes," said Monsieur Rougeron sadly, "we were obliged to house them here. Fifteen in all. On the whole they were correct, *mais au fond s'étaient de sales types*. They left suddenly this morning before daylight."

"How?"

"By car — several cars."

"In what direction?"

"Presumably in the direction of Rabat."

"In uniform?"

"Yes."

The Colonel put down his glass, wiped his mustache, glanced at his wrist watch, and addressed Monsieur Rougeron. "As of now the Hotel Miramar is the official headquarters of the United States Western Task Force."

Donning his helmet, he turned to Al and me. "Come on," he said.

Ten minutes later we were on the outskirts of the town. By the side of the road a German one-and-a-half-ton truck guarded by a young American lieutenant.

"Your name?" the Colonel asked.

"Lieutenant Dent, C Company, Seventh Infantry."

"What's the story?"

It seemed that in their flight the German Armistice Commission had split into two groups. The first had presumably made good their getaway. The second group had run smack into C Company, by that time across the Boulhaut Road, and had made the mistake of trying to shoot it out with them. Result: four wounded — three of them mortally — and seven captured.

"Congratulations, Lieutenant, on the first German casualties to be inflicted by American troops in World War Two," the Colonel said. "Where are the prisoners?"

"They were sent back to the beach."

"Get them up to headquarters at once," the Colonel said. "Also that truck."

High noon.

From the bank up which we had clawed our way — could it be only a few hours ago? — the beach appeared to have changed its personality. Gone was the early morning mist. Whitecaps sparkled on an animated sea whipped by the strong, gusty breeze. The long, insistent rollers broke high, boiling up the incline of wet yellow sand. Beached landing craft sidled helplessly in the swash of back-sucking waves.

Off shore, like newly risen volcanic peaks, the transports formed a group of dark islands, the intervening water a seascape of small craft doggedly chugging their loads of supplies and ammunition to the beach.

One is landing now, directly below us. It hits a runnel. The occupants, all but the helmsman, leap out into the swirling eddies. The helmsman reverses. The screw churns raucously. No go. Stuck fast. The ammunition bearers pull and haul at the cases, heaving them up onto the dry sand. Leaving the helmsman to his own devices, they load the cases on their shoulders and are making their way across the beach.

A fast Navy crash boat heading for a point about twenty yards away hits the same runnel and shudders to a halt. A tall figure vaults over the side of the crash boat and splashes ashore.

"Come back here!" he roars. A couple of ammunition bearers turn their heads uneasily.

"Yes, I mean *you. All* of you. Drop that stuff and come back here. Faster than that, goddam it. On the double."

Once more he is waist-deep in the water, his shoulder to the bow of the beached landing craft.

"Take hold here. You two, over to the other side. Wait for the next wave. Lift and push. *Now! Push,* goddam it, *push.*"

The screw churns, bites the water, and the landing craft backs away.

The bearers gaze incredulously at the tall dripping figure.

"Don't you realize that boat has other trips to make?" he snaps. "How do you expect to fight a war without ammunition? Now go and take that stuff up to the dump. On the double."

A shell whistled high overhead, exploded dully in the town beyond. Near the embankment an infantryman, his Tommy gun beside him, lay face downward on the sand. With a speed surprising in so large a man, the tall figure raced to the recumbent soldier, snatched up his Tommy gun, and leaning over him, shouted, "Yea-a-h."

The soldier half turned over, shielding his face with his arms. "Go 'way and lemme sleep," he said.

"Yea-a-h."

The barrel of his own Tommy gun was boring insistently into the pit of his stomach as the soldier decided to open his eyes. His glance climbed slowly up the cavalry boots, the wet trouser leg, the pearl-handled revolver, the deep-chested torso. Behind the butt of the Tommy gun, gray eyes blazing from an inexorable face surmounted by the dripping helmet with its two stars.

"Jesus," he said simply.

Stepping back, General Patton examined the lock of the Tommy gun. O.K.

"Get up, boy," he said gently.

The soldier scrambled to his feet, swaying uncertainly.

"Are you hurt?" the General said.

"No, sir."

"I know you're tired," the General said. "We're all tired. That makes no difference."

He put his hand on the man's shoulder. "The next beach you land on will be defended by Germans. I don't want one of them coming up behind you and hitting you over the head with a sockful of silt." Only that was not quite the word he used.

The man grinned.

"Here's your gun." The sharpness returned to the General's voice. "Now, get going."

Beyond the eastern extremity of the Casino's sea wall, a small bathing cabana had been rigged up with a field telephone. On its diminutive piazza overlooking the ocean, General Patton was receiving reports from the Beachmaster and a 3d Division liaison officer.

As we approached this hastily improvised command post, a French Dewoitine banked steeply over Cap Fedala and, straightening out, made a leisurely run down the beach. Opposite the Casino a bunch of ammunition bearers were assembling a supply dump. Dipping slightly, the French plane's machine guns rattled a slow burst. A crackle of retaliatory rifle fire. One or two of the boys, obeying their reflexes, flattened themselves on the sand. The distance from cabana to dump was perhaps a hundred yards. The General made it in ten flat.

"On your feet!" he shouted. "What the hell's the matter with you men anyway? What do you think you've got guns for?"

The faces of the recently prone expressed equal parts of sheepishness and incredulity.

"You heard me," the General said. "You've got guns. Use them." And as he turned away, a parting shot: "If I see another American soldier lying down on this beach I'll court-martial him."

As the General turned to regain the cabana, the Dewoitine made a U turn over Fort Blondin and headed once again for the beach. Higher this time. Along the line of flight a sustained tattoo of rifle fire. Here and there an imperceptible sagging of the seat of the pants, but no one lay down. The General did not even look up. Over the dump the plane waggled its wings, then with a left bank turned inland. From the forward window a gloved hand waved.

Standing straight and tall on the piazza, the General was in high spirits. "A bit of cussing-out always does me good," he said. "Should have come in sooner. Would have if I hadn't got caught in a goddam naval battle. Quite a show. A *great* show. Hello, Ratay, what's the dope?"

"Sir, your headquarters have been established at the Hotel Miramar. It is undamaged except for the kitchen." Indicating Al and me, the Colonel added, "This is Major Morse and Major Codman." Even on D day the Regular Army remains punctilious.

The General nodded twice. "All right," he said. "Tell them to have cold supper and accommodations for forty at six o'clock. And now" — turning briskly to the Chief of Staff — "I want to go up to Anderson's C.P. and find out what the hell's going on around here."

At the Miramar things seemed to be looking up. Behind the reception counter Madame was verifying the row of heavy keys, each hanging from its individual letter slot. At the counter itself Monsieur Rougeron was leafing through the hotel register.

"Glad to see you are opening up for business," Colonel Ratay remarked. "This evening you will have forty guests."

"Ah, yes, forty guests." Monsieur Rougeron's tone was professional. "It will be a little difficult — so near the end of the season. We will do our best. But, alas, there is no water."

"Why not?"

"The tank on the roof, the entire water supply, *foutu*. Two shells. Your Navy. Direct hits."

Outside on the spacious veranda under the watchful eye of one of our M.P.'s, a dozen or so French prisoners, officers and noncoms, sat primly erect about the small cane tables.

"Codman, get their stories," the Colonel said. "I have a priority matter to attend to." And he went down the steps.

Seated cross-legged on the lawn *below* the veranda, the half dozen oddly assorted Germans whom Al Morse had herded up from the beach to the hotel grounds formed a glum, nondescript circle. Individually and collectively they presented no distinguishing feature — except one. Their rumpled uniforms. Familiar. The sickly gray-green, the cloth headgear with the little round insignia, the Iron Crosses. Twenty-five years ago, on taking French leave of a Bavarian prison cage, I had hoped not to see that uniform again. It just goes to show, one never knows.

So these were members of the celebrated German Armistice Commission, the enforcers of the humiliating terms of June, 1940, the presumed forerunners of the *Wehrmacht* and of total German occupation of North Africa. Since the fall of France their number had increased to around two hundred — two hundred locusts diligently engaged in stripping North Africa bare. The main group in Casablanca had by now almost certainly flown the coop, but the gentlemen of the Fedala chapter had miscalculated. They had, in fact, made a serious error. And now they compounded it. Intent on registering an admixture of indifference, boredom, and defiance, they failed to note the approach of Colonel Ratay. At ten paces the Colonel stopped short. His mustachios bristled. His eyes flashed dark fire.

"Achtung!" he roared.

During his years of service as Military Attaché the Colonel had not wasted his time. For the next fifteen minutes the members of the German Armistice Commission responded as good Germans should to the staccato peals and guttural chimes of their native *Manual of Arms* — close-order drill, a lesson in snappy saluting and military courtesy. And when, to the enchantment of Monsieur Rougeron and his staff, the Colonel marched them through the lobby at regulation goose step, and up the stairs to their second-floor quarters, there remained in the minds of the erstwhile star boarders of the Hotel Miramar no doubt whatsoever as to the authenticity of their master's voice.

Throughout the Colonel's review of troops the conduct of the French on the veranda had been exemplary. By not so much as the flicker of an eyelid did they evidence awareness of the Teuton presence. The absent treatment. The same technique which over the past two years had baffled and infuriated the German Armistice Commission. Had not General von Wulisch in exasperation complained to Weygand that the entire French North African Army were deliberately attempting to create a vacuum around the persons and activities of his commission with consequent impairment of said commission's efficiency?

"They behave," Consul General Auer had fretted to Monsieur Laval, "as if they didn't like us, as if we weren't there."

The senior officer of the French group, who appeared to be a lieutenant colonel of Artillery, arose at my approach. I saluted. He saluted. The rest got up and stood at attention. A short exchange of civilities and they sat down again. Polite. Noncommittal. The Lieutenant Colonel and I made for a small table at the extreme end of the veranda, the circling-around and sitting-down process allowing each of us to take discreet inventory of the other's ribbons. Unlike the British, the French make no bones about their predilection for ribbons. Napoleon saw to that.

"I see, *mon commandant,* that you also have fought with us," the Lieutenant Colonel said, accepting a cigarette. The use of the formal *"mon"* and the barely perceptible stressing of the next to the last word were nicely managed.

The next two hours, while adding little to our store of strictly military intelligence, served to illumine — at least in part — a state of mind shaped by two years of humiliation, wounded pride, conflicting loyalties, and clandestine struggle — two years during which the banked fires of revenge burned low but steadily.

On June 22, 1940, the Armies of Metropolitan France capitulated, and at Rethondes before the ancient railway carriage of 1918 the *Führer* danced a jig. Within forty-eight hours there sidled into the Casablanca dock a small vessel, the *Massilia,* and down the gangplank marched Monsieur Mandel and the diehards of Bordeaux, bent on transferring the Government of France to North Africa and from there continuing the war. Their efforts failed. In the heart and mind of General Auguste Paul Charles Albert Noguès, disciple of the great Lyautey and since 1936 Resident General of France in Morocco, the flame of patriotism flared for a moment brightly. But his plea to the homeland for continuance of hostilities — *C'est avec mon coeur de soldat que j'addresse cet appel à mon chef"* — had fallen on deaf ears and he had now resigned himself to carrying out his oath to the aged marshal to defend North Africa against *all* aggressors. With more than half of France occupied by the Germans, *Liberté, Fraternité, Égalité* were replaced by *Travaille, Famille, Patrie*. Like Lord Gort and Duff Cooper, Mandel and his colleagues were brushed aside, and Noguès settled down to his long battle of wits with the German Armistice Commission. The silent struggle for North Africa was on.

In respect to another struggle, that for the French Navy, the British were neither inactive nor silent. In the general confusion the *Richelieu* had managed in 1940 to slip away from Brest and safely reach Dakar. The uncompleted but formidable battleship *Jean Bart* had been surreptitiously moved to Casablanca. At Mers-el-Kebir, the naval harbor of the Mediterranean port of Oran, rode two battleships and the 26,500-ton cruisers *Strasbourg* and *Dunkerque*. Within a fortnight of the fall of France — it was July 3 — their commander, Admiral Gensoul, was handed an ultimatum. He was then and there given the choice of (1) sailing his ships to British ports or to a French port in the West Indies, (2) placing them under U.S. trusteeship for the duration of the war, or, finally, (3) sinking them. The ultimatum was backed up by the grim silhouettes of His Majesty's *Hood, Valiant, Resolution, Ark Royal,* two cruisers, and eleven destroyers. Unfortunately for everyone concerned, Admiral Gensoul refused and twelve hundred French sailors lost their lives. Two months later General de Gaulle's ill-fated expedition to Dakar rubbed salt into French wounds and strengthened the conviction of French-African governors that automatic resistance to aggression from any quarter was preferable to having the Germans take over the job for them.

The U.S. approach was more subtle. As yet we were not, of course, in the war, but the importance of keeping North Africa out of German hands was obvious. Accordingly, in the autumn of 1940 the able and wily counselor of our embassy at Vichy, Mr. Robert D. Murphy, was dispatched to North Africa. There he conferred with General Weygand, recently designated by Vichy as Delegate General to North Africa with an over-all directive to organize and strengthen the defenses and economy of the entire area and to maintain cordial if firm relations with the Moslem population. From their meeting of minds flowered the famous Murphy-Weygand Accord of February, 1941, the somewhat moot policy of U.S. economic aid to North Africa, and the activities of our attendant control officers, familiarly known as "Bob Murphy's Vice-Consuls."

Shortly before Pearl Harbor, the Germans, suspicious of Weygand's activities, had effected his recall. Murphy's men had meantime made contact with the French underground resistance movement in Algiers. Through them, in the spring of '42, liaison was established in southern France with General Giraud, recently escaped from the German fortress of Koenigstein. To their necessarily veiled hints in regard to possible U.S. intervention in North Africa, Giraud responded by appointing as his undercover representative in Algiers his friend General Charles Mast, another alumnus of Koenigstein. In Morocco he named as his proxy General Émile Béthouart, leader of the French expedition to Narvik and presently commanding the Casablanca division. One thing, however, was evident. General Béthouart's plans had gone awry.

"Do you know the General commanding the Casablanca division?" I asked the Lieutenant Colonel.

"I know him," he replied stiffly.

It was slow going, but a piecing together of the talk on the veranda and subsequent conversations produced a scenario something like this:

Early in the summer General Béthouart was informed by the Algiers underground that an American expedition to North Africa was in the making. No mention of places. No date. On the evening of November 4 he received word that the moment was near at hand. On November 6 at 7 P.M. a scrap of paper left on his desk announced, "The operation will take place during the night of the seventh-eighth."

Short on time and information, Béthouart went to work. Assuming that the principal landing would take place at Rabat, the capital and nerve center of French Morocco, he lost no time in dispatching to Rabat a battalion of the Colonial Infantry Regiment, commanded by his friend Colonel Magnan, with instructions to be prepared to sur-round the Residence. He hoped to talk Noguès over to his side, but he wasn't taking any chances. Or so he thought.

November 7. Midnight. Before the headquarters of the Casablanca Division, General Béthouart's car was in readiness. At 12:02 the General and two members of the underground stepped into it.

"If anyone attempts to stop us my orders are to shoot," the General said.

After leaving les Roches Noires and the sea, the Casablanca–Rabat road winds through hilly country before descending again to the plain and paralleling the shore line. To the General's eyes, straining westward, the dark Atlantic revealed exactly nothing. And now the outskirts of Rabat, the double-arched entrance through crenelated walls, and soon General Béthouart was sweeping up the main stem of the capital. Beyond the palace of the Sultan of Morocco, and a few hundred yards below the Residence of General Noguès, the car came to a stop. Followed by his companions, General Béthouart entered the *État-Major,* military headquarters of General Lascroux, commander of all Moroccan ground forces. Earlier in the evening Lascroux by prearrangement with the underground had been kidnaped and spirited away to Meknes. Meantime Magnan's men had quietly infiltrated the gardens of the Residence, which was now surrounded. At the *État-Major* all military and civilian telephone lines had been rendered inoperative. So far so good. The time was 2 A.M. Béthouart was in charge and Noguès virtually a prisoner incommunicado. But was he?

In his pretty villa hard by the Rabat Cathedral, Colonel Jean Piatte, Chief of Staff of General Noguès's Military Cabinet, was peacefully asleep when the telephone by his bedside jangled. The voice of General Noguès. "Come up at once to the Residence."

Within three minutes Piatte was on his way downstairs.

"Be as quiet as possible when you come back," Madame Piatte murmured sleepily, "and don't wake the children." In reply, the click of the front door, followed by the dull clang of the grilled gate.

At the end of his street Piatte turned left up the main boulevard. As he passed the second palm tree, two men stepped from behind it. One of them stuck a gun in his ribs.

"Come along quietly," the other said.

At the *État-Major* Colonel Piatte stood at attention before General Béthouart.

"You are out late, Colonel," the General said.

"I was on my way to the Residence, *mon général.*"

"I will see that you get there," the General said. "Sit down."

Colonel Piatte sat down.

"At five this morning," the General said, "the Americans will make landings in force on all the beaches of Morocco."

"Splendid," Colonel Piatte said. "What do we do now?"

"You will go to the Residence," the General said. "In his heart Noguès is a patriot. He will listen to reason. He must be made to see the light."

Colonel Piatte, flanked by his two chaperons, made his way up the gentle incline of the curving boulevard. On either side the windows of the white administration buildings stared blankly as he passed. Fifty yards from the rear entrance of the Residence four armed figures barred the way. The password was given and received. A whispered consultation. His escorts stepped aside, motioning him to proceed.

At the rear entrance, no one. Colonel Piatte entered. Passing his own office, he followed the narrow corridor, with its straw wall matting, through the orderly room and the small double doors giving access to the office of the Resident General of France in Morocco. Except for the light on the spacious table-desk, the large high-ceilinged room was in semidarkness.

General Noguès pushed away the papers he was examining and leaned against the high back of his chair.

"Ah, it is you, Piatte," he said. "You have taken your time."

"I was unavoidably detained," the Colonel said.

To Piatte's account and to his presentation of the case the Resident General listened stonily. As the Colonel paused for breath, Noguès, with a sudden movement, leaned across the desk, his pale face now contorted with ill-suppressed excitement.

"So Béthouart thinks I should join his movement. Well, just take a look at these," he rasped, shoving the papers in Piatte's direction. "I am 'cordially invited to join in the liberation of my country.' On the strength of what? Documents without signatures, without dates, without places, names. 'The Americans are landing in force.' *What* force? No indications, no figures, nothing. A commando raid? Another Dieppe fiasco? Another Saint-Nazaire? A trap? And tomorrow the Germans on our necks. Ah, no. It would be too stupid."

"Who brought these?" Piatte asked.

"Captain de Verthamon, aide to General Béthouart — and," General Noguès added bitterly, "my nephew."

"He is here?"

"In the next room. Under arrest."

The muscles of General Noguès's face were twitching as he reached for one of the two telephones on his desk. There was no response. He put back the receiver.

"Still dead," he said. "For a dissident General, Béthouart is efficient in his way, but there is one thing he has overlooked."

Picking up the other receiver, General Noguès spoke crisply. "Get me Admiral Michelier." And during the ensuing pause added, "He seems to have forgotten the private line."

Another minute and Vice-Admiral F. C. Michelier, in command of all the naval forces and coast defenses of Morocco, was on the wire.

"Michelier" — Noguès's voice was tense — "have you anything further to report?"

"Nothing, *mon général.*"

"You are sure?"

"For a hundred miles out in the Atlantic there is nothing, absolutely nothing."

General Noguès carefully replaced the receiver.

"You see?" he said.

At the *État-Major,* General Béthouart looked at his wrist watch. One hour and twenty minutes to go. Further down the boulevard the black guards at the entrance to the Méchouar gazed impassively across the empty square. Within the vast walled enclosure the palace of the Sultan slumbered, dark and inscrutable, as twenty miles off shore, the

have confidence in me as I have confidence in you. We have but one goal, that of final victory.' You are listening to a broadcast of the American Forces, Moroccan Sector."

Giraud in Algiers. O.K. With communications virtually nonexistent, Algeria might have been on the other side of the world. Only later did we learn of General Eisenhower's stormy session with Giraud in the Rock of Gibraltar and of the fortuitous appearance in distant Algiers of Admiral François Darlan, Commander in Chief of all military, naval, and air forces under Marshal Pétain. For the time being, Western Task Force in Morocco was on its own.

A jeep flying the colors and a white flag swung into the hotel driveway, crunching to a stop before the entrance. Colonel Hap Gay, General Patton's Chief of Staff, slapping the dust from his uniform, came briskly up the steps. Close behind him, Colonel Wilbur, Chief of Special Activities G-2, appropriately named, since they already included during the past twelve hours two dashes to Casablanca and the capture of that noisome battery of 75's out on the end of Cap Fedala.

In answer to Ratay's inquiries, Colonel Gay shook his head.

"The French Navy seems determined to slug it out with us," he said.

Colonel Gay is the laconic type. It took time to piece together his shorthand account of their wild ride through the French lines into Casablanca, where enthusiastic crowds engulfed the flag-bedecked jeep and showered its occupants with sincere if incoherent tributes in French, Arabic, and Berber; of the call at French Military Headquarters only to learn of Béthouart's arrest; of the visit to the Admiralty, where Admiral Michelier refused even to receive them; of the scene in the outer office, the Admiral's aide standing stiffly at attention, while, to the rumble of our naval guns, the Chief of Staff of Western Task Force, unarmed and a dozen miles behind the French lines, stated the case for Reason and Common Sense.

"No use," Colonel Gay said. "I had just about finished talking when the big eight-inch guns of the El Hank coastal battery let go with a salvo that damn near blew out the windows. 'That,' said the Admiral's aide, 'is your answer.'"

CHAPTER II

Hotel Miramar
(November 8–25, 1942)

The over-all command in joint operations involving an amphibious landing rests with the naval commander, regardless of rank, until such time as the ground commander has his command post firmly established ashore. Thus, Patton naturally was most anxious to get established in the Miramar. However, the relations between Patton and Admiral Hewitt were of the best. Each highly respected the other. Both were fighting men of the highest order.

November 11, 1942. Armistice Day, and the first opportunity since we came ashore to get off a letter.

Our first evening (November 8) as nonpaying guests at this once fashionable seaside hotel — one of the few in Morocco at which you and I did *not* stay — was in the nature of a reunion of the staff, which for the ocean crossing had been split up among half a dozen transports. By nightfall most of us were ashore. Those not engaged in special tasks on the beach had gravitated to the Miramar, whose darkened lobby, dimly lit by a small kerosene lamp on the reception counter, suggested the preliminary activities of a hotel convention held during a power failure.

In the dining room Monsieur Rougeron, the hotel proprietor, was superintending the setting of the long table and the securing of the blackout curtains. Near the entrance Lieutenant Colonel Paul Harkins, Deputy Chief of Staff, was talking to Colonels Maddox and Hammond, G-3 and Signal Chief respectively. Standing by the head of the

table Bob Cummings, the Adjutant General, and Colonel Wilbur listened attentively as General Keyes, Deputy Commander of the Task
Force, briefed them on tomorrow's plans.

Near the foot of the stairs young Dick Jenson, the General's junior
aide, was talking animatedly to his senior colleague, Lieutenant Al
Stiller, veteran of the General's tank outfit in World War I, Arizona
cowboy, and a very handy man with a gun. A study in contrast, the
springy sapling and the sturdy oak.

Quick, firm steps on the landing. Jenson shouts, "Attention," as
General Patton makes his entrance. The soaked uniform, reconditioned
by the resourceful Sergeant Meeks, the General's colored orderly, fits
like a glove. The lamplight glints from the newly polished cavalry
boots, the ivory-handled pistols, and the remarkable headgear — a
gleaming white casque emblazoned with the Prussian double eagle —
the dress-uniform helmet of the German Armistice Commission's late
chief. It got a big hand.

"Considerate of the so-and-so to leave it in my room," the General
said as the staff gathered around him. "I shall wear it for our entrance
into Berlin."

Followed by his two aides, the General swept into the dining room.
"Sit anywhere," he said, pulling out the chair at the nearer end.

Food. For the last twenty-four hours no one had seen, smelled, or
even thought of food. I found myself halfway down the table between
Colonel Ratay and Major Robert Henriques, Combined Operations
Headquarters, commando, author, and valued adviser, the only British
member of our expedition.

"What, no insignia?" I said.

"Hush," Henriques said. "Out of consideration for the susceptibilities
of the French Navy I came ashore in the guise of an American officer
out of uniform."

"Don't let the General catch you."

"It was his idea."

The General was in high spirits. Considering the dangerous surf
conditions, the landings had been accomplished more successfully
than anyone had a right to expect. At Safi, one hundred and forty miles

south of Casablanca, General Harmon and his 2d Armored Division tanks were ashore, between six and seven thousand troops in all. Our own Center Attack Group, roughly nineteen thousand troops, was moving inland behind Fedala. A hundred miles to the north, General Truscott's 9th Division landing at Port Lyautey had met with bitter resistance from the French ground forces and his troops, numbering around nine thousand, were suffering considerable casualties. With a view to parleying with the local French commander, Pier Hamilton (Major Pierpont M. Hamilton) and Nick Craw (Colonel Demas Craw)* had volunteered for an early morning dash through the lines. Less fortunate than Colonel Wilbur, their gallant attempt ended tragically. Colonel Craw was killed outright by a trigger-happy *tirailleur marocain* who disregarded the white flag of truce, and Pier was taken prisoner.

From where I was sitting I could not hear everything the General said, but it was evident that his unscheduled participation in the morning naval battle had proved enjoyable.

"The *Massachusetts* and the carrier planes were pounding away at the *Jean Bart,*" he was saying, "when suddenly six French destroyers came streaking out of Casablanca Harbor and took on the whole goddam U. S. Navy. It was quite a show. The Frenchmen were full of fight. They were actually within a couple of miles of the beaches here, and shelling our landing craft before our Navy really took over. One of their shells landed close enough to the *Augusta* to send up a geyser which soaked Hewitt and me to the skin. The French sailors were fine but very foolish."

For some time the signal officer directly across the table from me had been silent. Between mouthfuls his head nodded, hitching forward in short, progressive jerks. Eyes closed, his face came gently to rest in his plate. His two neighbors got him under the arms and removed him.

"First sleep in three days," one of them said. "He's earned it."

A few minutes later a familiar apparition knifed into the room, long legs hurrying to keep up with the forward-thrust body, dark eyes

* Both these officers were awarded the Congressional Medal of Honor.

darting quick glances from side to side. Trig, nervous, conspiratorial. Twentieth-century *condottiere,* out of Groton by West Point, Colonel Black, Assistant Chief of Staff G-2. He seated himself in the vacant chair opposite.

"Hello, Bunny," he said, looking me straight in the eye. "Where is Codman?"

"Wait a minute, Percy," I said. (He is always mixing up our names.) "Do you mean Charley Carter or Bunny Codman?"

He laughed and looked less haunted.

"Bunny Carter is on the *Dickman* where he is supposed to be," he said. "What I want to know is how did *you* get ashore?"

"With Colonel Ratay."

"Oh," he said. "I might have known." Pouring himself a cup of coffee, he inquired, "Have you got a room?"

"No."

"In that case you had better move in with me. Ground-floor wing. Last room on the right. Last room in the hotel."

"Thanks."

A wonderful character, Percy. And a great G-2. Fun to work for. Exciting, too. You never know what he's up to. One long guessing game. As far as I am concerned he can do no wrong, since it is largely due to him — and of course our good friend Ralph Stearley* — that I am not still languishing in the Munitions Building.

The General was pushing his chair back.

"What is this I hear, Wilbur, about your taking a French battery singlehanded?" he asked.

Colonel Wilbur looked embarrassed.

The General turned to Colonel Gay.

"I want the facts by tomorrow, Hap. We might as well get him decorated *before* he gets himself killed."

In that last room, securely barricaded against high-ranking late arrivals, Percy extinguished his flashlight and burrowed deeper into his sleeping bag.

* Now Major General, USAF (Ret.).

"Tomorrow we'll get the G-2 Section properly set up," he said. "Yes, Colonel, sir."

"Incidentally" — a deep yawn — "remind me to remind you to go into town and get me some civilian clothes. Tweeds. Leggings, beret, sporting-squire effect. I'm thinking of running up to the Spanish Zone."

"Yes, Colonel, sir."

The following day, November 9, was almost as busy as the preceding one. In the morning I accompanied Percy to the command post of the 3d Division in the woods outside Fedala. With its trench system and barbed wire it resembled a World War I C.P. Our mission was to collect front-line intelligence, but owing to bad communications between the sub-task forces and ourselves, there was very little available.

Our own troops had moved inland, assuming positions from which to attack Casablanca from the rear. In the north Truscott's forces had taken the Port Lyautey airfield, providing our P-40's with a base from which to operate, and in the south we believed General Harmon to be progressing satisfactorily. So far, so good. But we are not yet out of the woods.

France's newest battleship, the *Jean Bart,* tied up in the inner harbor of Casablanca to the Môle du Commerce, remains a potential fortress. So do the big El Hank batteries. The city and vital port are holding out. No signs so far of German or Spanish reaction, but off shore our still heavily loaded transports and cargo ships offer tempting submarine targets. Sitting ducks with no place to go.

Afternoon and evening were spent at the hotel trying to get things straightened out. Bunny has now checked in and practically all the interpreting — further interrogation of French officers, *contrôleurs civils,* shopkeepers, householders, etc. — falls to him and me. One Capitaine de Frégate, picked up between Rabat and Casa, told me with a perfectly straight face and undoubted sincerity that he had it "on good authority" that the chief objective of our landing was to foment uprisings of the Jews against the Arabs and in the ensuing confusion assume control of Morocco. He was hard to unconvince.

"After all," he said, "your President Rosenfeldt is a Jew."

Such is the efficacy of Nazi propaganda. The French Navy's decision to fight is a double tragedy, since it has not only precipitated open warfare between Americans and Frenchmen with casualties on each side already running into four figures, but has also resulted in the total destruction of the valuable French Casablanca fleet.

November 10. Sure enough, early today the *Jean Bart* started lobbing shells at our covering group. In answer, nine bombers from the *Ranger* plastered her with thousand-pound bombs. That does it. Despite yesterday's stiff resistance and counterattacks by the Foreign Legion and French-led native troops, the French Army seems more disposed to call it a day. This morning, Lieutenant Colonel Métral of the Casa garrison came to Fedala and conferred with General Patton and Colonel Gay. As a result of their deliberations General Patton entrusted him with a letter to the Sultan in which he emphasized that the purpose of our expedition is to protect His Majesty's throne, his people, and the people of France in Morocco from enslavement by our common enemy, the Nazis; that we demand nothing other than friendship; that shedding the blood of friends is most painful, but that if by midnight the French armed forces have not desisted from the present fratricidal strife, it will become his — General Patton's — unpleasant duty to attack His Majesty's beautiful city of Casablanca by land, by sea, and by air with the utmost violence known to modern war.

Whether the letter will be delivered or not we have no way of knowing, but it seems worth a try. Meantime the plans for the all-out coordinated attack on Casa are set for 7 A.M. tomorrow morning. That it will be violent and bloody no one can doubt.

The night of November 10-11. A pull at the blankets of my cot. A flashlight shining in my eyes. Percy Black's voice. "Get up, Codman, you're wanted in the front office. An interpreting job."

Boots, helmet, where's that goddam gun? Under the cot. Within two minutes we were hurrying down the corridor and through the lobby.

My wrist watch said ten minutes of four. Percy pulled open one of the double doors of the smoking room and we went in.

The only light was from a candle stuck in a champagne bottle on a small table. Seated behind it on the banquette which curved around the oval end of the room, General Patton appeared to be studying a small irregular-shaped sheet of paper which he held flattened before him on the table. Standing at his right in the shadows, General Keyes, Colonel Gay, and Colonel Ratay. To his left and some distance away from the table, sitting very erect on a small straight-back chair, a French major wearing a black leather helmet. His khaki uniform was white with dust, his chalky face streaked with sweat and grime. The General motioned with his head to the empty chair beside the Frenchman.

"Sit down, Codman," he said, then added, "Commandant Lebel of the Third Moroccan Spahis, Major Codman of my staff."

The General looked up and handed me the paper.

"What exactly does that say — in English?" he said.

It was tissue-thin, badly crumpled, and contained only a few lines in French, hastily scribbled in soft pencil. It was dated November 10, but the time and addressee were both illegible. "On receipt of this order," it ran in substance, "French troops will cease hostilities with American troops. French commanders will take immediate steps to notify American outposts." It was signed "Lascroux." *

According to Lebel, General Leyer, Commander of the Meknes-Rabat Sector, had ordered him to convey this message to the French front-line commanders in the area. Unable to locate the senior troop officer, Lebel decided — it was 10 P.M. November 10 — to go himself to the front lines and transmit the order to as many battalion commanders as he could contact. This he did and found that in several sectors the French withdrawal had already begun. Five miles north of Fedala he was informed by some Arabs that an American patrol was approaching from the nearby river.

Lebel got out of his car and preceded it on foot so that the headlights would show him up clearly. A minute or two later the Ameri-

---

* General Lascroux, commander of all French ground forces in Morocco.

can patrol crossed the road ahead of him and he was challenged by a young lieutenant.

"What are you doing here?" the lieutenant asked.

"Looking for the first American outpost I can find," Lebel said. He was escorted to the headquarters of 30th Infantry and thereafter to the Hotel Miramar.

Following Lebel's statement and its translation, the General was silent. His face in the flickering candlelight was thoughtful, not unkindly, a little tired. He looked at his wrist watch.

"Lebel," he said, directly addressing the Frenchman, "you are a staff officer, are you not?"

"*Oui, mon général.*"

"Then you naturally realize the difficulties inherent in calling off at short notice a highly coordinated attack."

"*En effet, mon général.*"

"If I accept this cease-fire order at its face value, what is to guarantee that it will be obeyed by the French Navy?"

Despite his obvious physical fatigue, Lebel's voice was vibrant. "Will the General permit me to make a suggestion?" he said. "I am personally known to General Desré, now in command of the Casablanca Division, and to Admiral Ronarch, Chief of Staff of the Navy. If you will authorize me to go *now* to Casablanca I will guarantee the French Navy."

For about three seconds General Patton's fingers drummed on the table. Then sharply, "Ratay."

"Yes, sir," the Colonel said, stepping front and center with alacrity.

"You will accompany Major Lebel to Casablanca," the General said. "Unless the French Navy immediately signifies that it is bound by this cease-fire order, the attack on Casablanca jumps off as scheduled. It is now 4:15. I shall be at Anderson's forward C.P. Do you understand?"

"Yes, sir," the Colonel said, swinging the webbed belt of his 45 around the ample circumference of his trench coat and reaching for his helmet.

"And don't get yourself shot," the General added, pushing away the table and rising to his feet.

To Lebel, standing at attention, he extended his hand.

"I wish you the best of luck," the General said.*

6:45 A.M. Fifteen minutes to go. From the roof of the Hotel Miramar we watched the pinkening horizon over Fort Blondin. In the lee of the splintered water tank General Keyes was talking to Colonel Hammond, Chief Signal Officer.

"Are we still in contact with the *Augusta?*"

"Yes, sir."

Dawn creeping up the blue-black vault of the sky. The outlines of the motionless transports visible now, and to the west, slowly moving in for the kill, the ghostly silhouettes of the covering group.

Ringing the metropolis of Casablanca, our artillery is in position, the city's water supply is in our hands, one can almost hear the rumble of General Harmon's tanks rolling up from Mazagan.

General Keyes looks at his watch — 6:52. His face is impassive, but around his eyes there are lines of strain.

The hum of engines. Louder. Streaking across the sky directly overhead a squadron of fighter planes. Colonel Lauris Norstad's† P-40's from Port Lyautey. Out at sea a glint of wings — the Navy bombers taking off from the *Ranger*. Twelve miles distant the sleeping city of Casablanca, under whose white roofs half a million souls lie mercifully unconscious of the terrible engines of destruction closing in on them from the land, the sea, and the air.

Colonel Hammond's walkie-talkie comes to life. "Third Division C.P.?" "Yes. Just a minute." He hands the receiver to General Keyes.

"That you, Geoff?" The sharp, incisive voice of General Patton.

"Yes, sir."

"Call it off. The French Navy has capitulated. Ratay has just been here. You are still in touch with Hewitt?"

"Yes, sir."

"Good, but you'll have to work fast."

---

* Immediately General Patton had a radio message sent in code. "If you receive message from me in clear 'Play ball' cease all hostilities at once."
† General Norstad, presently commanding NATO.

At General Patton's first words a vigorous nod from General Keyes to Hammond, and a second radio set is already crackling its message across the water. Aboard the *Augusta* Admiral Hewitt and his staff get busy. Very busy indeed.

Outside the Casa breakwater, the covering group, big guns elevated, is now plainly visible. Over the city the Navy bombers circle and circle and circle. The seconds and minutes tick off. No one speaks. Without warning the leading bomber banks and peels off. The next, the next, as the circle dissolves into a long serpentine line headed for the open sea, where the *Ranger* is poking up into the wind to receive them. Once again the roar of engines over our heads as our P-40's hit the trail for home, 6:58.

General Keyes lowers his field glasses and with his handkerchief carefully wipes the lenses. Before starting down the stairs from the roof, he takes a last look in the direction of Casablanca.

"Thank God," he says.

In the lobby Colonel Ratay was conferring with Percy Black. Sitting erect on a bench along the wall, Lebel was staring into space.

"Let's go across the *place* and have breakfast," I said to him.

The Brasserie du Commerce with its cracked marble-topped tables and the flies buzzing around the stained lithographs over the *caissière's* desk resembles any and all of those countless places you and I have stopped at all over France for an omelet and a bottle of wine. After a second round of *oeufs sur le plat* and several *cafés filtre* Lebel began to relax.

"All the same," he said, "it was a close thing."

"Two minutes to spare," I said. "The least the Casablancans can do to express their gratitude is to rename the Place de l'Horloge after you."

"Getting into Casa was not difficult," he said. "It was almost dawn when we approached the railroad bridge where I knew our troops were, and our white flag showed up clearly. At division headquarters we explained the situation to General Desré and he accompanied us to the headquarters of Admiral Ronarch, in command of coastal defense.

Ronarch is a big man, over six feet. He speaks excellent English. However, I pointed out to him in French that the Americans questioned the intentions of the French Navy in regard to the Army cease-fire order. The Admiral read the order carefully and turned to Colonel Ratay. 'This order goes for the French Navy as well,' he said.

" 'That is all I want to know,' the Colonel said.

"As we recrossed the city the streets were filled with people going to work as usual. From where the road passes the Roches Noires we could see your bombers taking off from a carrier. Colonel Ratay kept urging the driver to hurry. No one bothered us until the very last lap when some of your boys took a few pot shots at us from the woods outside Fedala. Arrived at Third Division C.P., Colonel Ratay rushed in to report to General Patton. You know the rest."

For a while Lebel was silent.

"Earlier last night, how did you make out with our boys of the Thirtieth R.L.G.?" I asked.

Lebel swallowed the last of his coffee, wiped his mouth, and, for the first time, smiled.

"They couldn't have been nicer," he said. "The lieutenant offered me cigarettes and said we must at once get to battalion headquarters with the good news. Then he seemed a little embarrassed. 'I'm afraid we'll have to blindfold you,' he said. 'Orders.' Nobody had a blindfold so I offered them my handkerchief. 'That will be fine,' he said. 'If you don't mind, just blindfold yourself.'

"Pretty soon it became evident that the lieutenant had lost his way. As it happened, the Arabs had told me the location of your battalion headquarters — the same little shack in which we had our regimental *popote* during the summer maneuvers.

" 'If you will allow me to take off this blindfold,' I said, 'I will show you the way.'

" 'That will be fine,' the lieutenant said.

"At battalion headquarters they were very nice. Insisted on coffee and cigarettes. The captain there told the lieutenant he thought we ought to report to Task Force Headquarters.

" 'Where is that?' the lieutenant asked.

" 'I don't know,' the captain said.

" 'At the Hotel Miramar,' I said. The Arabs had told me that, too. 'If you will allow me, I'll drive you there.'

" 'That will be fine,' the lieutenant said.

"When we arrived there we parked the car at the foot of the drive. He was quite apologetic.

" 'I hate to ask you this,' he said, 'but you know how these higher headquarters are. Would you mind very much putting on your blindfold again, just to walk up the steps? Thanks. That will be fine.' "

A little later, when Lebel and I walked up the selfsame steps, General Keyes was standing in the entrance.

"Just the man I am looking for," he said to Lebel. "Have you got your car here?"

"Yes, sir."

"I want you to drive to Rabat as soon as possible and invite General Noguès and the Commanding Generals of the Ground and Air Forces of Morocco to come to the Hotel Miramar at three o'clock this afternoon to meet General Patton. O.K.?"

Lebel, who had been wiping his face with his handkerchief, replaced it carefully in his breast pocket.

"That will be fine, sir," he said.

Shortly before three o'clock General Patton ordered a guard of honor drawn up before the hotel entrance. At the prescribed hour a black limousine with motorcycle outriders swept up the drive. Out of it got General Noguès, trim, erect, ascetic, rather Spanish in appearance. He walked smartly up the steps, followed by General Lascroux, the compact, stoutish Commander of the Ground Forces, and General La Houlle, Chief of the French Air Forces, whose genial, forthright aspect made an immediately favorable impression.

At the top of the steps they were met by General Keyes, who escorted them to the smoking room, where General Patton received them.

A preliminary conference attended by Admirals Hewitt and Hall had taken place with the French Admirals, Michelier and Ronarch, who had arrived from Casa an hour earlier. Matters concerning the ports had been discussed. Michelier had been *pincé* and difficult, but thawed out more or less when Admiral Hewitt offered to shake hands.

General Patton now opened the full séance by expressing his admiration for the courage and skill shown by the French armed forces during the three days of battle.

"We are now met to come to terms," he said. "Here they are."

As the conditions of Treaty C were read aloud and the full import of their stringency began to sink in, the faces of the French grew more and more somber. At the end there was a strained silence, then General Noguès arose. "Permit me to point out," he said, "that if these terms are enforced it means the end of the French Protectorate in Morocco."

In the discussion which followed it became apparent that while Treaty C as drawn might reasonably be applied to a civilian setup such as exists in Algeria, its literal enforcement here would virtually cancel the responsibility of the French Military Protectorate to maintain law and order in Morocco. If, as provided by the treaty, the French forces are disarmed and disbanded, to us will fall the entire task not only of preserving order among seven million Arabs and Berbers, but of securing the Spanish Zone frontier, the port of Casablanca, and the long and vulnerable lines of communication to far-off Tunisia — now our immediate goal. Communications with General Eisenhower in Gibraltar and with General Clark in Algiers are nil. General Patton is on his own.

It did not take him long to decide. Rising to his full height, he picked up the familiar typescript of Treaty C and tore it into small strips.

"Gentlemen," he said, "I had the pleasure of serving with your armed forces throughout two years of World War I. Needless to say, I have implicit faith in the word of honor of a French officer. If each of you in this room gives me his word of honor that there will be no further firing on American troops and ships, you may retain your arms and carry on as before — but under my orders. You will do thus and so. We will do this and that. Agreed?"

It was.

"There is, however, an additional condition upon which I must insist."

The faces of the French delegation, which had brightened considerably, lengthened.

"It is this," General Patton said, signaling one of his aides, "that you join me in a glass of champagne."

November 13, 1942. Yesterday was a black day. I hope never again to see the sights we saw from the roof of the Miramar and in the gaming rooms of the Casino. The conclusion of the three-day war with the French seemed a legitimate cause for rejoicing. But we had not reckoned with the Germans.

November 12 dawned bright and sunny. At the Miramar the staff busied itself with the detailed application of the cease-fire arrangement and with preparations for moving our headquarters from Fedala to Casablanca.

Beyond the breakwater the remaining unloaded transports rode lazily at anchor. The question had been raised as to whether to move them into Casa Harbor, but Admiral Hewitt decided that it was essential to reserve the limited Casablanca docking space for the D-5 convoy due to arrive in a matter of hours. It was a reasonable and logical decision but, as it turned out, a tragic one.

It was close to six o'clock in the afternoon when the seaward windows of the Hotel Miramar were shaken by two muffled explosions, followed minutes later by a third. From the veranda clouds of black smoke could be seen issuing from the decks and hatches of two of the transports. I went up to the roof. General Keyes and several members of the staff were training their glasses on the burning ships, which now numbered three. A terrible spectacle. Inspiring, nevertheless, was the magnificent rallying of landing craft from all the other nearby transports and cargo ships, and the orderly disembarkation of those aboard the doomed vessels who had not been killed by the initial explosions or trapped below. It was a grim night in the town of Fedala. Quarters for the hundreds of Navy personnel brought ashore were hastily commandeered in hotels, churches, private homes. In the incongruous surroundings of the beach Casino an emergency first-aid station was set up. There, throughout the night and the following day, Army and Navy medical personnel worked around the clock to bring what alleviation was possible to the badly shocked and horribly burned survivors.

When late that night those of us who had been helping out in town returned to the Miramar, two of the three transports, the *Edward Rutledge* and the *Hugh L. Scott,* were no more. But not until almost three in the morning did the red puffs of smoke above the now invisible hull of the *Tasker H. Bliss* die away as the waves closed over the sturdy old ship.

Rutledge, Scott, and *Bliss* — throughout the planning period in the Munitions Building, increasingly familiar names. During the ocean crossing they assumed tangible, visible identities. It was sad that in the deceptively peaceful-looking waters off the Fedala beaches, their mission all but accomplished, these three good friends should at the last fall prey to the German submarine wolf pack which together for fifteen days and nights we had successfully challenged and evaded.

CASABLANCA

Western Task Force Headquarters are now located in the very modern office building of the Shell Oil Company in Casablanca. The General and most of the staff, including yours truly, live in a far from modern hotel, inappropriately named the Majestic, from which we daily march to the office and back armed to the teeth with 45 automatic and Tommy gun — total weight 18 pounds.

It was exciting to get your first letters, three of them together. Yes, they have been interesting weeks. Yes, I do realize that the Darlan deal and the retention of Noguès have raised quite a stink at home. They have here, too. Casablanca is teeming with O.W.I. boys, journalists, and assorted visiting firemen, clamoring for immediate solution of the Jewish question, the democratization of the Arabs, and the turning over of North Africa to de Gaulle. The hearts of these enthusiasts are doubtless in the right place, and in the long run they are likely to get their way, though the wisdom of prematurely forcing their objectives remains to be seen. For the moment their demands appear impractical to, and will be resisted by, the military.

Why? Well, you already know most of it, but here goes. French North Africa today: At the eastern extremity, Tunisia, a Protectorate of France since 1881. Into it the Germans, since our landings, have been pouring troops with which the retreating Rommel is attempting to form a juncture. The elimination of the German Army from Tunisia is the immediate Allied objective. It is proving to be a toughie. In the center, Algeria, the largest of the three North African areas and the longest under French control. Divided into three *départements,* with *préfets, députés,* and specialized bureaucrats, it is technically part of France. Actually, its capital, Algiers, is the seat of the Allied High Command under General Eisenhower. To the west, forming the strategic northwest corner of the African continent, stands Morocco, a rugged country of some six or seven million Arabs and Berbers whose tribal civilization and local feudalism are centuries behind the present era. With the exception of the international city of Tangier and a narrow Mediterranean coastal strip opposite Gibraltar under Spanish control, the whole of this vast and restless territory is administered and kept in order by the French Protectorate centered at Rabat, the Moroccan capital.

The French are here by virtue of the Treaty of Fez of March 30, 1912, negotiated by the French Government and the then Sultan of Morocco with the assent of the Algeciras Conference nations, i.e. twelve European powers and the U.S.A. The treaty was frankly designed to allow the French a free hand in restoring law and order to a territory which throughout the nineteenth and well into the twentieth century presented, at Europe's threshold, a spectacle of unbridled violence and anarchy. Colonization, pacification, by whatever name it is called, France's undertaking in Morocco originated as a necessary job of policing. Fortunately for France and for Morocco its prime mover happened to be no ordinary policeman but a man of genius. You and I, together with all those who had occasion to visit Morocco during his administration, are well aware that Marshal Lyautey's policies were a brilliant synthesis of intelligence, humanity, and a passionate creativeness, and that the chief beneficiaries of his extraordinary gifts have been the Moroccans themselves. The Arabs know it. Eight out of ten Americans do not. The Arabs know that, too. They are watching current events, cautiously but with great interest, and biding their time.

Morocco continues to be ruled, administered, and policed, nominally by the Sultan, actually by the French Resident General, in whose person is vested all the powers of the French Protectorate, which is primarily a military protectorate, hence authoritarian, hence a convenient and expedient instrument for our purposes at the present time. Noguès guessed wrong in resisting us and in the long run he will probably pay dearly for his mistake.

Meanwhile General Patton's enlightened armistice terms have produced what appears to be a genuine cooperation from the Protectorate, in helping us bring order out of chaos in the port of Casablanca, in the furnishing of valuable military intelligence in respect to Spain, Spanish Morocco, and German troop dispositions north of the Pyrenees, and in many other ways.

Incidentally, each day uncovers new evidence as to the determination and skill with which Noguès managed to bamboozle and frustrate the German Armistice Commission. This, together with a loathing for the Germans which fully equals your own, should appeal to you. Yes, Noguès bears watching, but he knows his Morocco, his Arabs, his Sultan, and his job. To take over the last would require the services of a good many more U.S. divisions than are at present available. To those, therefore, who taunt you in re our dealings with Vichyites, fascists, pro-Germans, turncoats, and traitors, suggest a look at the map of North Africa, and, if the figures are available, the present Allied military strength on this continent. From the fighting front in Tunisia run your finger along the four or five hundred miles of the single railroad line backtracking through wild country peopled by twenty million unpredictable Moslems to the port of Casablanca. In the event of the neutralization of Gibraltar and the closing off of the Mediterranean, Casablanca becomes virtually the sole mouth for the feeding and supplying of the entire expedition. In view of our highly vulnerable lines of communication a simple question is, I think, in order. Should the responsible military commanders on the spot be guided by political considerations or military expediency? From those obsessed by visions of overnight political reforms you may get a dusty answer, but that of General Patton insofar as Morocco is concerned is short and to the point: "Let the French police the country, and let *us* get on with the war."

The Darlan argument I beg leave to duck until I know all the facts. However, it seems reasonable to suppose that General Mark Clark, who, as General Eisenhower's deputy, made the deal, found in the Admiral a ready and perhaps the only immediate answer to the question above propounded. All I know is that Darlan, an unmitigated S.O.B., did produce a cease-fire and a rapid win-over of General Boisson, meaning French West Africa including, of course, Dakar, not to speak of the *Richelieu,* half a dozen Air groups, and over fifty thousand trained troops. The present setup which emerged from the deal does seem a bit messy. Darlan, head of civil government for all North Africa. Chatel remains local civilian governor of Algeria. Noguès remains Resident General of Morocco. (O.K. with us.) Giraud, in command of French armed forces and responsible for the organization of an enlarged French Army to serve under General Eisenhower. Poor Giraud. It seems he was under a complete misapprehension as to his role in Operation Torch. He is a good soldier, a fine man, a political zero. Yes, there is certainly room for improvement in Algiers, but the burning question is, or was, what Frenchman could get his orders obeyed by the African Army? Giraud couldn't, Juin wouldn't, Darlan could and did. Which brings us to the Vichy-Gaullist hassle.

To date there are virtually no de Gaullists per se in Morocco. There are naturally quite a few Frenchmen who are not in power who would like to be. These, invoking the name of de Gaulle, clamor on the doorsteps of our consulates, the hotels housing the newspaper boys, and our own G-2, vilifying the Vichyites, the fascists, the pro-Germans, the turncoats, and the traitors; that is to say, the present administration. I hold no brief for any of the above categories, but one of them, the first, should be defined. In North Africa a Vichyite is one who at the time of our landings believed that Marshal Pétain was still the legally constituted chief of the French state. If the term Vichyite were synonymous with the rest of the above sobriquets, then the entire French Navy and the overwhelming majority of the French Army of North Africa are fascist, pro-German, etc., etc. The *reductio ad absurdum* is obvious. Except for the die-hard Navy, the majority of the French armed services wanted to come over to our side. The sticking point, and unfortunately it was underevaluated, was, and is, the rigidly legal conception of duty and honor almost universally held by the professional officers of all the French armed services. Unlike the blind subservience of German military discipline, this deeply ingrained characteristic is a specialized, not to say paradoxical, reflection of French individualism. It was cleverly capitalized and exploited by Vichy. Every officer was required to take, and did take, a solemn individual personal oath pledging himself to honor and obey for better or for worse the orders of Marshal Pétain as transmitted by *the legal chain of command*. Thus military disobedience involves the breaking of one's oath and personal dishonor. That it may also terminate career, emoluments, pension, and imperil one's family in the enemy-occupied homeland are other factors, but these are secondary. Dueling is no longer prevalent in France, but the "code" has left deep grooves in the individual military make-up, and to a French officer "personal honor" is not just a phrase but a four-dimensional reality. General Clark during one of his early hectic days or nights ashore is reported to have said that if one more Frenchman mentioned his "honor," he would slug him. General Patton, on the other hand, made an investment in French honor which is paying dividends.

The African Army is made up of professionals — the best in the entire French Army. Their commanders were asked, on the strength, incidentally, of very meager information, to break their oath and furthermore risk overwhelming German reaction to violation of the 1940 armistice terms. Men like Mast and Béthouart, who took a chance with the full knowledge that their brother officers would label their actions as out-and-out dissidence — in the French military calendar a crime more heinous than mutiny on the high seas — showed rare moral as well as physical courage. In civilian Algiers, Mast's plans met with considerable success. In Rabat, capital of the Military Protectorate, Béthouart's plucky try was a fiasco. Why? Because from the point of view of his superiors he was merely another dissident General. General Clark presumably came to the conclusion that his choice lay between continuing bloodshed and enlisting the services of the highest link in the French legal chain of command. That this link should be personified by the unsavory Darlan is unfortunate, but as a temporary expedient he has been effective. To make a long story short, the Army's position — I mean our Army — is as follows: primary active object, to get on with the war in Tunisia with the least possible loss of life; primary negative object, not to upset the precarious North African apple cart. It is just as simple — and as complicated — as that.

November 21, 1942. Have been appointed liaison officer from Western Task Force to the Protectorate of Morocco, and will leave for Rabat, the capital, in a few days to report to a Colonel Guillaume, who is head of the Direction des Affaires Politiques, known as "la D.A.P." All the other "Directions," i.e. Ministries, are obliged to consult and correlate with D.A.P. all matters directly or indirectly concerning native affairs. Since this is tantamount to *all* matters, Colonel Guillaume's influence is second only to that of Noguès himself. D.A.P. will provide me with an office and clerical assistance and my job will be to transmit General Patton's wishes to General Noguès, see that they are executed, and keep Percy Black informed "as to what the hell goes on up there." In addition to the above, I am to cooperate with our "local troop commanders," which presently means General Anderson, whose 3d Division is encamped in a cork forest north of the capital. Should be interesting, and since I am the first and only liaison officer at Rabat from this headquarters, I will be entirely on my own, always a desirable feature in this or any other Army.

CHAPTER III

Rabat

(November, 1942–January, 1943)

November 25, 1942. The Casablanca road, you will remember, enters Rabat down near the native quarter. The large ogive portal seemed pleasantly familiar and the storks still perch on the crenelated walls. Once inside, however, you would hardly recognize the place. The Medina and the Casbah des Oudaias are, of course, unchanged and unchangeable, but the old Transat Hotel is no more, having been superseded by the Balima, in whose imposing lobby, immediately after the fall of France, Lord Gort and Duff Cooper cooled their heels while waiting for the interview with Noguès which never materialized.

The fields and *terrains vagues* which, when we were here, sprawled up to the hardly completed Residence of Lyautey are now a solidly developed residential district of fine and beautifully kept-up villas — out of California by Moorish Spain.

The D.A.P. headquarters is close to the Residence and, like most of the other administration buildings, surrounds a colonnaded courtyard. The turbaned Berber sentries saluted smartly and an elderly *chaouch,* or orderly, conducted me up the stairs to the outer office of the *directeur.* The latter's Chef de Cabinet, Commandant Pantalacci, received me with great politeness. "The Colonel is looking forward to welcoming you," he said.

Through the open door I could see a part of the large corner office. On one wall a huge three-dimensional relief map of Morocco. Through the window, a fine view of the Chella, necropolis of former sultans, and, like the Acropolis, a "must," you will remember, by moonlight.

We went in. A compact figure in khaki arose, hand outstretched across the enormous desk. Black hair swept back from a high forehead. Aquiline nose. Intense dark eyes, aware, penetrating, luminous. Colonel Augustin Guillaume, Chief of the D.A.P., instantly recognizable as the type of officer responsible for the greatness of the French Army in its heyday. Later that afternoon I learned from Pantalacci something of Guillaume's record to date. Born 1895 in the Hautes Alpes, graduated 1914 from Saint-Cyr just in time to leave for the Vosges with an active combat unit, naturally a battalion of *chasseurs alpins*. Taken prisoner November, 1914. Three escape attempts landed him in a German disciplinary camp near the Russian frontier, where in company with a certain Captain Charles de Gaulle he improved the idle hours by mastering both German and Russian. Immediately after World War I he embarked on the determining course of his career by applying for and being received into the elite corps of les Officiers des Affaires Indigènes of Lyautey in Morocco. From then on his advance was rapid, his distinctions and citations numerous. Appointed to his present job in 1940, one of his important contributions to the war effort has been the clandestine organization, under cover of his official position and the noses of the German Armistice Commission, of those indefatigable partisans and extracurricular mountain fighters the Berber *goumiers* of the Atlas. He should be fun to work with.

Have been assigned an office across the hall with a lovely stove. Important, as there is no central heating and winter is practically upon us. My billet has been arranged for *chez* le Capitaine et Madame de Battisti, who have a villa in the Orangerie section of Rabat outside the walls. Am on my way there now to meet them and get bedded down, and tomorrow morning will call on General Noguès. I think I'm going to like this job.

November 30, 1942. Yes, I *do* like this job, which incidentally keeps me good and busy. A typical day? No such thing, since each day raises problems as diverse as the disposition of the Loyalist Spanish internees and the new tariff to be established for 3d Division by the local Association of Bordel Madams. However, here is how most days start.

Am awakened at 7 A.M. by Mohammed, my Berber orderly, who enters my comfortable room on the second floor of the Villa Mon Repos with a tray on which is a cup of tea brewed by Madame de Battisti, who is dark, decorative, rather shy, and very nice. From across the hall, Capitaine de Battisti — a dashing young cavalry officer, amusing and attractive — sings out, *"La salle de bain est à vous, mon commandant."*

Mohammed has brought my Citroën — furnished by D.A.P. — to the door. It was a week before I discovered by accident that since I had not told him he could drive the car by himself, Mohammed and a *copain* each morning had been pushing it by hand from the garage a mile or so away.

Now we are rolling through the quiet streets, under the arched portal, and up to the Balima, at which an American mess has been established in the basement. Breakfast, usually with one of our consular officials, Mayer or Hooker Doolittle or both. By 8:30 am driving up the broad boulevard past the arcades of shops, the Poste et Télégraphe, the Méchouar, through whose entrance the palace of the Sultan can be glimpsed, up to the D.A.P., which is only a few yards from the rear, or working, entrance of the Residence.

The morning grist: from Guillaume's office, the French translation of yesterday's German propaganda broadcast in Arabic. "The Anglo-Saxons have decided to deliver you to the Jews as they have your brother Moslems in Palestine. . . . In North Africa hundreds of Moslems have gone before American firing squads for expressing hostile sentiments against the Anglo-Saxon aggressors. . . . American requisitioning of food reduces Moslems to starvation. . . . American violation of native religious customs," etc., etc. Unfortunately, the technique of the "big lie" is quite successful among the Arabs.

Bulletin issued by the "Front National de Libération" — unsigned, no address: "Inhabitants of Morocco! The enemies of America and her Allies are still solidly installed in North Africa. Darlan, Noguès, and Co., the apostles of Nazism, responsible for leading France to the abyss, for the pillaging of her soil and that of her colonies, for the massacre of our soldiers and sailors, these men at the head of a powerful Fifth

Column in the pay of Germany are still in power. They must be pitilessly exterminated, death to the spies, traitors and adventurers."

Memo from the Sûreté: "I have the honor to inform you that last evening at 19:00 an American soldier accompanied by a Mauresque woman was pursued down the Avenue Moulay Hassan by four hundred enraged natives including thirty of the Sultan's Black Guard. The soldier and the woman finally eluded their pursuers by taking refuge in a house of prostitution. Investigation of the incident indicates that the anger of the crowd was directed not specifically against the United States Army but rather towards the Mauresque woman, her manner of dress, particularly the absence of a veil, and the company she was keeping. I remain, with highest consideration," etc.

Finally, a note from Percy Black: "Find out why the hell they haven't released the 'de Gaulliste' prisoners. Get a list of all inmates of Moroccan work-camps. Am sending Lt. Auberjonois to Rabat to take charge of censorship of Radio Maroc and the French Press."

Report from the Deuxième Bureau on enemy units north of the Pyrenees and enemy capabilities in re Spain and the Spanish Zone.

Conference with Pantalacci, Guillaume, and Noguès — the last polite, affable, cooperative in certain matters, procrastinating in others. His vast office in the Residence is next the salon in which you and I once had tea with Lyautey. Noguès was then a *capitaine* on his staff, he told me, and it was he who delivered to the Marshal the telegram announcing World War I. "They are mad, mad, mad," the Marshal cried. "A war between Europeans is a civil war and that is the worst kind of all."

Leading from the Resident's office to the rear entrance is a corridor whose walls are hung with straw matting. Off this corridor are the bureaus of the Resident General's Cabinet, whose Chief is Monsieur Hardion. I stop in to tell him, together with his assistant Lalouette and de Carbonel, who oversees Radio Maroc, of the censorship plans.

"If our press and radio are to be taken over," Hardion said, his intense dark eyes flashing, "I shall resign." He would like to. Almost any excuse to get back to his tank outfit and fight Germans would do. A tough guy, Hardion, but an able one and likable.

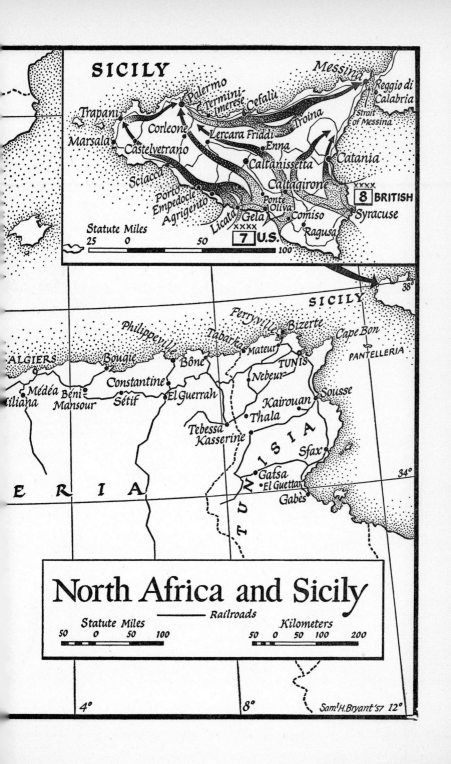

SICILY

Messina
Reggio di Calabria
Trapani
Palermo
Termini-Imerese
Cefalu
Troina
Strait of Messina
Marsala
Corleone
Lercara Friddi
Castelvetrano
Enna
Catania
Sciacca
Caltanissetta
Porto Empedocle
Caltagirone
XXXX
Agrigento
Ponte Olivo
8 BRITISH
Licata
Gela
Comiso
Syracuse
XXXX
Ragusa
7 U.S.

Statute Miles
25   0   50   100

SICILY   38°

Ferryville Bizerte
Philippeville Tabarka
Cape Bon
ALGIERS   Bougie   Bône   Mateur   PANTELLERIA
Médéa Béni Constantine TUNIS
iliana Mansour Sétif El Guerrah Nebeur
Kairouan   Sousse
Tebessa Thala
Kasserine   T U N I S I A
Sfax
E R I A   34°
Gafsa
El Guettar
Gabès

North Africa and Sicily

——— Railroads

Statute Miles   Kilometers
50   0   50   100   50 0 50 100   200

4°   8°   Sam¹ H. Bryant '57 12°

"Don't be hasty," I said. "You will find Auberjonois quite reasonable."

He looked glum.

Across the hall to the office of Colonel Piatte, Chef du Cabinet Militaire — crisp, nervous, intelligent, competent. He fills me in on some additional Deuxième Bureau stuff and I depart.

Next stop, Direction des Communications, Production Industrielle, et Travaille, which is halfway down the boulevard just below the impressive Finance Ministry, presided over by the brilliant and talented Ludovic Tron. Monsieur N., director of DCPIT, is neither brilliant nor talented. Furthermore he has a tendency to stall. He is doing it now over the matter of the work-camp internees.

"It will take some time, several weeks, to assemble the complete list," he says.

"We require it today."

"Impossible."

"In that case" — rising and looking sad — "my usefulness here is at an end. I shall ask to be recalled from Rabat. It will be necessary, of course, for me to explain not only to General Patton but also to General Noguès, whom I have this moment left and who assured me of your cooperation, exactly why I am leaving."

"Let me see what I can do," he says nervously.

"Fine."

Lunch at the Balima with our Lieutenant Cameron, who has recently set up our Counter Intelligence office in a nearby building. He passes on some dope which tends to confirm certain of our misgivings in re the Chief of the French Sûreté.

Back to Colonel Guillaume's office to meet the impressive and picturesque Caïd El Ayadi El Hachemi. His territory extends from Marrakech to the Oued Oumer Ribia, his followers number over one hundred thousand rifles. In southern Morocco he is second only in importance to the Glaoui, whom incidentally I visited a fortnight ago when he was *de passage* at Casablanca. We reminisced about General Daugan and the old days and I have a date to see him again in Marrakech. Ayadi professed warm friendship for the U.S.A. and will be glad to welcome the commander of any American troops that may enter his region.

I was halfway through my written report to Percy when a *chaouch* knocked and entered bearing a bulky envelope. Outside, the initials DCPIT. Inside, the list of work-camp internees with a polite covering note from Monsieur N. It would seem that with the French, the mournful veiled-threat technique is preferable to shouting and desk-pounding, at which in any event I am deficient.

Well, that was today. Tomorrow may be entirely different.

P.S. The evening "Vigie" has a paragraph about an *"incendie au Grove Coconut, boîte de nuit populaire de Boston dans la Massachusetts. Plusieurs morts ont été signalés."* Anyone we know?

December 19, 1942. Yesterday drove in to Casablanca to make a verbal report on a number of things to Percy. In order to have a place where he may interview such shady characters as would hesitate to come openly to our headquarters, Percy has acquired — by the simple process of evicting a rich collaborator — a fine apartment of neo-Chinese décor on an upper floor of a modern building at 227 Boulevard de la Gare, complete with a white-coated houseman, formerly an Austrian spy. This comfortable hideaway he shares with Bunny Carter and Piggy Warburg,* the latter presently engaged in confecting for Washington a voluminous report to be entitled "Morocco and the Jewish Question."

Around ten or so, as we were preparing to turn in — yes, there is an extra bedroom — the telephone rang.

"Shall I answer it?" I said.

"It's tapped," Percy said. "Makes a difference what you say. I'll take it."

He listened with mounting exasperation. "Algiers again," Percy said, hanging up. "They have ordered General Patton to take over Radio Maroc *at once,* by force if necessary. Reason given, antidemocratic broadcast yesterday to the effect that an authoritarian government was still necessary in Morocco. Real reason, British annoyance over Radio

---

* Captain Paul Warburg.

Maroc beating the B.B.C.'s daily news bulletin by one hour due to some mix-up over double daylight-saving time."

Percy got up, fixed me with a beady eye. "Sorry, Piggy — I mean Bunny —" he said, "you will have to return to Rabat immediately and take over the station."

"O.K., Percy," I said, "but in case force becomes necessary, give me something in writing."

"The Supreme Commander," Percy scribbled on a half sheet of scented notepaper, "has directed General Patton to take over full control of Radio Maroc. Major Codman will take charge of the station tonight. He will have full authority to designate whomever he may detail to represent him. By order of General George S. Patton, Jr., by Colonel Percy Black, A.C. of S. G-2, Western Task Force."

"It would be better on green or pink paper with at least one seal," I said, "but maybe it will do the trick."

During dinner it had started raining and now it was pouring. The drive back to Rabat was something of a nightmare. Sheets of solid water lashed at the wiperless windshield and dimmed headlights. A close call at the jutting bridge abutment over the ravine. Another at the crossroads in Boulhaut. A relief to pass through the dripping Rabat archway and limp up the streaming boulevard, two cylinders out of four missing, to the darkened front door of Monsieur Hardion's villa.

A ring. A long wait. Footsteps on the stairs. The door opens a crack. Monsieur Hardion, an overcoat over his pajamas.

"Sorry to bother you at this time of night, but I bear an important message."

"Come in. Come in."

"My instructions are to take over Radio Maroc as of now." I handed Monsieur Hardion Percy's perfumed note. As he read it, his mouth became a straight hard line.

"That settles it," he said. "I shall resign."

"Not until tomorrow," I said. "There is work to be done."

"One moment," he said. Telephone. A number. A wait. A voice. "Is that you, Carbonel? Here, Hardion. Sorry to bother you at this hour, but your presence is required here immediately." Click.

"Are you all right, Bernard?" A silvery mellifluous voice from the stair landing. Leaning gracefully over the banisters, Madame Hardion, her blond good looks becomingly set off by the diaphanous scarf thrown carelessly over her negligee.

"Yes, quite all right. But you, Nellie, you must not take cold."

She starts down the stairs. "Ah, it's the Commandant Codman." Surprise. Business of rearranging scarf. A good entrance.

A knock on the front door. Madame Hardion opens it. Carbonel enters breathing hard and dripping pools of water. Conference. Hardion and Carbonel agree to accompany me to Radio Maroc. We sally forth into the torrential night. Silhouetted in the doorway, Madame Hardion, in beautifully modulated phrases, beseeches Bernard to be careful, to be prudent.

Radio Maroc is situated on an upper floor of the huge Poste, Téléphone et Télégraphe Building halfway up the boulevard. The rain-sodden sentry presented arms in dispirited fashion. In the vast marble-floored rotunda our footsteps echoed hollowly. No one about. The mezzanine offices dark, empty. We march on up the stairs to the floor above. Empty, dark. Next floor, ditto. Through a closed door on the top floor the sound of violins. We enter. A phonograph plays softly. Standing before the microphone, Monsieur Godefroy, *"le speaker,"* French for announcer, declaiming like a *sociétaire* of the Théâtre Français, *"Ici Radio-Maroc, vingt-trois heures trente. Les nouvelles sont bonnes. Sur le front russe trois cent chars allemands anéantis. . . ."*

Sitting at the control board, intently following the script, a familiar, if unexpected, figure — Lieutenant Auberjonois.

"Fernand," I said, "how come?"

Still following the script, Auberjonois, as I sat down beside him, hissed in my ear, "Algiers called up about an hour ago to ask if Radio Maroc had been taken over, and, if not, to take it over immediately, by force, if necessary. There was no one around, so I took it over."

"Fine." Monsieur Godefroy was signing off. I stood up and in solemn tones read, once again, Percy's note.

"Postscript: Under the authority vested in me by virtue of the above order, I designate Lieutenant Auberjonois, G-2, Western Task Force, to take full charge of Station Radio Maroc, and to remain in full charge, by force, if necessary, until further notice. And now," I said, not into the mike, "let's all go over to the Balima and have a drink."

P.S. Next morning bright and early I called the ever-cooperative Colonel Lauer, Chief of Staff of the 3d Division, and outlined my need for an Arabic scholar to cover the Moslem broadcasts.

"I have just the man," Colonel Lauer said. "Lieutenant Archibald Roosevelt."

"Of course, why didn't I think of it?"

We got Archie on the phone.

Lieutenant Roosevelt is hereby designated to take over censorship of the Arab broadcasts. By force, if necessary.

> *Christmas Day, 1942 — Rabat. Admiral Jean François Darlan, originally representative of the Vichy Government in Algiers, had arranged the general armistice between the French and American troops in early November. With Anglo-American approval, Darlan remained French Chief of State in North Africa until his assassination on 24 December 1942. General Henri Giraud succeeded him.*

Have just come from a memorial service at the cathedral for the late Admiral Darlan, who was shot on Christmas Eve by a young man named Bonnier de la Chapelle, who in turn will be shot tomorrow, having been tried and convicted this morning by the French authorities. All the officials, the wealth, and the beauty of Rabat were there in their Sunday best. All behaved with decorum, but I have seldom attended a less funereal gathering. After the service the congregation gathered in groups under the palms in front of the cathedral exchanging amenities and gossip.

To forestall what I feel may be your next question, NO, I do NOT think the Darlan solution might well be applied to the local picture. Besides my weakness for Madame Noguès, I have grown quite attached to the General himself, and anyway am against assassination on general principles. As a matter of fact, Madame Noguès, nee Delcassé, is full of charm. She asks, as always, after you.

Seriously, I am still convinced that General Patton is right in preserving, at least for the time being, the present administration in Morocco and making the French responsible for law, order, and our communications. Like every capital, Rabat presents a veneer of superficiality and *inconscience*. Beneath the not wholly misleading surface, a lot of hard, conscientious, and patriotic work has been and is being accomplished. For those who judge Rabat chiefly in terms of its continuous round of intramural dinner parties, its bickerings and flirtations, the formal lunches and Sunday-afternoon receptions at the Residence, it might prove something of an eye opener to accompany General Noguès on one of his frequent trips into the interior or merely as far as the Sultan's palace.

Smooth functioning of the Protectorate is premised, as Marshal Lyautey* pointed out, on close working cooperation between the Sultan and the Resident General. Since the days of the great marshal some Residents have lost sight of this elementary principle. The present Sultan, His Majesty Sidi Mohammed Ben Youssef, whom you and I met when he was a delicate and seemingly ineffective youth of fifteen or sixteen, is now in his middle thirties. He is still fragile in appearance but has acquired real dignity and considerable charm. He is intelligent, sensitive, willful, and clever. A clumsy Resident could find him quite a problem. Noguès has handled the relationship with consummate skill. Understanding, flexibility, personal warmth, firmness, in exactly the right proportions. El Glaoui, Pasha de Marrakech, almost the last of the great feudal overlords, is still the most powerful individual Moslem chieftain of Morocco. His entire career has been closely identified with the French and he well knows where his bread is buttered. The same is true of the vastly erudite Chérif Kitani, head of the important religious brotherhood of Kitanya. Surrounded by the rare books of his famous library in Fez, he chuckles and smiles, and rumbles — a benign, portly, white-whiskered Moslem Santa Claus. But despite the surface geniality, he, like the Glaoui, must be kept in line.

Throughout the entire complex native pattern of friendly, semi-friendly, and potentially hostile tribes of Arab, Berber, and Arabized

* The first Resident General in French Morocco.

Berber collectivities of city, plain, and mountain, their caïds and pashas, their individual peculiarities, their local customs, their deep-seated xenophobia, continuous control and a very sure touch is essential. Noguès has it.

So there it is. Noguès guessed wrong, tragically wrong, in resisting us. Since the landings he has been, and continues to be, useful to us. I am quite aware that in addition to the de Gaullists, most of our own press and consular representatives are out to get his scalp. They will probably succeed. I only hope that by the time they do, we shall have passed on to other fields of action. Merry Christmas.

December 29, 1942. Well, Christmas is over and so is Admiral Darlan. Giraud is in — you probably heard his speech, or rather interview, last night and everything seems to be going along fairly well.

Yesterday was a sort of typical quiet Sunday. It went something like this: 7 A.M., tea in bed — Sidi's own minted tea. Up. Shaved before the Captain now instead of after. Brahmin, my orderly, brings the car around. It is still dark, but the east is getting pink. Drive through the villa quarter, threading my way among bicyclists, natives, and children, through the old walls — the storks are not back from Alsace yet — and through the center of the town, which is already awakening. *Porgy and Bess* themes — Arabs hawking their morning papers. Breakfast at the hotel with the division officers. American breakfast — eggs, real coffee, sugar, cream. Up the hill to the lazy Residence. Sunrise.

Work, reports, interviews, Sunday lunch at the house of the father-in-law of my Corsican captain. Father-in-law is Alsatian and a doctor — his wife Belgian. He came here the year I was born. In those days an Arab family paid the doctor one hundred francs a year to keep them in good health, but they kept running in eighth cousins on him, until finally he struck.

Tending the Sultan paid better but had certain inconveniences. He, the doctor, came down with typhus on one occasion when visiting *Sa Majesté* up in the hills somewhere. The local medics pronounced him dead and Father-in-law came out of a two weeks' coma just in time to prevent the coffin lid from being nailed down on him. Then he told about tending one of the royal wives. He was only allowed to use his stethoscope through a slit in the harem door — but even today Mrs. Father-in-law looks rather prim and says, "I have the impression you profited by your visit just the same."

There is a helluva lot of work to do here and I thoroughly enjoy my end of it, which is liaison of various and very varied kinds with the Residence. Of course, I don't know how long my job will last, as things are in rather a state of flux.

I am in somewhat of a dither. Who should blow in here but Ted Curtis and Harold.* They flew up here to say that they had been cabling the Pentagon to send me right over in a bomber to do liaison work. They were astounded to learn that I *had* come over "the hard way." They stopped in on their way up to see my General, who said, "Certainly *not*," so now the tussle is on.

My General arrived here today — in fine form. "The aviation people are after you. I told them that, as always, they were too late. Moreover, you will go further and see more with me." Maybe he's right, I really don't know, but nothing I do or don't do would have much to do with deciding it. As a matter of fact, the whole trip from the very beginning has been and *is* wholly fascinating, not to say amazing.

January 13, 1943. My General has just made me his Assistant Deputy Chief of Staff and says he has no intention of giving me to the Air. I imagine you saw the piece about him in *Life.* Yesterday he got the Grande Croix from the Sultan. The citation in Arabic translates *"Les lions dans leurs tanières tremblent en le voyant approcher"* ("Lions in their lairs tremble at his approach") — and so does everyone else. He has been swell to me and, as a great treat, promises us all a warm summer.

January 24, 1943. The news of Alec Woollcott's death came out in this morning's news flash and I find myself feeling immeasurably sad about

---

* Colonel Edward C. Curtis, General Spaatz's Chief Executive Officer, and Major Harold Willis, in charge of liaison with the French.

it. In a queer but fundamental way he was very much engraved in our lives. In the last year or two I had grown really fond of him and from his last letter I gathered that you and he were getting to be fairly close buddies. It is this aspect I mind the most, since now, of all times, I hate to think of the disappearance of anything or anybody that you and I share in common. Of our "public" friends, I think that I shall miss him more than anyone since George Gershwin.

Speaking of which, last evening I found myself for the first time since landing actually *alone* for a couple of hours. We have an excellent Steinway in the apartment and I surprised myself by remembering — the last time I tried I hadn't been able to, so it must have been telepathy or something — a lot of George's old tunes, including, naturally, "Cousin in Milwaukee" and "You Can't Take That Away from Me," and thinking more than ever of our funny house in Marion, of George's cigar and fur overcoat, and of 53 Pinckney Street, and hoping that latter song title hadn't any catch in it and was basically sound. Of course it *is* and I must have a touch of the good old African *cafard* or I wouldn't write this way.

CHAPTER IV

Anfa Conference

(January–April, 1943)

January 25, 1943. Now that it can be told, or at least some of it, here are a few minor side lights on the three-ring circus which yesterday closed a successful engagement at the Hotel Anfa.

To go back a bit, on New Year's Eve I made another trip to Casablanca to report to Percy. Dinner at his Chinese apartment with Bunny and P. Warburg. After dinner, Percy having (1) got rid of the cloak-and-dagger butler for the remainder of the evening, (2) carefully closed the doors of the salon, and (3) inspected the chandelier, among whose ornate convolutions he had the previous week discovered an ingeniously concealed microphone, motioned us to gather around him.

"Here is the dope," he said. "Top Secret, naturally. The Hotel Anfa, in the suburbs of Casablanca overlooking the ocean, together with a certain number of villas to be requisitioned, has been designated as the location for a very, very high-level conference to begin in about ten days and last about ten days. General Alfred Gruenther, General Clark's Chief of Staff, is responsible for organizing the party. General Patton will be responsible for military security. Plans are already drawn for surrounding the Anfa and satellite villas, in fact the whole hilltop on which they are situated, with rings of barbed wire and gun emplacements. Washington feels that this is as safe a place as any, and that the main problem will be to conceal the presence of the V.I.P.'s from local spies and enemy agents."

"The V.I.P.'s?"

"The President" — Percy lowered his voice — "Churchill, possibly

Stalin, the Joint Chiefs, the Combined Chiefs, everything but the kitchen stove. Oh, yes," Percy went on, "also de Gaulle and Giraud. This is where you come in, Codman. You are to report here for the duration of the conference and be available for interpreting or other odd jobs in connection with the French visitors."

It was past the witching hour and the arrival of the New Year when we finally turned in. We were all sleeping soundly when the sirens began their insistent wail. My wrist watch marked 3:10. Slipping on overcoats, we went out onto the balcony. Searchlights prodding the overcast. The antiaircraft guns making an unholy racket. The Casablanca acoustics seemed to amplify them out of all proportions. Two dull explosions, quite far off. Nothing more.

"I wonder how Washington will feel about that," Warburg said.

At breakfast we got the complete if meager report. Four four-engined German bombers had dropped a like number of medium-sized bombs. Very little damage to military personnel or property. One bomb landed in the Medina, killing more than a score of Arabs.* The A.A. people think they got one enemy bomber over the harbor. Not confirmed.

A few days before the conference was due to start I was having family supper with Captain and Madame de Battisti and their son Christian, a nice, if rather shy, boy, in his teens. I had been trying to think of an explanation consistent with security as to why I was leaving the Villa Mon Repos for a week or ten days. No explanation was necessary.

"Ah, you are off to Casa," Battisti said with a twinkle. "Doubtless you will be attending the Anfa Conference."

"The what?" playing dumb.

"*Ah, non,*" Madame de Battisti laughed, "do not bother to pretend. It is no secret, not even Polichinelle's."

"What is no secret?"

---

* General Patton went to the Medina the next afternoon and presented fifty thousand francs to the Chérif for distribution to the families of the dead. This made a great hit, and Patton became a man of fame, next in importance to El Glaoui.

"That Anfa is soon to be the meeting place of everyone in the world of any importance." Suzanne was really going strong now. "Your President, Monsieur Churchill, Generalissimo Stalin, His Holiness the Pope, General Marshall, General Eisenhower, everyone, even de Gaulle."

"*Voyons,* Suzanne," Battisti said, "let's not exaggerate. Of course," he continued, "once you started requisitioning the villas, every one of which has Arab servants, the cat was out of the bag. Mohammed sees your people installing ramps for a wheelchair in the best villa on the hilltop; he compares notes with his friend Mahmoud of the villa across the way, who has been watching with interest the arrival of cases from England containing the favorite brandy of the Prime Minister. Soon the news is all over Casa and half a day later every servant in Rabat has a complete list of all the *vedettes*. Our Amar recited us his list yesterday."

"You all know a lot more about it than I do," I said, attempting, doubtless unsuccessfully, to hide my discomfiture.

On the tenth I moved into Casablanca, i.e. Percy's apartment. Paul Harkins arranged for some desk space for me in his office at the Shell Building and from there I commuted daily to Anfa. Paul himself, responsible for setting up practically the entire conference, was out there early and late, ministering to the at times temperamental needs of the V.I.P.'s. By the twelfth, most of the big shots, except the President and his party, had dropped from the sky and been whisked from the airport to the hilltop in limousines whose windows, heavily plastered with mud, concealed the exalted personages from the gimlet eyes of Mohammed, Mahmoud, and Amar. On the fourteenth the President's C-54 slid into the field and he was conveyed swiftly, smoothly, and without incident to the star villa, Dar es Saada ("House of Truth"), complete with a huge sitting room, air-raid shelter, protective steel shutters, and swimming pool. Dar es Saada also lodged Harry Hopkins, Elliott Roosevelt — and a few days later young Franklin Roosevelt — together with a bevy of secret-service boys. Mr. Churchill's abode, the Villa Mirador, only slightly less luxurious, housed his son Randolph and certain members of the P.M.'s staff. Next morning General Eisenhower arrived, looking and sounding as though he had a very bad cold — he had — and in the afternoon, direct from his desert headquarters, General Sir Harold R. L. G. Alexander, Commander of the Middle East Forces, whose fiery sunburn and three-day beard in no way impaired the fine features of his arrestingly attractive face.

Seated in one of the deep leather chairs of the Anfa Hotel's lobby, a very familiar figure, Freddy Wildman,* talking earnestly to an Englishman in shorts and a two-day beard.

"Well, for God's sake." We pump one another's hand, and Freddy introduces me to the pleasant, unassuming Britisher, Air Marshal Sir Arthur Tedder.

The Air Marshal listens attentively and apparently sympathetically to Freddy's sales talk on close air support. After a while he passes his hand over his chin, looks at his watch, gets up. "Meeting with the Combined Chiefs in ten minutes. Better go and shave this thing off. Cheerio."

"What is your function, Freddy?"

"I am the eyes and ears of General Arnold," Freddy said. "The old man is upstairs taking a bath. After this shebang we fly on over to the Pacific theater."

A harassed waiter, French, dashes through the lobby with a tray. In hot pursuit, Paul Harkins, who catches him by the coattails and signals to me.

"Tell this bird that Admiral King has again complained that for the third day running his breakfast coffee is undrinkable."

"What's wrong with it?"

"Cold and weak."

I explain to the waiter.

"*Entendu, plus chaud, plus fort,*" he says, releasing himself from Paul's clutch.

That was my first job at the Anfa Conference. My second was interpreting for General Somervell, top Supply Chief, and General Giraud.

* Colonel Frederick S. Wildman, airman and wine man par excellence.

Had just got the latter installed in a nice pink villa halfway up from the compound entrance to the hotel when the call came from General Marshall's assistant, Colonel Frank McCarthy. "General Somervell will come there," he said. "Thinks it will be quieter than up here."

General Somervell is quite an impressive figure. If he weren't a General he would be a big business tycoon. I filled in General Giraud on who he was and by the time he arrived Giraud's eyes were gleaming in anticipation of the equipment which would be forthcoming for the newly formed French forces. General Somervell made a brisk, business-like entrance, shook hands all around, then in a genial but down-to-brass-tacks tone turned to me. "I want you to begin," he said, "by telling this Frog that Uncle Sam is no Santa Claus."

"Mon général, le Général Somervell voudrait établir qu'en principe l'Oncle Sam et le Père Noël, ça fait deux," I started. No, that would merely puzzle him. Taking a chance on General Somervell's knowledge of French, or rather lack of same, I transposed things a bit, trying to get across to Giraud that he would be wise to be modest in his demands and build up gradually. After a few exchanges things went well and you could see that both Generals were getting to rather like one another. Upshot, General Somervell said he would recommend virtually all of General Giraud's requests — subject, of course, to confirmation by the Joint and Combined Chiefs.

The next job, on the following day, was a good deal more formidable. Memo from Frank McCarthy: "General Marshall presents his compliments to General Giraud and invites him to attend formal session of the Combined Chiefs of Staff at 5:30 today in the conference room of the Hotel Anfa. General Somervell will call for you both at 5:25. Explain to General Giraud that those present at the meeting will be the following: General Marshall, Army; General Arnold, Air; Admiral King, Navy; General Brooke, Army; Admiral of the Fleet Sir Dudley Pound, Navy; Air Chief Marshal Sir Charles Portal, Air; Vice-Admiral the Lord Louis Mountbatten, Combined Operations.

At 5:25 to the second, General Somervell's car drew up to the entrance of the pink villa and at 5:29 we entered the conference room of the Hotel Anfa. The Combined Chiefs, already assembled, rose to greet General Giraud, who was then placed about halfway down the long conference table, with General Somervell on his right and me on his left.

General Marshall opened the meeting. "On behalf of the Combined Chiefs of Staff, General Giraud, allow me to welcome you to this conference and to express our pleasure at your being here."

Why the hell can't *I* think of the word for welcome? A pause. Across the table Lord Louis smiling quizzically.

"What is the French word for welcome, sir?" I said in what was supposed to be a whisper but which was perfectly audible up and down the table.

"Bienvenue," Lord Louis said, his smile broadening.

"Of course. Thanks. *Mon général, le Général Marshall vous souhaite la bienvenue et tient à vous exprimer de la part des* Combined Chiefs of Staff *tout le plaisir qu'ils ressentent,"* etc., etc.

After that it went fairly smoothly except for one impassioned harangue towards the end during which the General galloped along for five minutes without drawing breath. My translation of what I could remember of it took only two minutes, but if there were a few omissions — and there certainly were — no one seemed disturbed, least of all *le généal*. I think Giraud made a good impression on, and will obtain favorable action from, this exceedingly meticulous and realistic jury.

The next day I accompanied General Giraud to the Villa Mirador, where the Prime Minister wanted to see him alone. We rang the garden-gate bell and almost instantly Mr. Churchill emerged from the front door and hurried down the path, at a trot. Why is it that if one is familiar with the likeness of a great man only from photographs, the great man himself invariably seems smaller than one had imagined him? It is fair to say that if Giraud towered over the Englishman like a colossus, it was, as expected, Mr. Churchill who, in a matter of seconds, completely took over. *Soyez le bienvenu, général, entrez, entrez.* Very affable, full of steam. The evening before he had given his own Security Police heart failure by escaping from the compound.

Eventually he was found strolling by himself in the moonlight along the beach in the direction of the El Hank lighthouse.

"Interesting sea shells in this part of the world," he chortled, patting his bulging coat pockets.

Most of the Anfa evenings were taken up with dinner conferences at the President's villa or in the hotel. On a number of occasions a group of the top-layer V.I.P.'s dined with General Patton at the sumptuous Villa Mas, into which he had recently moved. It is situated on the slope below the Anfa compound and reflects the dubious taste — and character — of its owner, Casablanca's richest newspaper magnate. Percy, for his part, played host to various old friends or conferees momentarily out of a job. In the former category we had last evening Brigadier General A. C. Wedemeyer. He has come up fast and reportedly enjoys the high esteem of General Marshall, whom he accompanied to the conference. I liked him immensely, and so will you when — as he has promised to do — he looks you up on his return to the U.S.A.

Standard procedure for visiting firemen is a carefully guarded tour of the famous Casablanca *bousbir* — red-light district to you — conceived and constructed by Lyautey.

"If there must be a *quartier réservé*," the Marshal had observed, "and I suppose there must, let it at least be a thing of beauty." It is.

Situated in a corner of the Old Medina, or native quarter, it constitutes a complete walled city in itself with its own police, hospital, prison, shops, and all the rest.

Self-contained and containing, the *bousbir* engulfs its citizenesses in perpetuity. Only two possible ways out, by purchase or by marriage. Curiously enough, both occur not too infrequently.

Well, here we are at the arched portal. Another sight-seeing party, headed by Lord Louis Mountbatten, arrives simultaneously. We join forces, led by a French supervisor, and closely surrounded by an armed platoon of M.P.'s of the United States Army, we march down the gentle incline of the stone-paved street curving between shadowy houses whose ogive doors and windows are blankly dark. And now an open square, dimly discerned, silent but for the splashing fountain at its center. A cloud passes from before the face of the moon. Did Lyautey arrange for this too — the silvery rings of the fountain into which the unveiled Arab girl is dipping her earthen jug, the slender shimmering columns of the enveloping arcades against which robed figurines out of *Scheherazade* lean, watchful, waiting, one eye on the lookout for the potential client, the other appraising the ghostly couples gliding through cobalt shadows?

"By Jove" — Lord Louis's voice — "this is *something,* as you Americans say."

The supervisor leads the way to the other side of the square to the arched entrance of a narrow street plunging steeply downward. The moon is now framed in the center of the arch, doing unearthly things to the descending colonnades and the roofs spread out below. The street twists and turns. A light behind a shaded window. "Shall we take tea?" the supervisor says. No one demurs. The supervisor enters. We follow. A small bare room devoid of any furniture save the heavy floor matting and a low table set for tea. Seated behind it on the floor, an Arab girl in simple white robes. Very young, seventeen, eighteen perhaps. Pretty, except for the scar on her left cheek. Big brown eyes, frankly curious but traditionally diffident. The supervisor rattles along as she prepares the customary sweet mint tea. Statistics, tariffs, the special police problems involved. She hands us our glasses one by one, prettily, with complete self-assurance, simplicity, and dignity. Through the supervisor we ask her questions, most of them foolish, all of them childish. She smiles easily, cheerfully, quite contented with her lot, it would seem. The gaze she turns on each questioner is frank, open, but she never holds it long. A matter of politeness. Time to go. She does not rise. We bow and thank her. She smiles, keeping her eyes down.

The moon is in and out. Halfway up the street in the angle formed by two houses a couple of girls are chattering together. At our approach they burst out laughing, throw their skirts over their heads, and go into a violent invitational pantomime. "They are kidding us," Percy said. And why not? Surrounded by our armed guards, we must, in our beribboned uniforms, look fairly silly.

We recross the square and approach the entrance. The supervisor is reeling off more statistics. "Disease, yes, a serious problem. Before our arrival the venereal rate in all Moroccan reserved districts remained absolutely steady."

"What *was* the rate?" General Wedemeyer asked.

"One hundred per cent," the supervisor said. "However, by applying heroic measures we have reduced it — slightly."

"Bully for you," General Wedemeyer said. And to the M.P. sergeant, "O.K., Sergeant, you can dismiss your men now."

We made our way to Percy's car. Behind us the incisive tones of Lord Louis again. "Good show," he was saying. "Scenically, the finest I've ever visited — except, of course, Bhamawaddy in Upper Burma."

"Quite." In the darkness another very British voice. "For sheer purity of line nothing can touch good old Bhamawaddy, can it?"

Last Thursday, January 21, a trip to Rabat was organized for the President so that he could review, and be seen by, the U.S. divisions in that region. Security in and about the compound, already very tight, was stepped up several more notches. The presidential party had left without untoward incident, and it was midafternoon. In the office of the Deputy Chief of Staff at the Shell Building, where I was covering for Paul Harkins, the telephone jingled.

"This is Corporal Brundage, Corporal of the Guard at the Anfa compound entrance. There's a Frog officer here, big guy, says he's a General, wants to go in town to do some shopping. He is unable to show the new pass, the blue one. Wants us to contact Major Codman. He's kinda sore."

"General Giraud?"

"That's him."

"Send someone up to the Anfa, on the double, and have his pass issued. Meantime, let me talk to him on the phone."

General Giraud was fuming. "No one told me of a new pass," he said. "I arrive here at the gate to go into Casa to buy a pair of babouches for my wife and find myself virtually under arrest. It is inadmissible."

77

"I agree, *mon général*. A most unfortunate mistake. All of us are desolated. In a few moments everything will be arranged."

After a while he calmed down. All things considered, he was pretty nice about it.

Detailed written report to Percy on the incident. 5:45 P.M. No one around. Quiet day. Lock up desk preparatory to leaving for Percy's apartment. Lock office door. Start for elevator. Back in the office the telephone rings insistently. Return and pick up the receiver.

"This is the Anfa entrance gate. Corporal of the Guard speaking."

"Corporal Brundage?"

"No, this is Corporal Farino. We relieved Corporal Brundage and his guard about fifteen minutes ago."

"What's on your mind, Corporal?"

"There's a French General here, big guy, big mustache, says he lives here. Wants to be passed in but is not in possession of the new pass, the brown one."

"The *brown* one, what's the matter with the blue one?"

"That expired with Corporal Brundage's guard — fifteen minutes ago."

"Listen carefully, Corporal. This is Major Codman, Acting Deputy Chief of Staff. I order you to pass General Giraud in immediately."

"Sorry, Major, no can do. My orders are from Colonel McCarthy in writing. No one other than U.S. personnel to be admitted during my tour without the new brown pass."

"Where is the General now?"

"In the guardhouse," the corporal said, "and he's good and sore."

Motor pool. A car. Step on it. By the time I got there matters had been clarified. Nevertheless, the corporal was right. General Giraud was not pleased. *"Je sors pour faire des emplettes, on m'arrête. Je retourne, on m'arrête. Je me demande si je me trouve au Maroc, Protectorat Français, ou en Allemagne."*

It took longer than the first time, but finally he calmed down and we proceeded up to his pink villa, where we had a Pernod. Under its influence he told me all about his escape from Germany. It's a good story and telling it made him feel much better.

This week the Anfa Conference really went into high gear and most of the future military naval and air operations are being assigned their various priorities. Overhanging the immediate picture like a cloud, however, is the bedeviling question of French politics. It would seem essential to get Giraud and de Gaulle together to form a Provisional French Government, but Giraud is hazy as to what basis would be acceptable and de Gaulle has withdrawn into a deep freeze.

During the evening of January 21 we received a signal announcing General de Gaulle's arrival by air the following morning. It was laid on that Colonel Wilbur, who had been with de Gaulle at the École de Guerre, would meet him and escort him to Anfa. About ten minutes after Wilbur had left for the airport I happened to be walking down the Shell corridor past General Patton's office. Was a few feet beyond it when the door was thrown open with violence and the General himself hurried out into the hall.

"Codman," he shouted, catching sight of my back, "where is Wilbur?"

"He has gone out to the airport to meet de Gaulle, sir."

"Pursue him, overtake him, catch him. Tell him to drop everything and report to Anfa *at once*," the General said. "The President is waiting to present him with the Congressional Medal of Honor."

"Yes, sir."

"You can take over de Gaulle," the General added.

A good peep and a good driver. We are really making time. Approaching the airport there is a long straight stretch of dusty road. Sure enough, there is Colonel Wilbur bouncing along at a fast clip. But what the hell is that procession of rather disreputable civilian cars, their windows plastered with black mud, coming from the opposite direction? Did de Gaulle and his party get in ahead of time? If so, there was no one other than the civilian drivers to greet him at the airport, another snafu due to that damned double daylight-saving business.

Have caught up with Colonel Wilbur and together we come to a stop, bumper to bumper, directly in the path of the now halted cortege. I jump out and deliver General Patton's message to Wilbur.

"All in good time," he says, striding up to the leading limousine. No mere order, whether from General Patton or the President himself, is going to rob the Colonel of his big moment. Seizing the door handle, he opens it and leans into the darkened interior.

"Mon cher camarade" — the Colonel's rather rigid French is tinged with genuine emotion — *"quelle joie d'enfin retrouver mon vieux copain de l'École Supérieure de Guerre."*

A pause. A long-fingered hand removes a pipe from beneath a dimly perceived mustache. From the recesses a very British voice. "I'm afraid there's some mistake," it says. "Here, Harold Macmillan." *

Slamming the door shut, Colonel Wilbur rushes to the second car, opens its door, leans in.

"Mon cher camarade, quelle joie d'enfin retrouver mon vieux copain de l'École Supérieure de Guerre."

This time from the further corner a French voice. *"Pardon,"* it says. *"Il y a peut-être erreur. Ici le Général Catroux."*

At least the Colonel is getting warmer. The third car proves to be the jack pot. *"Mon cher camarade,"* the Colonel begins. At which point two long legs emerge through the door and seconds later we are in the presence of General Charles de Gaulle. We salute, he salutes, stiff as a ramrod — and, I may say, twice as grim as General Giraud in the guardhouse.

Wilbur apologizes for the mishap in meeting him. From de Gaulle no answer other than an imperceptible inclination of the head. Wilbur offers to ride with him in his car. With one hand on the door handle, de Gaulle, with the other, indicates the blacked-out windows. "I do not like to think," he says, "that the purpose of this camouflage is to conceal my presence in North Africa from my compatriots and from the people of Morocco."

"No, no, *mon cher camarade,*" the Colonel puts in hastily. "Entirely for your protection. It was the same with the President, Mr. Churchill, all the really important ones."

* At the time, Mr. Macmillan was top British political adviser in North Africa.

Finally we get going. Wonder how long the President has been waiting. At the Anfa entrance the guards throw back the gates and we sail through. No passes required today, blue, brown, or otherwise.

The villa assigned to General de Gaulle is a hundred yards or so above the entrance gate. Before it the procession stopped and everyone got out. Nose in air, the General looked about him. With a cold eye he viewed the barbed-wire barriers and the Army guards. He didn't say anything, but a rather officious member of his entourage came up and hissed in my ear.

"Is the General to conclude that for the time being he is virtually a prisoner here?" he asked.

"No more so than the President of the United States, the Prime Minister of England, and —" I added injudiciously — "General Giraud."

General de Gaulle must have good ears. His nose tilted higher. "And where, may I ask, is Giraud's billet?" he said.

"The pink villa, *mon général,* almost immediately across the way."

With care and concentration de Gaulle's steely eye measured the distance from the pink villa to the Anfa Hotel, or rather to the entrance of Dar es Saada. A like estimate of the distance between his own villa and the throne didn't help things at all. Barking a few sharp words to an aide, he turned on his heel, folded his arms, and in haughty silence surveyed the fields of the plain below.

The aide, the same hissing guy, stalked up to me again. "The General will be unable to occupy the villa assigned to him."

"Why?"

"It is not satisfactory."

"Why?"

"It is inadmissible that General de Gaulle should accept lodgings that are inferior to those occupied by some casual French officer."

"As a matter of fact, his villa is larger and in much better condition than the pink one."

"Nevertheless, in the hierarchy of villas its location is secondary, if not inferior, to that of General Giraud."

"An optical illusion. I am prepared to furnish you with blueprints showing that General de Gaulle's white villa is, in fact, two and a half meters nearer our headquarters than is the pink villa of General Giraud. Furthermore, at any moment now, the President will be sending his special representative to escort General de Gaulle to the Villa Dar es Saada. The President would be deeply disappointed if his envoy should find General de Gaulle's villa empty."

The hissing boy approached the solitary figure still studying the landscape. The confab lasted for some minutes. Finally the General turned with a shrug and started towards the white villa.

"Dans ces conditions, j'accepte," he said.

Sunday, January 24, 1943. Midmorning: ran into Bob Murphy, Averell Harriman, and Harry Hopkins strolling together near the Anfa Hotel. Murphy seemed pleased.

"The President has been talking turkey to both Giraud and de Gaulle," he said, looking at his watch.

"It shouldn't be long now."

"What shouldn't be long now?" I asked.

"The strains of that old-fashioned shotgun wedding," Harry Hopkins said.

By now you have probably seen the pictures of the bride and groom's "chalorous" handshake.

So that's that. The Anfa Conference is over. The President and the Prime Minister are off for a day or two of relaxation at the Villa Taylor in Marrakech. Bunny is down there now conferring on security.

January 26, 1943. Went back to look at Rabat today and had a lovely time — in fact, was rather overwhelmed by the reception I got. General Noguès put me next to him at lunch and said some very pleasant things. He *is* attractive and Madame even more so. She, full of life, very downright, forthright, and maybe upright for all I know, as against his almost native subtlety and finesse. Just a bit player, of course, compared to the *vedettes* I have been bumping into lately, but quite a boy nevertheless.

February 4, 1943. Local note: Fast car driven by nicely turned-out Moroccan in European clothes is stopped by American M.P. on the main road.

"Pull over to the curb. Where's the fire?"

The Moroccan takes it calmly.

M.P.: "Your name?"

Moroccan: "Sidi Mohammed Ben Youssef."

M.P.: "Your profession?"

Moroccan: *"Fonctionnaire."*

M.P.: "What function?"

Moroccan: "Sultan of Morocco."

Tableau.

February 25, 1943. I am still at Rabat as liaison officer to the Protectorate, though technically I am farmed out to General Clark's Fifth Army, which has taken over all liaison business in Morocco. Have been joined by two associates — very congenial ones — my classmate Trevor Swett, and Ridgeway Knight, formerly one of Bob Murphy's viceconsuls, and now a major in the Army.

Have seen very little of General Patton. Once at a lunch at the Residence, for Governor Boisson, again at a lunch for Juin, and during a couple of visits to the Sultan's palace. Among my side jobs seems to be that of setting up audiences with the Sultan for visiting V.I.P.'s, ranging from General Clark to Archbishop Spellman. The last is perhaps a typical example, since at the final moment the audience was called off. Reason, Sultan and Archbishop each being a spiritual leader and a prince of his respective church, the protocol experts were unable to arrive at a clear-cut decision as to who outranked whom.

One of General Patton's visits to the Sultan — I think it was on the occasion of the fifteenth anniversary of His Majesty's ascension to the throne — was enlivened by the following alarum or excursion. We had been through the business of being received at the palace entrance by Si Mameri, Chef de Protocol — and incidentally my favorite Arab — ascending the marble stairs to the long, narrow throne room on the top floor, marching the length of same with three halts and three bows from the waist before reaching the royal dais. At this point the Sultan goes democratic, rises from his throne, shakes hands with everyone. Greetings over, he slips back — eight or nine centuries — onto his throne again, indicates with a gracious wave of one hand that we are to be seated in the stiff-backed chairs adjacent to the dais, and with a peremptory gesture of the other, lets it be known that he is prepared to receive the homage, together with the customary gifts (i.e. customary, or better, or else), of his pashas and caïds. This ceremony, which must be seen to be believed, consists in each pasha and caïd being individually hustled and rushed the length of the throne room by a couple of the gigantic black palace slaves, who, arrived at the dais, hurl the supplicant sprawling at the feet of the Sultan. If the sprawl is not sufficiently ignominious to suit the slaves, the visitor's head is pounded, repeatedly and hard, on that portion of the floor where the rugs end and the bare marble begins. A suitably chastened frame of mind having thus been induced, the prone pasha, or caïd, as the case may be, is then allowed to kiss the Sultan's toe and withdraw in a backward crawl. Meanwhile, his nervous retainer, bearing a tray loaded with interesting-looking sacks of various sizes and shapes, delivers same to the Sultan's retainers, who disappear with it behind the curtains. I imagine each sack is very carefully checked before the donor is allowed to take off for his own domain in town, plain, or mountain fastness.

It was after the last chieftain had made his crablike exit and General Patton had bid the Sultan adieu that the unprogramed incident occurred. Those remaining were standing around in small groups exchanging small talk. I was conversing with the Grand Vizier, El Mokri, who is now in his middle nineties, bright as a button, and, except for rather thicker spectacles, unchanged since we met him here in Rabat over fifteen years ago.

"He is *formidable,* your General Patton," the Grand Vizier was saying.

"*C'est le cas de le dire.*" Si Mameri, who had joined us, bared his golden teeth in a twenty-four-carat smile. "Doubtless your Excellency has heard of his fantastic exploit at the Glaoui's boar hunt last week. *Formidable,* yes. The Glaoui and General Patton are waiting for the beaters to drive the ferocious animals from their lairs. There they come. Three huge beasts with blazing eyes and dagger tusks break their way through the bushes and charge across the open space directly at the waiting huntsmen." With a pantomimic gift second to none, Si Mameri in turn becomes the Glaoui, the General, the beaters, and the wild boars.

" 'You first,' the Glaoui says to the General. General raises his gun and takes aim. He waits. Nearer and nearer hurtle the terrifying brutes, their gleaming fangs flecked with the foam of madness. The General is impassive. So, too, the Glaoui, but you can feel the itching of his trigger finger. Has something gone wrong? The spectators are petrified. Bang. Bang. Bang. Three shots. Three hideous bodies sliding and slewing in a cloud of dust. A moment of frightful uncertainty. The dust settles. Three dead boars. The bloody head of the largest is resting on the toe of General Patton's boot." And as Si Mameri, invoking the classic image of sleep, places his palm-joined hands to one cheek and gently closes his eyelids, there are seen to rise from the corner of his mouth one or two discreet bubbles of delicate froth.

Then it happened. Two rifle shots. Each sharp crack seemed to come from above and not too far away. In a flash, Si Mameri was at the Sultan's side. I don't remember seeing him move. One instant he was talking to us, the next he was at the elbow of his sovereign. The Sultan, perfectly composed, whispered a few words to his Chef de Protocol and together they disappeared without hurry through the curtains behind the throne. The Grand Vizier, the other viziers, and the attendants behave as if nothing had happened. Minutes went by. Five, perhaps. The curtains rustled. The Sultan and Si Mameri reappeared. The manner of each was calm, leisurely. The Sultan reascended his throne. Si Mameri rejoined us. The politeness of the cultivated Arab is boundless. How natural it would have been for him to draw the Grand Vizier aside or at least to mutter a few private words in his ear. Not at all. Pulling with thumb and forefinger at his rather sparse white beard, he beamed his high-priced smile upon us both. "It was nothing," he said. "All is well."

We murmured our relief.

"These things are bound to happen from time to time," he continued. "One of the ladies of the royal harem was taking the air on the roof. She failed to notice that the breeze had partially unfurled her long silken scarf and that the end of it was hanging down through the ventilator which aerates His Majesty's zoo. The panther is a playful creature. Zikah is no exception. Seeing the pretty silk dangling from the hole above, Zikah leapt. A superb leap, since it carried him to the level of the roof. No lion could have done it, nor any of the other panthers. Hearing screams, Mizpah, the eunuch, hurried to the roof with his rifle. Rolling over and over, locked in close embrace, were Zikah and the lady of the harem. With great presence of mind, Mizpah confined both shots to the moments when Zikah was on the rise. The second shot accomplished the necessary." Si Mameri nudged me gently in the ribs. "General Patton would certainly have dispatched the matter with a single shot."

"How is the lady?" I asked.

Si Mameri seemed surprised. "Why, very well," he said. "A few scratches, a few weeks in the hospital, and she will be none the worse for her play hour with Zikah."

"His Majesty will be sad about the passing of Zikah," the Grand Vizier murmured. Si Mameri's mien momentarily took on the expression of a bereaved bloodhound.

"Ah, yes," he said. "It is indeed a sad loss." Then, brightening, "It is the will of Allah. And besides," he added, "I have already suggested to the Pasha of Mogador that the gift of a pair of fine young panthers would be in order."

PLANS FOR SICILY

On 5 March, General Patton, who was then at Rabat, received a telephone message from General Eisenhower to depart at once for the front to take over temporary command of the II Corps. Conditions were not good in the area of Faïd Gap, Kasserine Pass — in fact, all along the line. Gafsa had been abandoned by the American forces. The difficulty was not with the Commanding General of the II Corps, but rather in that the Army commander, General Anderson, British Army, had insisted on splitting the American forces into little groups and scattering them on a 150-mile front. General Patton's job was an unenviable one, but in the end it worked out very, very well. The key battle was at El Guettar. Victory went to the American forces. A strange incident made this possible. An enlisted man in the Signal Corps of the United States Army picked up a message in German stating that the German attack would be delayed six hours. This enabled General Patton to shift a battalion of tank destroyers (antitank) and two battalions of artillery, so that when the German attack took place, they were stopped before they got started. Then the 1st Infantry Division, under Major General Terry Allen, completed the rout of the German forces.

On 14 April at Gafsa, General Patton turned over command of the II Corps to General Bradley, this in accordance with a prearranged plan made by General Eisenhower. This plan had been made at the Anfa Conference in January 1943, when it was decided that an amphibious landing would be made on Sicily. The American forces were to be under the command of General Patton and to be known as the Seventh Army.

Just prior to departing Gafsa, General Patton, Colonel Gay, and Sergeant Meeks stopped at a little barren cemetery, and there General Patton placed a very small wreath of wild flowers, which he had picked, on the grave of his aide, Captain Jenson, who had been killed just a few days before. The night of the fourteenth was spent in Constantine. The next day, General Patton, accompanied by General Spaatz, flew to Algiers, where a conference was held with General Eisenhower, and on the next day he flew to Rabat and took charge of planning the invasion of Sicily.

March 2, 1943. Did I write you that I had gone to see the Glaoui? I did — alone, with a Moroccan lawyer friend of mine. For the first ten minutes he pulled the business about not speaking French, then broke down and was charming. He's aged quite a lot.

To your last question, has the sun helmet from Abercrombie and Fitch arrived, the answer is No. On the other hand my promotion (to Lieutenant Colonel) came through last week. With the African spring and summer just around the corner the helmet may well prove more vital than the promotion. The wearing of any unorthodox form of headgear requires special authorization. My immediate superiors at Fifth Army Headquarters, Colonels Arthur Sutherland and Charley Saltzman, two very fine and friendly guys, are going to take care of this with the understanding that no mention will be made of my Limited Service sun allergy, since I do not want to suddenly find myself back in the shade of the Munitions Building.

"Perfectly simple," they said. "We'll just say that you get sunstroke at the drop of a hat."

April 6, 1943. Big news. Stunning news. Yesterday Colonel Gay sent word that he wanted to see me at the Rear Echelon Headquarters of I Armored Corps. An interpreting job probably. Guess again.

"Sit down, Codman." The Colonel's manner was brisk. As usual he came right to the point.

"You have heard about Dick Jenson?" he said.

"No, sir."

"He was killed in action in Tunisia on the first day of April," the Colonel said. "He was killed instantly, a direct hit by a German plane. General Patton is returning from Tunisia to continue with the planning and preparation of the next amphibious assault, which, as you know, was decided upon at Anfa. He would like to have you for his A.D.C."

Surprise, combined with a tingling of the spine at the thought of trying to keep up with the human dynamo that is General Patton, left me stuttering rather incoherently.

Colonel Gay eyed me with a certain wintriness. "Want time to think it over?" he said.

"No, sir" — pulling myself together — "I am deeply honored and accept with pleasure. When do I start?"

"That's better." Colonel Gay smiled. "I will communicate with Gruenther and you will probably receive orders within a few days to check in at Oujda and from there proceed to Mostaganem, where you will report direct to General Patton."

"Mostagancm?"

"Between Oran and Algiers. Headquarters of First Armored Corps Reinforced. Within a reasonable distance of the training centers and beaches."

April 28, 1943. I've had a sort of strange day, wistful, exhilarating in a way, and instructive too. It's been a day of good-bys and I've been a little overcome by the unquestionably sincere regrets of quite a number of the boys and girls. In some cases the downright disbelief in the *possibility* of my displacement was almost comic, and in others, some of the things that were said — and God knows how well the French can say things when they really mean them — got me once or twice off balance.

I'm afraid that with all its superficialities and shortcomings I am attached, or was becoming attached, to Rabat. Hence, if for no other reason, I am sincerely glad I'm going onward and upward. Not that this phase has all been lotus eating. Some of the things that came out today made me realize how much the *trait d'union* of us *"anciens de la dernière guerre"* means to the sincerely patriotic boys. So there it is. It's simply time to move on and I'm glad of it, though I'm a trifle ashamed to say I shall miss it. What will *really* be fun will be to come back here with you.

My first visit was to General Noguès, who was so upset that on behalf of His Majesty he decorated me on the spot, so that from now on I will circulate Inchallah with a rather noticeable rosette on my Abercrombie and Fitch tunic. It doesn't mean much, but it's probably good business all round.

So here I am in bed at the Villa Mon Repos for the last time and thinking of some people who touched me quite deeply by some of the things they said today.

CHAPTER V

Mostaganem
(May–July, 1943)

On 26 April 1943, Headquarters I Armored Corps (Task Force 343) moved from Rabat to Mostaganem, which is on the Algerian coast some thirty to forty miles east of Oran. Headquarters was established in a French battalion compound. It made a very suitable place, in that it was completely walled in, and there was only one entrance which had to be guarded. Here planning was completed for the invasion of Sicily, which was scheduled to take place on the morning of 10 July with the attack to be made on Palermo. Early in July the place of attack was changed from Palermo to the southern coast, centering on Gela. It took some doing to change those plans, and the change was preceded by a plant; that is, a body was dropped out of a submarine off the coast of Spain. He was dressed as an officer of the British Army, given full identification, carrying papers stating that there was to be an attack made on Corsica and Sicily with the main attack on Corsica and the feint at Palermo. This was carried through so expertly that it not only fooled the Germans but fooled a great many of the Allied Force commanders.

Headquarters of the I Armored Corps remained in Mostaganem until the morning of 29 June, when it moved to the harbor of Algiers and went aboard the Monrovia, the flagship, or sometimes called the command ship. This was a reunion once again of Admiral Hewitt and his staff, the

have now arrived and my only annoyance is that since I have written to you about each one in detail it looks as if some of my letters have gone astray.

I can't get over how much I like my boss. Have never seen anything to equal him and I guess I haven't seen the half of it. What I don't understand is why he wanted me — well, I do in a way, but it's all pretty amazing.

This afternoon after what I would call a full day — incidentally we ran into Teddy Roosevelt,* who was in good form — the boss stopped the beflagged chariot about two miles from home and said, "How about stretching our legs? I hate walking, but I've got to do something. There's an order out about maintaining field fitness at all times."

Needless to say, we walked. At his approach, trucks would practically run off the road and countless officers' cars would come to a squeaking stop and ask if they could give him a lift. He waved them imperiously on with a "What the hell do you mean, a lift? Do I look decrepit?"

After dinner, over three cigars, he gave a talk on the history of armor and recited textually, and well, too, "At Florés in the Azores Sir Richard Grenville lay," two long poems of Kipling's, and one of his own.

May 25, 1943. You'll be surprised to hear that the sun and I get along fine. With helmet and dark glasses I seem to be able to take on old Sol with impunity, and with liberal smearings of that invaluable cocoa butter, the bout is so far at least a draw. Today has been a rousing day on land and water. With my boss and two top Britishers, General Sir Harold Alexander, commander of all forces, British and American, and Major General Richardson, and a lot of other people. It was all pretty fascinating and I learned a lot, though invariably I shudder to think of how little I do know about this particular kind of thing. General Alexander and his Number Two stayed on at the villa for the night. He was evidently much impressed by what he had seen of our setup, and that is saying quite a lot, because he has had over ten years of

---

* Brigadier General Theodore Roosevelt, Assistant Division Commander of the 1st Infantry Division, veterans of Tunisia, which was to lead the assault on Gela, Sicily.

solid fighting, not just military service — God knows how much he has had of that — but actual fighting. A very pleasant fellah. Will be seeing more of him, I fancy.

Well, as Archie Alexander* said the evening I dined with him, "In this rather fascinating transcontinental train we managed to catch I'm not exactly in the caboose, but *you,* goddamit, seem to be riding up in the engine cab." Somewhat exaggerated — but still I can't complain of being bored.

June 2, 1943. Since life now is all work and no play and since work nominally lends itself to being written about I will do a little reminiscing. Have been looking at the records of our early days here. It is really, when the time comes, a swell story. The action part — the landing in Morocco, the naval battle, and all that — has been pretty well covered, I guess, or will be by lots of people, but I know now what I want to develop and it is something that not so many people know about, and that is my boss's "foreign policy." His letters — and there are hundreds — are a gold mine, and knowing what I now know of the inside, I am more deeply impressed than ever by his sagacity and correct intuitions at and immediately after the armistice. I knew it was a good job — our columnist friends notwithstanding — and was glad to be able to contribute a small part of it, but it was not until I had seen the records that I realized just how good it was. And also what might have happened if it had *not* been good. On this aspect I can bring quite a lot of Rabat evidence to bear and it ought to be rather good fun to do. The nub of the whole matter was this — to listen to the "outs" and kick out the people who were and are running the place and know *how* to run it, or keep the latter in and run them. Expediency certainly indicated the latter course. In the early days in Rabat, the ratio of Moroccans to Europeans was somewhere between five and ten million (nobody knows exactly how many) to a couple of hundred thousand. Even up to 1934 there were still *"poches insoumises,"* plenty of chance for trouble. Therefore, the maintaining of

* Captain Archibald S. Alexander.

the prestige of the boys in the saddle, who obviously knew their stuff, was essential, otherwise we ourselves would have been in for an enormous policing job instead of going ahead with the war.

Listened this evening for an hour and a half to the most engrossing talk on the world situation by one who probably knows more about it than any living person I have ever heard (General George C. Marshall). It was both fascinating and encouraging. Harvey is right. He is a great man.

Have just been bathing and anointing myself with cocoa butter. Thank God, or rather you, for *that* idea. Am now the color of old mahogany, or maybe one of those redwoods would be closer.

June 17, 1943. You must have had my letter saying that *all* the packages have arrived, including my Shubert uniform, which got here yesterday. Thanks a million. The boss likes wool, hence we are to be in wool this summer, hence my request for three very light wool shirts — did you get *that* letter — size 16.

Regarding the sun helmet: It arrived, as I wrote you, and the next day (which was a blisterer) seemed just made to order. Was in a hurry and forgot to bring it to headquarters — fortunately, as it turned out. That evening the boss launched forth in his most picturesque vein about a guy he disliked above all others — a crook, a coward, a pimp, a bastard, a complete S.O.B. — "but those," he said, "are not the *real* reasons I disliked him on sight — the *real* reason is that he turned up at *my* headquarters in an *elephant* hat."

"Do you mean a sun helmet, sir?"

"Call it what you like, but if any misguided so-and-so turns up here with one I'll throw him in jail for the duration."

So naturally the helmet has been carefully put away for the duration. The only thing he likes *less* than elephant hats are closed cars — or open cars with tops — summer uniforms, unless they are wool, and caps with visors.

Don't worry, everything is O.K. and I'm doing fine. As a matter of fact, the steel helmet liner is the best sun helmet there is and that's what we are wearing. Furthermore, in spite of some of our tastes and habits being somewhat different, I'm crazy about the boss. He is really superb.

"Love will find a way, love will find the cocoa butter."

P.S. In the letter you didn't get — to date — I described saying au revoir to Rabat and to General Noguès, who then and there created me a Commandeur of the Ordre Ouissam Alaouite. Since then at my approach preceded by a luxuriant orange rosette the local cats tremble instead of purring. As a matter of fact it's a rather nice thing to have in this part of the world. Will send you the diploma, in two languages, when I get it, which may be several months as it takes the Sultan (Sidi Moulay Youssef) a long time to get around to affixing his seal. The moon or the tides or something — maybe his wives — has to be just right.

June 19, 1943. Yes, yes, there certainly appears to be an inevitability or something in the way our lives have followed a predestined pattern. You speak of that trip you and I made to Nancy three years ago. It is a queer thing but that last trip of ours is to me almost indistinguishable from our first trip — you and me — to Amanty.* Basically it is all of one piece. I guess everything is. The reason the Rabat chapter, now very definitely finis, remains sort of poignant is that underneath the often superficial surface of things every activity, every job, the little fantastic ones as well as the two or three bigger ones, all the pleasurable things and the sad things, every conversation even — and God knows the wordage was terrific — every single thing that happened to me and that I did and was had a root or a branch or a twig or a leaf in the river that has been our life — yours and mine — since first we ambled around the countryside in that little green car. Our *old* world war stuff, the wine business of course, our dealings with all sorts and conditions of people, silly ones, theatrical ones, angry ones, mean ones, and occasionally good ones — all that came into play. I have said before and I say again, you will perhaps never realize — though I wish you would — how vividly, almost tangibly, present you were every minute of

---

* Amanty was where his squadron, the 1st Day-Bombardment Squadron, was stationed in the First World War.

every day of that particular chapter — it was so much your stuff. The only wrench, really, about leaving there was that in some strange, paradoxical way it was like leaving you all over again. Fortunately I don't have much time to think. When I do, it is of all the wonderful things you have been and are and will be to me, and of how to people like you and me the Germans have a special accountability — one which I must say I look forward to being in on.

One of the things I like about my boss is that he is a great hate builder, and believe me, when the time comes, the Axis boys are going to be very sorry to meet him and his boys — I think. Well, that's that for the moment.

June 21, 1943. As I wrote you yesterday, I thought my farewells to Rabat were for good and all. However, in the Army one never knows. Last evening the boss suddenly thought of a message he wanted to send and said, "Take my plane and go." Raced out to the field early this morning with the pilot. Strapped ourselves into a lovely little air-sedan job and were (presumably) off. But no. The self-starter ground for quite a while and exactly nothing happened. At the moment a crew of mechanics are swarming over the little bastard — practically concealing it — and I am up in the tower writing to you.

The tower is run by a silvery-haired captain who must be considerably older than I am. He works all day in the tower and eats there and sleeps there — seven days a week. This field is remote and his only contact with the outside world consists of the crackling messages that he gets through his earphones from the ships that slide in and — as quickly as possible — *out*. The temperature in the tower is — let's see — exactly 103°. Well, the Captain is a West Coast newspaperman, *has* been for over twenty-five years, and like all good newspapermen he's got an insatiable appetite for going places and seeing things. In the spring of 1917 he went to his boss and said, "Boss, I want a leave of absence."

"What for?" the boss asked.

"I want to see this here war."

The boss, according to the Captain, was a pretty understanding sort of guy. "O.K.," he said with a shrug. "If that's your idea of getting ahead and you want to take a leave of absence without pay, I'll see what I can do about holding your job open."

So the Captain was all pleased and because he likes planes he joined the Air Corps and went to ground school and all the rest of it and finally got his wings. Did a good job, instructing. Organized one of the new fields in the south. Was disappointed, though, because when the armistice finally came round, although he had tried out every conceivable lead, he had *not* got to France.

Well, you remember the boss was a pretty good guy and the Captain after a while *did* get his job back, though the pay was somewhat less, of course, because the boss had had to hire someone in his place and couldn't very well fire *him*. The Captain worked hard and along about the middle of '41 it seemed from something the boss let drop that he had a good chance of being reinstated as to pay, perhaps around Xmas time or anyway by the first of the year.

Came Pearl Harbor, and shortly after, a severe recurrence of that itch to go places and see things. The Captain gave it a lot of thought. He wasn't as young as he used to be and maybe this time the boss wouldn't be able to keep *any* job open. But somehow the afternoon before Xmas he found himself knocking on the boss's door.

"Boss," he said, "I want a leave of absence."

"What for?" the boss asked.

"I want to see this here war."

The boss pushed his eyeshade up and his spectacles down. "What do you want to do *that* for?" The boss seemed a little hurt. "You saw the last one, didn't you?" he said.

"Sure, sure," the Captain said. "You were very white about that, boss, but even so I'd like to see this one — maybe from a little closer."

The boss shrugged. Shrugging was the way the boss signified that a conversation was terminated. At heart, though, a pretty understanding sort of guy. He pulled his spectacles up and his eyeshade down. "O.K.," he said, "if that's your idea of getting ahead and you want to take a leave of absence without pay, I'll see what I can do about holding your job open."

And so the Captain rejoined the Air Corps and, at about the same time as we did, he found himself in a convoy and he landed on these shores. He was immediately put in charge of this tower and here he works, sleeps, and eats, twenty-four hours a day, seven days a week. He thoroughly enjoys it. It makes a change and anyway the point is he likes *planes.* He sees quite a bunch of them and as they slide in and (as quickly as possible) *out,* each one of them crackles a few words to him over the earphones. He is a happy man. After the war? Oh, that will work out somehow. The boss at heart is a pretty understanding guy. Meantime the Captain is going places and seeing things.

Looks as if our plane is ready. The Captain is giving me an envelope for this and I will mail it — or rather *he* will mail it — here. I like the Captain.

June 24, 1943. Well, I am up in the control tower again, waiting this time for my boss, who is coming in from another direction. Within the forty-eight hours since I was here last the elderly captain has become a major and expects to move on, presumably to a bigger, better tower. He is pretty pleased about it.

Having a little time on my hands and knowing your love for detail, I will amplify my last letter a little. Had lunch in Rabat with Ridgeway Knight and Trevor Swett, who, together with myself, were made honorary *goumiers,** which is not unflattering and gives one the right to wear the saber of the *goumier* — in miniature fortunately. Next morning called on your boys (Cigogne),† particularly Captain and Madame de Fouquières — they are really good — and then took off in my private plane amidst a lot of agitation of handkerchiefs.

June 28, 1943. Yesterday we had the decorating ceremony I mentioned. It was very French and involved a few minor last-minute changes; i.e. the colonel of the division lined us up and with some good sonorous phrases initiated us as members of the 69th Régi-

* *Goums* are irregular companies of Berber mountaineers organized, equipped, and officered by the French. They are primarily useful for mountain fighting, as was later proved in Sicily. They existed before the war.

† The Cigogne Pursuit Squadron, which fought in both world wars. Mrs. Codman was their *marraine.*

ment d'Artillerie d'Afrique and then proceeded to bind us up, not in red cord but with the *fourragère* of the *Médaille Militaire,* which, as a matter of fact, goes better with our uniform. Bunny was off on a short trip, so I accepted his for him and have forwarded it to him with a note saying that when and if we have occasion to stroll together into the Travelers' Club, *ça fera bien,* and that anyway we will get our pictures taken in a Barrel of Fun or riding a Crescent Moon and send them to our wives, leaving the latter in no doubt whatever as to our state of illumination.

Worked this morning with the boss on a speech which he will make and which you will eventually hear — it's damn good, too. I may say my contributions were infinitesimal. He is a great man and I am not unproud of being along on his party.

Curiously enough, because he is so *very* young in spirit — and, God knows, physically too — the combined ages of his two aides, Captain Stiller, a former enlisted man who looks as if he were made of solid hickory — and is — and I, total exactly one hundred and one years.

Last night after the others had gone to bed the boss told us both just what he expected of us, and of himself, in the days to come. In a way it is quite simple.

Must stop now and pack.

July 2, 1943. Yesterday the boss and I having bid farewell to our local friends took a long and very beautiful drive. Come noon we picnicked by the roadside. After lunch the Corniche Road became even more winding and lovely. The driver got drowsy and I offered to spell him. The boss said:

"Codman, do you drive *well?*"

"Yes, sir."

"Well, then, go ahead and drive, but I don't want my neck broken at this stage of the game."

"Yes, sir — I mean no, sir."

One turn in the road was particularly reminiscent and I told him that there existed a villa* on the Riviera, formerly owned by the Queen of

---

* La Leopolda, near Nice, then owned by Ogden Codman.

the Belgians which might have been designed for him — the boss —
and that when and if we got there I would take particular pleasure in
requisitioning it for him. He seemed to like the idea. That evening we
arrived at Algiers.

July 3, 1943. Spent the morning working on the boss's very private
papers and sorting them away with various bigwigs' so that they will
be properly disposed of — just in case.

This afternoon went swimming with Red Slocum and others — sort
of little dingy Deauville. Lots of gobs and doughboys. Some good
numbers, viz. a local belle very dignified in her beach chair — dark
glasses — sun oil — intent on her knitting. A gob in nothing but a Lee
string (Gypsy Rose) steals up behind her, puts his arm around her
while a friend gob snaps the striking picture. Same to be sent back to
the girl friend of gob number 1 in Iowa? She ought to be impressed —
maybe not too favorably.

Dinner in town and a loge at the Casino Music Hall. The same show
we've seen all over the world — the same bum orchestra, the same
aging *chanteuses,* a fifth-rate Chevalier and eighth-rate Dranem, an
archicommère and a pansy *compère.* In the funny little *balcons,*
fauteuilles, baignoires, and *strapontins,* a wonderful entertainment,
hungry burlesque audience of all nations, soldiers and sailors — all this
and an air raid too.

July 4, 1943. Am up in the cool again, watching through the greenhouse of a fast bomber the parched earth crawling brownly past. The
boss is sitting in the engineer's seat on the level above. He is in very
good form. We are taking a trip which in a way marks a milestone.
There are quite a good many things to think about, not so much the
immediate present but the past and the future. It is characteristic of him
that he refuses to worry about either. I believe that in his way he is a
great man and that his profound conviction in his destiny is based on
a sure and valid instinct.

Having no feelings of my own with regard to destiny, my thoughts
are entirely occupied with lovely times we have had and the lovely

times we will have together again. I know that this part between campaigns has irked you with a sense of events piling up of which you are not a part. As I have tried to say before, this is simply not so. I am just over here taking movies for both of us; and when we have got them developed and screened they will be just as much yours as they are mine, for as you surely know, if it hadn't been for you I certainly wouldn't be functioning in this show at my present capacity and by that I mean that while what I'm doing or trying to do may not amount to a hell of a lot it would amount to a goddam sight less if it weren't for you — so you see this war is just as much yours as it is mine. Yes, all this was just as it was meant to be and viewing the whole picture from the stimulating freshness of the greenhouse — I do like altitude — I feel that all in all I'm a very lucky person. Everything that has happened so far has been exactly right — the big things and the little things. There is even a quaint rightness that up in the greenhouse of this bomber a copy of today's *Stars and Stripes* should be tacked on to the radioman's board with the following important *items:* "Pretty Simone Simon looked extremely happy while dancing with George Raft, who is still wearing the wrist watch Betty Grable gave him. . . . Caesar Romero, now in the Coast Guard, celebrated his last evening in civvies by holding hands with Virginia Bruce. . . . Betty Grable will break George Raft's ticker in a couple of days when she becomes the wife of the trumpeter Harry James. . . . Frank Sinatra, the former Tommy Dorsey vocalist, who is making feminine hearts beat faster with his lilting arrangements, is laid up with a sore throat. . . . Meanwhile gorgeous Dinah Shore remains the doughboys' favorite songstress. . . . The rubber girdle, part of the wardrobe of the late John Barrymore, was bought at auction by a steel jobber for $4.50."

And come to think of it, this is the birthday of the great Mr. George M. Cohan.

It's a funny world and an interesting one.

Later, on our return this evening, I dropped in to le Bosphore to get a vermouth. Coming downstairs, three shots rang out and a small dark civilian just behind me crumpled up with three bullets in his stomach. With the greatest dispatch he was rushed by two waiters to the sidewalk so as not to embarrass the clients by dying on the premises. Just a little squabble between *"ces messieurs du milieu,"* it seems. The lady pianist appeared a trifle worried — kept looking over her shoulder and hit several false notes. Otherwise hardly a ripple.

"Will they get the bird who did it?" I asked the *patron.*

"Oh, *vous savez,"* and he shrugged in the direction of the somewhat leaking form in the gutter.

"Celui-là c'était un type peu recommendable."

CHAPTER VI

Sicily

(July, 1943–January, 1944)

Plans for the invasion of Sicily had been made at the Anfa Conference. At this conference, Mr. Churchill very much wanted to delay the invasion of Normandy and bring the war up through the Balkans. The United States was definitely against this proposition; thus a compromise was arrived at, and plans were made for the invasion first of Sicily and then of Italy, with the invasion of France to be delayed for approximately one year.

The invasion of Sicily was to be made with two forces: the American forces, under General Patton, landing near Palermo; and the British forces, under General Montgomery, landing on the southeast corner of the island. Just a few days before the actual invasion, these plans were changed and the American forces made their landing with the center on Gela, which, in effect, placed them on the immediate left of the British forces. The objective, or the mission, of both forces was the complete subjugation of the Isle of Sicily to provide a springboard for the invasion of Italy.

At one minute past midnight 9-10 July 1943 the Seventh United States Army was activated, and General Patton designated as its commander. He stated most appropriately at that small ceremony aboard the command ship (Monrovia): "This is the first army in history to be activated *after midnight and baptized in blood before daylight."*

The American forces, the Seventh Army, moved rapidly, conquered Palermo, then turned east and captured Messina on 17 August. This campaign by the Seventh Army was one of the most successful campaigns ever made by an army in history. It was thought by the Seventh Army staff that great credit would be given to General Patton for this magnificent campaign, and at least some credit to his staff. Such was not to be the case.

July 14, 1943. Since I am not allowed to say anything about this operation and since by the time you receive this letter you will long ago have read about it — doubtless in great detail — I am more than usually at a loss as to what to say, except to take my first two letters to you of some eight months ago (the Fedala landings), magnify them slightly, and you should have a rough idea of the last few days. It seems so far to be a success. Our losses are small and the future looks good, so the experts say.

For the individual it has been spectacular and pretty strenuous and I imagine will continue in that tempo.

One rather nice number I think I can mention: Riding yesterday with the boss, we came suddenly at a turn in the road upon a unit of *goumiers* which has recently joined us, the only one of its nationality and race in these parts. The boss rose in the chariot to his full height and made a rousing speech of welcome. The captain at the head of the column saluted smartly and said, "We owe you a lot, *mon général,* to find ourselves here on the fourteenth of July."

Am afraid this is rather sketchy, but it is about all I can say. Bunny and Red Slocum are well.

July 17, 1943. We have been here just a week, which, measured by its crammed events, feels more like a month. A number of us, including the boss, are lodged in the former abode of a local party leader whose black silk shirt and emblems hang in my closet. Well, not exactly *my* closet since four of us are sleeping on the sofas of this particular salon, music room, or whatever it was. Splendor and squalor, rich tapestries, noble four-posters, tropical birds still slightly dazed in their gilded cages — yes, we feed them, I think. Will look into it. Modern plumbing (no water, of course). A whole armoire full of patent medicines — fascinating-looking labels which I can't read, goddamit — and over all inches of dust and armies of bugs.

Things are going well. The boys have been — and are — magnificent. It shouldn't be long now before the military end of this party is cleared up.

July 20, 1943. Every day continues to be a pippin. Yesterday, for example — or maybe it was the day before — I asked the boss if I could go up and see my *"indigènes"* buddies (the *goumiers*) — seeing as how I'm an honorary member of same. He said Sure; in fact, he had a special message for them. Accompanied by a Colonel Campanole whom you don't know, but I hope you will someday as he is a character — speaks eight languages and specializes in "Interrogation" of the Hemingway variety — I commandeered a peep and we set forth at 7 A.M. into some pretty rugged country. At an advanced C.P. we discovered — it was about noon — that my buddies had taken off an hour ago to capture a mountain town.

On *my* map there wasn't any road to it, but they told us there *must* be *some* kind of a road, so off we went. Well, there was a road of sorts, the kind you like when the main road doesn't do what you want it to — only this road was littered with a good deal of destruction and rather disconcertingly empty of any Allied traffic whatsoever. About five miles from where the town should have been, we came upon another peep parked behind a boulder. A lieutenant and two men were scanning the crest of the mountain. Asked what was cooking. The lieutenant said he was an advance reconnaissance with orders to progress along this road until he got shot at and then come back and report on what he had seen.

We borrowed his opera glasses — I mean field glasses — and observed that the town we were looking for was at that moment being entered by a company of something. The uniforms were undistinguishable at that distance. "Let's hope it's our buddies," the Colonel said.

"If they are buddies, why are they coming in from the *north* side?" the Lieutenant asked.

"That is what we'll have to go up and find out," the Colonel said.

Ordering the reconnaissance party to follow us (which they did at a respectful distance), we wended our way up the switchback road. Round the last shoulder the terrain flattened out. No cover of any kind and there was the town. We were about a couple of hundred yards from its entrance when out from the gateway there trundled towards us a truck — an *enemy* truck. We stopped, aimed, and with a magnificent gesture the Colonel challenged — in four of his six languages — the advancing vehicle. It stopped and for a while nothing happened at all. Then a trim figure stepped down from beside the driver and brought his hand up to his familiar blue kepi in smart salute. Well, it seems that one company of *goumiers* had circled the town (the one we had seen through a glass darkly) and just walked in. The Captain had commandeered a truck and was taking a look around this end of town.

"You're just in time to receive the keys of the city," he said.

He jumped in with us and we drove in and down the main street. That was *something*. From every window, balcony, and doorway the populace were waving sheets, tablecloths, drawers, anything *white*. We got a tremendous hand. In the principal *place,* the mayor and town notables, including for no particular reason a couple of Spanish priests — they were on a pilgrimage, they said — were assembled. Here we had quite a fascinating parley which proved highly satisfactory. The Colonel had a chance to use up two more of his languages, and flagons of wine — not very good wine — passed freely from hand to hand, except, of course, those of my buddies whose religion forbids the use of alky.

August 1, 1943. Am in bed with a cold, but sulfathiazole now seems to be getting the upper hand, and once that has been accomplished, all one has to do is to recover from the sulfathiazole.

The boss has been very nice about it. Comes in to see me twice a day

— takes my pulse — and orders the doctor to keep me in bed. It is the first time I've been laid up since being in the Army (except for a few days last winter at Rabat, but I was alone up there, so nobody knew about it); hence, I don't suppose I can complain, but it is a bit of a nuisance at just this moment. However, it gives me a few days of rest and a chance to read and do a little recapitulating.

Speaking of "firsts," my only one during the last war was to be with the first U.S. bombing squadron at the front. This time there are several: the first *and* second operations of their kind in the history of the world; a member of the first army to be born at sea and within twenty-four hours engage in an invasion operation; there are a couple of others, but I doubt if the censor would care for them. Also I guess there is a "first" in connection with the capture of the town with my *"indigènes"* buddies, the *goumiers*.

August 1, 1943. Seem to be entirely recovered from my little attack. Sulfathiazole is a wonderful thing, but like many other wonderful things it takes it out of you. And speaking of wonderful things, we had quite a show from the palace window last night. It was very noisy but colorful in the extreme. The high-water mark — and perhaps the most beautiful as well as satisfactory sight I have ever beheld — was a flaming enemy bomber spattering itself and its occupants against the side of a mountain. God, it was gorgeous — completely cured the sulfa hangover.

Took a tour around Palermo today and all of a sudden realized wherein this town and dozens of others we have been through add up to a (for me, as it would to you) *completely new experience*. Street after street of crumbled houses. Whole blocks of shapeless rubble; parlor, bedroom, and bath exposed like a scene from *Salvation Nell* by the fantastic projectile that strips away the façade and leaves intact the hat on the bureau, the mirror on the wall, the carafe on the night table; a whole ship blown out of the water and perched atop a comfort station.

All this familiar enough. You and I have seen it a hundred times. And *that* is the point. Our basic associations with this kind of destruction are inevitably with Gothas, Heinkels, Stukas — or rather the Boches. The new experience is adjusting to the fact that all this beautifully executed chaos is the result of our *own* bombs, our *own* planes, our *own* gunfire. It is pretty lovely. I can think of no one in this world who would appreciate it as much as you — but it's a little awe-inspiring. It's so goddam well done — and for the old-timer requires a conscious psychological readjustment from the days when it seemed as if we were always taking it rather than dishing it out.

Another new experience was loafing along the other day in the boss's comfortable plane surrounded by *an escort* of fighters — that was pretty satisfactory, and for me a decided novelty, as you know.

August 2, 1943. Went with the boss to the hospital this morning, where he distributed forty Purple Hearts, and, God, he did it well.

"Where did you get it, boy?"

"In the chest, sir."

"Well, it may interest you to know that the last German I saw had no chest and no head either. To date you have captured or killed over eighty thousand S.O.B.'s — that's the official figure, but as I travel round, my nose tells me that the figures are much bigger and before the end they will be double that. Get well quickly — you want to be in on that final kill. . . ."

To a very black Negro, "Where did you get it, boy?"

Negro perfectly seriously, "In de bivouac area, sah." That got quite a laugh.

A rousing collective speech to each ward, to the nurses, to the interns. The last guy he decorated was unconscious, oxygen mask, probably won't live. The boss pulled one of those quick switches of his — took off his helmet, knelt down, pinned the medal on the pillow, whispered in the guy's ear — stood up at attention. Elementary if you like, but I swear there wasn't a dry eye in the house, and — as you know — hospital doctors, nurses, and interns are not the most impressionable people in the world.

Afterwards he and I and the colonel I took that trip with went to Mass in the royal chapel — just the three of us. For lunch, General Alexander, General Miller, General Penney, etc., of the British Army. To-morrow a trip to the front. And so it goes.

Wish to hell I could speak the Italian language and still think that *after* the operations my greatest usefulness would be with the French picture. However, that is not for me to say, and anyway there is nothing I can do about it.

August 13, 1943. Seem to have a few minutes on my hands for a change so will take advantage of them to write to you. As I told you in my V-mail letter of yesterday, Cabot* was with us for a day. As usual his timing was unerring and he saw a good show including a satisfactory number of dead Boches. He and the boss together make up into quite a number and a good time was had by all. This whole thing is an amazing show. If you had told me even a few months ago that we would be pursuing Germans over hill and dale—and *what* hills and dales!—I would have thought you were nuts—and so would you—but that is just what we are doing.

The climate is *something* and apparently continues to be for some time to come, but I suppose it's just as bad for the other side.

A local hotel keeper back in the city—of course we are now in tents and bedding rolls—it was just as well I brought that bedding roll all this way—told me that it was unheard of for people to come here at this time of year. If you are asked if I have ever been to Sicily you can truthfully say, "Only once (what I mean), and then, out of season."

I must say it was nice seeing Cabot and getting some news of people. He's *quite* a boy—particularly at this back to nature phase.

August 17, 1943. As you will have seen by the papers, the boys have done it again and Messina has been entered—by our troops!

What a campaign this has been. We have been roaring and sweating up and down this island—especially up—and it looks like the party is pretty nearly over—locally, that is. After that, *qui sait?* Not I.

Have covered a lot of ground since leaving city life behind. Break camp before sunup. Shave by starlight and cold water with swarms of

* Major Henry Cabot Lodge, formerly Senator from Massachusetts.

yellow jackets zooming round and the ants working on your ankles. Wielding the old-fashioned razor requires agile blade work. Breakfast under an inch of dew. Off on the road as the sun comes up like a red-hot thunderbolt. Traffic, dust — unending clouds of dust with equal parts of sweat; it makes a curious gray paste all over — intermittent dive bombing, strafing, and endless mines.

Just the same the Boches have got a terrific licking and it is quite exciting to be — for once — on the pursuing end of the game. The boys — the doughboys, I mean — have really been superhuman and so have the Air and so have the Navy — a swell show.

August 18, 1943. For the first time in a long time things are relatively calm. We are still enjoying what might be called country life and for the moment the country is peaceful.

This morning after putting General Bedell Smith on a plane I went with another guy in a peep on the first purely sight-seeing tour I have made since our arrival, and I do see that the place has beauty and that the amazing mountain-perched towns are unique, but when we go on that extended voyage after the war I shall be quite happy to give this island a wide berth and that goes for the inhabitants.

And now, what next? If I knew I could tell you, but as a matter of fact I haven't the remotest idea.

This morning a letter came from your friend Wild William — Bill Donovan — requesting my services — also Bunny's. The boss promptly said *NO* and when he says no he means no — so there you are.

August 19, 1943. Just as I was thinking things were getting a little dull they got quite good again. A wire arrived saying that General Giraud with his entourage was on his way here to inspect, decorate, and embrace his baby *goumiers*. On the spot the boss made me a flight leader (for the day) and I hurried down the island to a prearranged meeting place with five planes — very small ones be it said — picked up the boys from their larger conveyance and shepherded them back here to our part of the world. It all went off very well, including a rather tense moment when a tight formation of pursuit planes rocketed by just underneath us. They turned out to be Spitfires. If they hadn't been, North African politics would have got quite active again and *I* wouldn't be writing this letter. A nice landing. Greetings from the boss. A long, tortuous drive up into the mountains. In a sylvan glade — the *goumiers.*

It was in the best French tradition with *"garde à vous"* and accolades and *"mes enfants"* stuff. Towards the end Giraud discovered he had brought one Legion of Honor too few. No whit disconcerted, he removed the medal he had just pinned on the next to the last *goumier,* saying in his grandest manner, "Allow me to borrow your medal for a moment," and with an extra flourish pinned it on the final recipient. Afterwards they probably tossed for it.

The ceremonies over, we proceeded to a small clearing where a divan had been installed — *goumiers* never heard of chairs — upon which Giraud gracefully reclined — he is *so* photogenic — while we fought this war and the last one all over again.

Finally a light collation, a bottle of cognac, lots of *trinqué*-ing.

On the way back he was treated to the charming old Sicilian custom of being bombarded with fruit — *faute de fleurs* — receiving from one picturesque but overenthusiastic peasant a full basket of apples and nuts in the face — we were going at a good clip, too. When he had recovered from this he remarked a little groggily, *"Pourvu qu'ils ne jettent pas de melons." You* would have liked it.

August 22, 1943. Last evening our guests at the palace* were none other than Bob Hope and Frances Langford.

On arriving yesterday, discovered they were playing this town, so naturally went to the show and then, employing the old Pinckney Street technique, kidnaped them — with the aid, I may say, of a personable young captain who had his eye on Langford — and rushed them through a mob of autograph hounds to the boss's car — thence to the palace.

It couldn't have been better. Supper with lots of *Asti spumante.* The boss was nothing short of terrific. With Hope was a guitar player, a

---

* The royal palace at Palermo.

tenor, Langford of course, and his script writer, a Mr. Block. He was fascinated by the boss — they all were, but he especially.

After about the second of the boss's sallies — in his best vein, Mr. Block just put down his knife and fork and gave.

"But, General, that's *beautiful* — Bob! Did you hear that reading? — and what *timing* — say, General, can we use that one in next Thursday's show?"

A little later, "You might as well bow out, Bob — he's topped your every line so far."

Hope: "He's right; from now on I'll just play it straight — and to-morrow I'll get a new script-writer."

And so on for hours.

Langford sang some old songs and also some of Cole Porter's new ones — then we got her on Gershwin and even you would have re-lented over her rendition of "Embraceable You." She is better in a room.

Romarro, the guitar man, is something. His arrangements are nearly as good as Cole's or even George's. Bob Hope and Pepper, the tenor (he said he would telephone you), were marvelous. Sketches, gags, songs, even some steps out of *Roberta*.

The boss gets eloquent again — then sentimental — has them in tears. Hope brings them back to normal with:

"Not the old blood and guts *I've* heard about."

The boss goes over the campaigns — is very modest about it — says he just prays he's done his job as well as he could.

Hope leans over — conspirator stuff. "Look, General, if you should ever be *out* of a job, I *believe* —" his timing *is* perfect — "I *believe* I can get you a solid week at Loew's State."

Good-bys — pictures (I saw to that).

The boss tells Hope that entertaining the soldiers is a fine thing. "It is wonderful," he says. "You can see how they enjoy *anything* in the way of entertainment."

Hope: "How do y'mean, *anything?!?*"

The boss thinks for a moment. "Well, let's say *everything*."

Mr. Block is practically cataleptic with joy. "It's beautiful — see what I mean, Bob? — it's beautiful. Now he's *double*-topping you."

September 7, 1943. I have rather belatedly discovered that there are many interesting and even beautiful things to see in Sicily. Yesterday I spent the day showing some of them to John Marquand, who has just turned up here. Towards the end of the afternoon on the outskirts of one of these amazing mountaintop villages I was communing privately, as I thought, when, from a balcony which I hadn't noticed, a pleasantly modulated feminine voice remarked, "Are you looking for anybody?"

Pulling myself together, I said, "No, just waiting for a streetcar," then realized it was quaint, to say the least, to be addressed in unaccented English — or rather American — from the balcony of a remote Sicilian cottage. The lady, it seems, was from Cleveland, Ohio, had come over here in June to visit the home folks, and got caught in the war. It ended up by our having tea with the whole family and hearing some quite entertaining stuff about how it feels to be looted by the Boches, abandoned by the Wops, and bombed by the Americans.

"You'll have quite a lot to tell the folks back in Cleveland," John said.

"Sure," the lady said, "but they won't believe a word of it." Which is life or something.

In the evening back here John dined at the palace with the boss, who was in rare form.

Later when I took John back to his hotel, in the lobby we ran into ex-Governor Poletti, Douglas Fairbanks, Jr., and John Steinbeck, which called for quantities of *Asti spumante,* with bismuth on the side for me. It's getting to be quite a tourist spot.

September 8, 1943. Yes, I did have a little touch of dysentery and have now, but it seems to be fairly well under control and the weather is getting a little cooler, so don't worry about my health, which is O.K. You have been and are very swell about this whole thing and if there is any justice in the world — and there is — it will all come out all right.

Was just putting this in its envelope when sounds of revelry, firecrackers, church bells came wafting through the palace window. Outside several hundred small kids with homemade band instruments —

mostly combs and tissue paper — are putting on a lively demonstration. Assorted pin wheels, firecrackers, and carbines are crackling all over the place. Italy has capitulated and the Sicilians are pleased. A detachment of kids is rushing off down the side street in pursuit of a woman — only it's not a woman, just a Fascist pansy. Stoning fairies seems to be an old Sicilian custom.

Time marches on. This has certainly been an eventful summer.

Bunny has just got his lieutenant colonelcy, which delights everyone. Nobody has ever deserved it more.

September 12, 1943. The tourist trade continues brisk. Yesterday Norman Davis and the entire Red Cross flew in. Opening of the Red Cross Clubhouse — speeches. The boss, incidentally, made one of the *best* speeches I've ever heard in my life. Just four minutes. When he got up, there was a prolonged ovation. His opening line as he stepped up to the microphone was, "There are certain moments — and this is one of them — when I think that possibly I've not been such a sonuvabitch as I thought I was."

That wowed them of course. Then one of his famous quick changes — the old switcharoo. Four minutes of electrifying homage to the American doughboy, ending up with, "The American enlisted man in this campaign has accomplished the impossible against the unspeakable" — only somehow it was better than that — anyway, there was not a dry eye in the house.

Afterwards he said, "I hadn't the slightest idea what I was going to say. As a matter of fact, what *did* I say?" I told him.

"That sounds all right," he said. "I should have written it down."

"No," I said. "If you had, it wouldn't have been nearly as good."

He agreed.

More speeches. Opening of the theater, the doughnut bar, the bathhouses, the yacht club. Was standing on the piazza of the latter when without warning something small in a blue uniform popped up under my arm and embraced me. It was none other than Louisa Groody! Later there was a dance and when I cut in on her she was with an

engineer colonel who kept proudly introducing her as "Miss Rooney."
Sic gloria!

Tomorrow am lunching with Al Jolson. This place is becoming just
a branch of Broadway.

September 15, 1943. At dinner one evening — this was back in North
Africa before the present party started — the boss lit a cigar, leaned back
in his chair, and said, "Everything is going to be all right. Colonel
Campanole is on his way here."

Some of the old-timers smiled and the rest of us looked blank.

"Colonel Campanole," the boss continued, "is a great man — and an
artist."

In the last war he showed remarkable talent for making people talk
— Mata Hari, for example — and in Mexico some very stubborn Mexicans who remained mute under ordinary interrogation just talked their
heads off after a short session with the Colonel. Perhaps that was because he is himself partly Mexican, as well as many other things. He is
sixty-two, has no scruples of any kind, and is afraid of nothing. When
he arrived, instead of the formidable — even sinister — character indicated, the Colonel turned out to be a mild, courteous-mannered gent
who stutters slightly when he talks, which he does incessantly, and always with the pained, bewildered air of an Italian baritone who has just
missed a cue. Personally I find him charming and have become greatly
attached to him. It was he who accompanied me in pursuit of the
Goums when they took that town.

October 17, 1943. Life goes on — most uneventfully. These between-
operations periods are pretty boring and I realize more than ever what
a wonderful break I got after the first one and that after all one can't
expect *all* intermissions to be as good as that.

Last week Colonel Campanole and I organized a little party for
the boss. We sat down, eighteen, at a flower-laden table. Goblets of
Kebir, which went very big. Music and dancing in the moonlit patio.
All very O.K. As the evening waxed, *Bunny,* in an expansive moment,

asked the champion girl swimmer (it was his first meeting with her) if she would like to go to the Saturday night U. S. Army dance. *Would* she just! Can a champion girl swimmer swim? For the rest of the evening a certain wistfulness on the part of the Flavias et al., but my deepest and surest instincts bade me keep everything *very* fluid and make no commitments. For an Army dance has some curious ground rules. Each officer is allowed to bring one "date," for whom he is rigidly responsible. The dances are numbered and, to keep the dateless free-lance wolf element from completely gobbling up a guy's Little Red Cross Ridinghood, there is *no* cutting in during even numbers.

Well, I noticed that during the day yesterday Bunny seemed a little thoughtful and when at about 9:30 P.M., as the boss and I were quietly enjoying an after-dinner glass of Kebir and a cigar at the palace, the telephone rang — for me — and Bunny's voice, hoarse with emotion, came quivering over the wire, I wasn't entirely surprised.

"Help," he said. "I'm down at the Grand Hotel, the dance is in full swing, and I'm in a jam."

Well, after a while I went down to the hotel. At the entrance to the ballroom I found Bunny — up to his armpits in Sicilians. It seems that he (and Red Slocum — for protection) had gone out to the country to call for the champion swimmer, and on ringing the doorbell of her domicile, was confronted by Popper and Uncle — *en smoking* — Momma (three hundred and ten pounds) and Auntie (three hundred and forty pounds) — *robe de soir* — not to speak of Gina, Flavia, and an anonymous *cousine*. Into the car they piled. No go. Just not enough cubic feet. Two shifts — back and forth from the suburb to the hotel. After a while it developed that they thought they were coming to a sit-down dinner — hadn't eaten — so sandwiches were run up. A little later the champion swimmer espied a light-footed captain across the room.

"That is the man I want to meet," she said.

Bunny — always the good feller — fixed it up. The captain seemed a little taken aback when she started to caper around him.

"Me, Ginger Rogers," she said. "You, Fred Astaire."

Eventually they put on a number which completely stopped the show. Towards the end of the evening I remember asking Uncle if our American Army hops resembled their Sicilian ones at all.

"Not at all," he said.

"In what way do they differ?" I asked.

"In *every* way," he said.

October 22, 1943. Here it is a year ago today that I left Washington. One always takes one's first war a little hard — and the funny part is that one's second war is infinitely harder to take. Well, the first year ends up for me more or less in the doldrums and more than ever I realize how lucky I was to get that liaison break between the two active operations. Looking back, that was by far the most satisfactory, if least exciting, chapter for the simple reason that *anyone* could have done the active stuff as well or better than I whereas Rabat required sort of special handling which happened to be up the old alley. However, one can't have everything all the time and I have an idea that sticking along with my present boss will prove anything but dull. Incidentally, he told me today that Mrs. Boss had written that there is a story current in Boston that Dick Storey and I were bombed out of a bathtub. He says that he is writing back to say that as far as he knows since being here I have never *been* in a bathtub — which is pretty nearly true — certainly not with Dick Storey.

Dined with Archie last night, who is a major now and is doing a superb job.

October 28, 1943. I am functioning again; my morale has gone up a thousand per cent.

There is no question in my mind that the boss is a great man. For some funny reason he has been very swell to me and one of the things that pleases me most about the outlook is that I think I can now make myself more useful to him than has been the case in the immediate past. Maybe he foresaw that, though not consciously. Next to you he has more intuition and a more continuous and progressive sense of destiny than anyone I have ever seen. Compared with his intuition, the much advertised exterior trappings — themselves quite good, as a matter of fact — are relatively minor characteristics.

C O R S I C A

In late October General Patton flew to Corsica on an inspection trip. Here, as on his later visits to Egypt and Palestine, it was expected that his whereabouts would be reported to the German High Command and help to confuse them as to the next move.

October 31, 1943. Today is your birthday and surely more than a coincidence that it should also be the most completely satisfactory day that I have spent since leaving you early one October morning. A day spent with congenial — oh, so congenial — people, traveling over the most beautiful countryside, without exception, that I have ever seen — beautiful not only scenically but mentally, morally, and symbolically.

Got here yesterday and had a wonderful lunch — real *frites — vin blanc — vin rouge* — very strong. Then a grand tour with a couple of Generals, both very good — one, General Juin, just about the best there is.

Frequent stops to inspect the snappy units standing at attention under the Tricolor. Songs — "Chant de Lorraine." Autumn foliage. Lots of old friends from Rabat. Spent the night at a lovely hotel. Grand dinner — *vin d'honneur.* Off again this morning through even more beautiful scenery — from one high point I thought I distinguished the French coast. Another lunch out of doors on a spectacular terrace with a view second to none. This evening another hotel — practically a palace — bath with hot water — *femme de chambre* — "*Vous voulez peut-être vous reposer un peu avant dîner.*"

Said Commandant Seyes, who rides with me, "*Mais c'est invraisemblable; on a presque l'impression d'être dans un 'hôtel.'*"

November 2, 1943. To continue. Two days of spectacular scenery and the kind of food and hospitality that you and I are accustomed to and above all the French soil — not to speak of the French kilometer stones.

My companions in the car consisted of two Commandants, Bernèd and Seyes, one of whom turned out to be a great friend of Bunny's. For two days they kept up a continuous rapid fire of informative and stimulating data — so good, especially about the Wops and their infinite capacity for retreating and how in really big moments the unit leaders bark out a sharp command such as *"Faccia feroce"* which is supposed to frighten the enemy to death. *"Alors,"* said Bunny's Commandant, the boys advance their chins, roll their lobster eyes, utter piercing cries, and retreat twenty kilometers.

But the one I like the most was in re an old Corsican peasant with a pushcart who found his progress blocked by an Italian tank which had backed up and stopped at the entrance of the tiny street from which the old peasant was trying to gain the main street. Walking round to the front of the tank, the old peasant removed his hat, bowed to the Italian officer in charge, and in a thick Marseilles accent — that makes it even better — he said, *"Pardon, monsieur l'invincible, mais pourriez-vous — pour une fois — vous avancer un* tout *petit peu?"*

Later in the day we stopped just below a little mountain village so that General Juin could visit his mother's birthplace. Big turnout of uncles, aunts, cousins, etc. — great excitement, general *embrassades.*

"Il n'a pas de chance, le général," the aide observed. *"Sont tous des vieux."*

At the end an old girl came up to our group and said, "We are proud that from our race has come a French General."

"Notez, madame, that he is not the first," concluded the aide.

Quite neat, under the circumstances.

We got a big hand through all the towns. Bunny's Commandant is quite a guy with the women, it seems, so every time the aide who was riding in front would sight anything in skirts he'd intone, *"Attention, mon commandant,* to the left."

The Commandant would then lean out of the window, calling, *"Bonjour, ma mignonne,* shall we take you with us?" but with varying reactions.

One promising silhouette turned out to be a fierce old girl with a full beard and a shotgun. To the Commandant's ritual of *"Bonjour,* shall we take you with us," we just missed a volley of lead through the rear window.

November 6, 1943. Well, I'm back in the palace again. Yes, the boss is often cozy, especially alone. In a crowd, and there nearly always is a crowd, one has to watch out for the thunderbolts that are apt to fly in all directions at a moment's notice. So far I have come off unscathed and I think in a way he sort of likes me. Certainly he has been damn nice to me.

There being no news since I wrote you last, will give you a slight picture of the "household" at the palace. Besides the boss and his Negro orderly Meeks — a great character — there is the Chief of Staff (Brigadier General Gay) and his aide — young George Murnane (Lieutenant) and smart as they make them. Then there is the man of oak, Captain Al Stiller, to whom I am much attached, and our doctor, Lieutenant Colonel Charley Odom of New Orleans, a helluva good guy and a real friend — tall, dark, good-looking Southern stuff and bubbling with energy and enthusiasm. Finally there's our pilot, Captain Otis Gunn, also a Southerner — silent hillbilly type — so I thought at first. Actually a great character and a marvelous flyer. All in all a very happy family.

November 14, 1943. You will be interested to know that the Opera season opened today at a matinee performance. The boss was supposed to grace the royal center box, but at the last moment and for sound diplomatic reasons — furnished mostly by myself — he did not attend, so I found myself with the royal box at my exclusive disposal. Hastily gathering a small band of music lovers from the Signal, Medical, and Provost Sections — everybody else already had seats — we rolled up in style to a special royal entrance, were escorted by the Prefect, Mayor, and other local dignitaries up the guard line, royal staircase, to the private antechamber of the royal box. Said antechamber being rather larger and certainly more ornate than the entire *rez-de-chaussée* of Maxime's — thence to the enveloping *fauteuils* of the royal box itself.

The entire auditorium — which makes the Metropolitan look like Tom Never's lodge — was of course completely sold out. The Army, the Navy, and all the wealth and beauty of the island — so many jewels in a vast tiara of red and gold plush. After bowing to Bunny and the three Red Cross girls who occupied his adjacent but more modest *baignoire* I gave the Prefect to understand that the show could go on. It did. And how!

For various reasons I will not attempt to describe the extramusical activities of the next couple of hours except to say that it appears to be an old Sicilian custom to air political differences at the opening of the Opera season. "Say it with arias."

I never knew Verdi could be so stimulating.

The intermission was pretty good too. As the *promenoir* was, to say the least, crowded, it seemed only hospitable to ask some of the citizens in to our antechamber and they didn't need to be asked twice.

More local dignitaries, an airplane manufacturer, a South American heiress, the Commodore of the Yacht Club, a big orange and lemon man, and an ancient diva. Puccini, she said, had written most of his operas for her. She remembered the time she had sung *Aida* on that very stage — with three hundred figurants and six elephants, which, considering her own weight and the fact that the basin is seventy feet deep, was not an unsporting proposition. More of this anon. Must get this off.

November 24, 1943. We and the British have quite a few great leaders, I think — General Marshall, General Alexander, and quite a few others that I wouldn't have missed seeing and hearing for a good deal, but I know of no one living who equals the boss in one respect, namely as regards that amazing capacity for instant rightness and lucid anger. It's a rare and invaluable quality — the Rector used to have it and so did Pa. You can't fake it. You either have it or you haven't. For the individual who blunders, of course, it's hard — it is *foudroyant* — but it has the inestimable virtue of making others fighting mad and God knows that's what we need.

One day during the latter part of the Sicilian campaign the boss was suddenly called upon, or felt that he was, to make a critical decision.* It was one of those decisions where if you guess right others get the credit and if you guess wrong you and you alone get the blame. Well, he was right and it wasn't a guess, either, but that sixth sense made up of intuition and conviction which goes to make a *grand chef.* After it was over he said, "Codman, I consider that yesterday was the first day of this war that I earned my pay as an Army Commander," and he meant it, too.

"If by that, sir, you mean that yesterday you earned a year's pay I'd be inclined to agree." He rather liked that.

Someday I am going to do a piece on the boss's modest, self-deprecating side.

E G Y P T

This trip to Egypt by General Patton and ten members of his staff was for the purpose of giving the Germans the impression that the Allies were contemplating an invasion of the "soft underbelly" of the Balkans. Consequently it was made with no secrecy — quite the contrary — in fact we were instructed to appear in as many night clubs as possible and were even provided with funds to do so.

December 13, 1943. For the last few days I *have* been having a good time, but doubt if you would disapprove as it is all pretty educational. A lovely trip here with the boss and Bunny and a number of others, passing over lightly a lot of history both ancient and modern. And the funny part is that this place, which I've always wanted to see, is just as the books describe it. Our program is pretty crowded, but today was listed by our host, General Sir Henry Maitland Wilson, as a day of rest, so the boss didn't get up till half *past* six.

Along about eight he decided he wanted to go shopping, so he and I were assigned a car and a shopping guide — Lady Ranfurly, a combi-

---

* The decision was whether or not to make an amphibious landing in the rear of the enemy line. Generals Bradley, Keyes, and Truscott were all against the maneuver. It worked perfectly.

nation of the Honorable Brenda and Ethel Barrymore at the age of thirty-six. It all went off very pleasantly.

This afternoon we inspected things and I have just had a stroll in a lovely garden followed by tea that *is* tea. Now a nap and this evening the boss and I will do some more shopping with Lady R.

December 18, 1943. You would have liked the boss's speech to our cousins, the British, and the picture I took of him in front of that rather disappointing desert lioness.

This letter from, or rather over, somewhere in Asia (Palestine) is written under rather crowded conditions and in slightly turbulent air. The scenery is most interesting and evokes to both Bunny and me some of our early school hymns — "Oh, Little Town of Bethlehem." We must send the Rector a postcard.

To the boss, however (it seems that he acted as Allenby's aide for a short time), the sun-baked slopes over which we are passing suggest cavalry rather than calvary, which is as it should be.

December 19, 1943. I wonder what you are doing this minute? Guess what I'm doing. I'm in bed with one of my classic colds, and rather enjoying it. Comfortable room in a comfortable villa. Lots of trays borne by two impeccable British batmen. The boss has just been up to say I mustn't get up for another day, so I did not make the snake-charmer party, but Bunny tells me that he turned out to be the son of Cole Porter's snake charmer and produced serpents from the most unlikely places. The boss let it be known beforehand that if any monkey business occurred, like draping a cobra round his neck, he, the boss, would shoot them both, i.e. the snake charmer first and the snake second. Everything went off pleasantly. The savant, Major Emory, who was conducting the party, was good about the snake charmer's even more famous father. "The poor chap came to rather a sticky end," he said.

"How's that?"

"Well, he was getting *on,* you know, and a bit nearsighted and one day he happened to cross a cobra he *hadn't* planted. Bad luck that."

S I C I L Y

December 21, 1943. Heigh-ho. Here we are winging our way back toward the palace. All in all a fascinating trip. Last night a very mixed and very good farewell party given by the RAF. Buffet, little tables, and afterwards a terrific Russian movie — not fiction — actual. Some very interesting gents present, including a French pilot who started on Bréguets-14's during the last war and has seven thousand hours at the front. The feminine contingent ranged from a British movie star and a bevy of South African WACs to a startling Yugoslavian lady who gave me a most engrossing account of her escape, her married life, her deep sympathy for Americans, especially Marines. It later turned out that she thought *I* was a Marine, but I'm afraid a disappointingly mild one compared to the last Marine colonel of her acquaintance, whom she was "obliged to *rebuke*," good word for being too quick, if you see what I mean. The payoff was when she caught sight of the boss and exclaimed, "And who is that splendid *French* General?" I dared her to go and ask him that herself, but just then the movie started.

Time out while we go over some pretty historic and, I may say, bumpy spots.

Lunch on another historic spot in the Libyan desert while we gas up. Off again. The countryside strewn with burned and busted-up German tanks. Nice sight.

December 24, 1943. Once more I am winging my way toward the palace after twenty-four hours in Algiers. Put in a day of hard work and learned some very interesting and very satisfactory things. Yes, I think that full-circle thing is going to work out O.K.

I *did* get hold of Henry Hyde, who was amazed at being tracked to his lair.

"How did you ever get my number?" he said.

"By the simple expedient of calling up Bill's (Donovan) local chapter," I said.

"But I'm not supposed to be connected with same," etc., etc.

Arranged to meet him for dinner and then dropped in, or up, on

Madame Tron for a recuperative cup of tea — in fact two — in fact three.

"I knew you were going to appear today," she said.

"How so?"

"Because FitzGeorge is giving the party of the year tonight — all the grand personalities — and your timing is always perfect. A small dinner here — just a few intimate friends — and we will all go on afterwards."

"How about transportation?"

"So-and-so and so-and-so have cars."

"No point in being crowded. I'll get another car." And right there is where I made a big mistake. You'll like this one.

Phoned my friend Leon Dostert. He gets the idea. "Will send you my French car at nine-thirty."

You see, in spite of the American rule against American cars carrying feminine freight, there is always the *Système D.*

Very pleasant dinner with Henry at an excellent little *marché-noir* hideaway. Passwords, booths, just like the speak-easy days. Henry good. Is having an interesting time.

9:30. "Henry, I've *got* to go, it's been great seeing you," etc., etc. *Addition,* long good-bys to the *habitués,* the *patron,* the beards. There's no hurry, what the hell. A stimulating drive in Henry's lightless car thru the black drizzling streets, H. driving with one hand, gesticulating with the other, talking six hundred to the minute. Finally he deposes me in a dank, wet square. See you again soon. Good night.

The Tron apartment. *"Ah,* enfin *vous voilà."* The party has shrunk to Madame Tron, Madame Something-or-other, whose name I can never remember, who lives with Madame T., and the young French captain who was there last time and who has just appeared again *en perm.*

The girls are dressed to — and including — the eyebrows. Final dabs of perfume, lipsticks, etc. *"Alors,* shall we go? The others have gone on in their cars."

"Has Leon's car reported in?" I ask.

Blank looks. "Didn't you *come* in his car?"

"No, it's supposed to meet us here."

"It *must* be there then."

We all go down. Outside, blackness and torrential rain. No car. *"Ah, ça, alors."* Up again. Phone calls, lots of phone calls. No good. Nobody home. Leon out. Henry, no answer. FitzGeorge is six miles out in the country and hasn't *got* a telephone.

"Haven't you any de Gaulle friends?" I asked.

"Well, there's the Ministre d'Épuration," Madame Machin says.

"Ah, ça, non." Madame T. says. *"J'aime mieux renoncer."*

"Et tous ces grands personalités··· *. . ."* Madame Machin gets plaintive.

"They say that D.* and the beautiful Diana arrived this afternoon and will be there."

"What!"

"No, they won't be here for another week."

Madame T. says, "Even so, something has *got* to be done."

Hold everything. Down and out into the night. Eleven blocks in the rain. Mother Red Cross. My idea is to wake up somebody — maybe Louisa's back — and borrow an ambulance with four stretchers. No good. Louisa is not back, and all the girls have gone to *another* party of the year — presumably in the ambulances. Back eleven blocks, still raining — up again. Thank God, anyway the *ascenseur* works. Madame M. asleep on the sofa. Madame T. nearly so. The Captain pretty sardonic about the whole thing. A drink, a great big drink. The Captain and I have a long argument about France. I like the Captain. Another drink and we have a long argument about Russia. From Madame M.'s corner a light, regular snore. In their gala finery both ladies are sound asleep.

"This is perhaps the moment to leave," the Captain says. We do, on tiptoe. And that is how I *didn't* go to the FitzGeorge party of the year.

December 25, 1943. Christmas Morning. Well, here I am in my familiar palace bedroom, of which I have grown quite fond; its brocaded walls, rococo ceiling, and Goldberg chandelier. My accumulated pos-

---

* Duff Cooper and Lady Diana, his wife; he was British Ambassador to the French Algiers Government.

sessions are strewn around in a disorder which would probably pain you, but it's sort of comfortable to me.

Last evening got back just in time for Christmas Eve dinner here followed by a movie — not very good. At a quarter to twelve I went with the boss to midnight Mass. The place was packed and the wind whistled through the glassless windows gutting the candles and swirling the priestly robes. It was an impressive service. Doughboys, gobs, Britishers — the straight Episcopal service — no funny business — so familiar, so *unstrange* in these strange surroundings.

When we got back everyone had gone to bed, so I revived the dying embers, got out a bottle, and had a very cozy hour and a half with the boss talking of things past and things to come. Of the former he said something which naturally pleased me and touched me very much. I had said something about what a wise and supremely difficult thing he had done in consistently maintaining complete silence in the face of grossly unfair allegations and misstatements.*

On that whole thing he said, "You have been sound and I have taken your advice — as a friend."

Of things to come I can only say life *does* seem to have an inexorable logic and that I find myself exactly where I ought to be and where you would want me to be — and that applies to Bunny too.

January 1, 1944. Happy New Year!

Well, here it is New Year's Day and I am sailing along with the boss over a floor of clouds that look like limitless stretches of New England snow — very seasonal up here.

Last night at the palace we gathered about us some of the local folk to see the New Year in — and what with the Christmas tree and an open fire and plenty of Kébir it all passed off very pleasantly. Yes, it's been quite a year all in all and this coming one bids fair to be no less eventful. Where, with whom, how, when, or what I now have not the slightest idea. The Army is a funny place. Last week I *thought* I knew exactly what was going to happen. Now it is just as much of a mystery to me as it is to you, probably more so. We can only wait and see.

* This is a reference to the famous "soldier-slapping" incident.

Bunny horrified me by showing me a letter from Red Slocum saying that you were sick in bed, though he also said that your vivid account of Washington activities belied your prone position.

Yes, the slapping incident, as such, seems to have blown over, though I hear that the ebullient Mr. Drew Pearson is now sounding off in re the boss — and, of all people, General Noguès. All that seems very long ago now, but if later on anyone would really like to know the ins and outs of the early Moroccan days just sing to them, "Come to Poppa, come to Poppa, do."

Here comes lunch. Sandwiches and hot coffee. What, no hostess?

That was salubrious and took the chill off and it was pleasant sitting in with the pilot just now and getting Fred Allen by rebroadcast. I hope you were listening too.

Must stop now and work out appointments with the boss. Will be seeing Algiers soon and maybe Diana. Again Happy New Year. *Buono anno* 1944, to me one great question mark.

January 4, 1944. Once again we are scudding along over the clouds, the boss, the man of oak, and I, after a full and for me slightly poignant Algiers day. Learning that Diana was arriving, I, yesterday morning, called our cousins' (the British) place of business. The dialogue went something like this:

Opening inquiry by me.

"Well, I'll see. Who wishes to speak to her?"

"Colonel Codman of Boston." Long wait.

"No, it will be quite impossible to speak with her. Resting. Very tiring trip," etc., etc.

"Let me speak to Mr. Cooper." Long wait. A new man's voice.

"Hello. Who is this?"

"Charley. Is that you, Duff?"

"No, this is Major Something-or-other."

"Well, now, Major, listen carefully," and I got quite dynamic.

Long wait. Very long. A cool, noncommittal voice, feminine. "Hello."

"Is that you, Diana?"

"Who is speaking?" Same voice.

"Charley Codman." And then everything got all right.

"Come here *immediately*," she said.

"Where's *here*?"

"I haven't the slightest idea. Where are *you*? I'll come there."

"This is the gent's toilet of the officers' mess."

"No, that won't do at this time of the morning. Isn't there a Ritz or something somewhere?"

"There is *not*. However, there is the Hotel X."

"Right, I'll be there in ten minutes."

Lobby of the Hotel X — ten minutes — another ten minutes and another.

Then Diana wanders in in a gray *tailleur* — just a suggestion of WAC influence. Gray shirt, yellow bow tie, golden hair surmounted by a green hat (out of Michael Arlen by the Brooks Uniform Co.). Same nose, same eyes, same voice, no change at all — amazing.

"I must have gone to the wrong place," she said. "A *very* large bar with very curious people." She looked around the dark, empty lobby.

"And what do we do now?" she said.

"Anything you say."

"Well, one *must* go to the Kasbah, mustn't one? One might as well get it over with at once. By the way, who is Captain Katzman?"

"*I* don't know. Who is Captain Katzman?"

"They told me that a Captain Katzman wanted to speak to me on the telephone. It didn't sound promising, but I thought I'd better investigate."

"Glad you did."

The Kasbah. The idea was to find electric light fixtures for the new house. You can imagine how successful *that* was. However, the conversations with innumerable shopkeepers in clipped, precise French were all good review material.

Also a certain amount of news. The last days of Singapore. "Such a perfect place, everyone so happy and so *rich,* and so well organized. Everything beautifully thought out — everything except defense. Overlooked somehow. A pity that."

Back to Diana's car and up to the new house, which has lovely grounds but no hot water and *few* electric fixtures. I doubt if there will be more of either, but, as I told her, it will make a nice summer place.

Dinner was fun. Duff in rare form. Harold Macmillan *good*. Hadn't seen him since Anfa when he was living with Bob Murphy and Averell.

Both D.'s particularly wanted to be remembered to you and we all wept because you weren't right there *now* — as Bunny would say. By ten o'clock everyone was exhausted from talking — hard and fast.

And so good-by to all that. And now what? I wish I knew.

MALTA

January 6, 1944. It's going to get so that I can't write a letter at all *except* in an airplane. Excuse the autograph but it is cold and I have on those nice woolly gloves you gave me.

The last two days have been interesting in the highest degree. A week end that for a long time the boss and I have been planning to make, and an enthralling two days it has been. Lord Gort a charming host. Gosh, how you would like him.

A seventeenth-century manor house, service impeccable. Tea in bed. Steaming hot water — pitcher on the kind of washstand that I remember as a child in Cotuit. Help-yourself breakfast. Kedgeree eggs and bacon, porridge, scones, the morning paper on a rack in front of you so you can use both hands for toast and marmalade. A staff of younger fellers, all out of the top drawer, *so* good. A day of sight-seeing — visible record of one of the great epics of the war. History — medieval and modern, some great "chaps." An appropriate cat — tea with the Navy, dinner with the Governor — billiards afterwards — *that* was a good number. What a race! Am now reconciled to *not* seeing the southern coast of France.

January 10, 1944. Once again we wing our way toward the palace. This time after a couple of vivid days at the Italian front. I must say the air, as always, is purer up there — also considerably colder. Somehow it was more reminiscent of the last war than of anything I have seen so far — and since it all passed off happily I may say I came nearer getting mine than at any time since September, 1918 — including the beach at Fedala and the first three days of our last campaign.

The first day was passed visiting General Clark and Colonel Saltzman in a palace* even bigger than ours. Next day, up the line. Endless camions, mud, all the old *mise en scène*. A cold night up forward in my — very different, I find — sleeping bag. Next morning some strenuous climbing amidst rugged scenery and reverberating cannonades. Lunch with an active unit and up again into the hills. More rugged scenery and some interesting echo effects.

Late afternoon. Just time, however, to go take a look at a recently captured point. Up we go. Very interesting.

"Well," said our guide, General Keyes, "I guess you've seen about all that there is to see."

That was a cue for the Boches on the hill opposite. Whiz bang, whiz bang four times. A shower of stones — those tin helmets do come in handy at times. Two hits against the cliffs right over our heads and just below us. Not more than ten yards away. Two nice new craters. Pretty good shooting.

The boss was delighted. "That set me up more than a bottle of champagne," he said when later we gathered at a convenient mess in a quieter area. "Proves that my luck is still in."

"It certainly is" — along those lines anyway.

It was rather exhilarating once you found you still had both arms and legs and a head, and I must say I slept longer and more soundly than I have in months.

And now back to wait around until Lady Fortune or someone tells us what the hell we are going to do. As you know, I like fluidity, but it would be nice to have a glimmering of where, when, and with whom.

January 15, 1944. In regard to the soldier-slapping incident, it now seems to be closed except for the continuous fan mail, which it is one of my jobs to handle and which is running rather better than the Gallup poll on the same subject — about 89% pro and 11% con. Taken as a

* U. S. Fifth Army Headquarters at Caserta, near Naples.

whole, it forms quite an illuminating human document. What you say is quite true about the importance of backing a leader, specially one who has the rare quality of making people *want* to fight.

In my letter before last I wrote you of a little session at the front. Apparently the boss has written to a couple of people about it. If it should get rather colorful in the telling don't worry about it since a miss is as good as a mile. It *was* a fairly close thing and if he (the boss) hadn't stopped for about thirty seconds to take a picture it would have been curtains all right.

January 16, 1944. After dinner last night the boss got going on Wellington, whose life he is very much immersed in at the moment. Illustrating Wellington's really lofty side, the boss particularly likes the one where Wellington's aide and lifelong friend, Lord Something-or-other, staggers mortally wounded into his tent gasping, "Milord, this time they've done for me." And Wellington, looking up for a moment over the top of his book, says calmly, "Egad, sir, *so* they have."

Well, here we are, waiting, waiting as the time just meanders along.

Have been doing a certain amount of reading for a change and I, too, have found particularly interesting the life of Wellington. From it I learned that those waiting periods are harder on army commanders than any number of strenuous campaigns, and what I never knew till now was that the Iron Duke had more than his share of frustrations — of being kept in ignorance, pushed around, passed over, and generally stymied. Being a great man, he managed through it all to retain that most invaluable of all assets — his self-confidence — and in the end came through magnificently. But it does seem queer that in war times a fighting leader should not be used to the fullest extent, particularly as his qualities are necessarily of a kind that become impaired with disuse, all of which is, of course, academic.

CHAPTER VII

England

(January–July, 1944)

On or about 22 January 1944 General Patton received orders to go to England without delay. He was authorized to take no one with him except his aides. Later practically all of his staff were released to General Patton and were flown to England. Headquarters, Third Army — General Patton's new command — was established in Peover Hall, Knutsford, England. His troops, consisting of the VIII, XII, and XX Corps, were widely dispersed over England and Ireland. The XV Corps, General Haislip commanding, consisting of the 2d, 5th, 8th Infantry Divisions, was bivouacked near Belfast, Ireland. These were the first troops visited and inspected by General Patton. His presence in England and his command were kept a secret in order that the enemy could be made to believe that the landing in Normandy was to be made in two different places, with the feint near Cherbourg and the real attack near the mouth of the Seine. General Patton himself did not move to the Continent until July.

MARRAKECH

January 25, 1944. It seems like a long time ago that I was sitting in this garden of the Villa Taylor with Bob Sherwood and my host Ken Pendar, but it looks very much the same and is certainly one of the beauty spots of the world. This evening it has a slightly hollow feeling, though, a little as if it had been sucked dry by all the *va-et-vient* and the famous people of immense vitality who, as they pass through, absorb and carry off a part of the garden's essence.

I had to go and take a look at the Mamounia Hotel for old times' sake and it is lovely, the snow mountains, the tropical verdure, the stateliest of all minarets and — that balcony where one breakfasts in the sun.

One way or another I've seen a good deal of this strange continent during the last year and maybe I got it a bit in my blood. Anyhow, this evening I feel the way I did on leaving Rabat for good.

January 26, 1944

> A groggy night o'er this old town
> It had me low and damn near down
> I viewed the morning with alarm
> Blind instrument flying had lost its charm
> How long, I wondered, must this thing last
> But the age of miracles hadn't passed
> For suddenly — Adele Astaire
> And in soggy so-and-so
> The sun was shining everywhere.*

L O N D O N

February 3, 1944. Yesterday, after spending two days at General Wood's headquarters near Badminton, where he inspected the 4th Armored Division, the General drove to London to see his old friend General Patch,† just in from the Pacific and on his way to North Africa to take command of the Seventh Army. In order to discuss impending staff changes in privacy, General Patch was to meet General Patton at the new Mount Street flat recently assigned the latter by S.O.S. for his personal use when in town. It was around 4 P.M. when

---

* This parody on George Gershwin's "A Foggy Day in London Town" indicated his arrival in London.
† Major General Alexander M. Patch.

Sergeant Mims brought the car to a halt before a low three-story build-ing on a quiet street back of Grosvenor Square.

"Is this it?" the General said as we got out.

"Yes, sir."

The entrance was unobtrusive, the vestibule small and dark.

"Since they mean to keep me under wraps, this should do fine," the General said.

But he was in for a surprise. The door of the second-floor landing was opened by an S.O.S. corporal who saluted smartly. Paneled hall-way. Exotic prints on the wall. Thick carpet. Soft indirect lighting. Pe-riod sitting room, more boudoir than salon.

"Who the hell picked this place?" the General said.

"General Lee himself, I believe, sir," the corporal said.

"I might have known," the General muttered. Then crisply, "Where's my room?"

We followed the corporal down another hallway leading to a closed door. The corporal threw it open.

"Your room, sir," he said, stepping aside and to attention.

Rooted to the threshold, the General surveyed the white bear rug, the walls and curtains of pink brocade, the triptych-mirrored dressing ta-ble, and beyond through an open door the glint of nickel fixtures and two-tone seafoam tile. Then, as his eye caught the reflection in the mir-ror on the ceiling of the enormous bed lying low and lascivious under its embroidered silk coverlet, the silence was broken by a single highly charged exclamation.

"JESUS," the General said.

It seemed like an appropriate time to ease back along the corridor and inspect the floor above. Three more master bedrooms. Two baths. Serv-ants' quarters. By the time I got down again, General Patch had ar-rived. Over a couple of Scotches he and the Old Man were deep in Gen-erals' talk.

"This morning at SHAEF," General Patch was saying, "Beetle claimed that particular matter was high-level stuff. He said I would get instructions in due course."

"That whole headquarters is so goddam high level you have to carry an oxygen tank to live up there." General Patton's voice rose. "To hell with Beetle, see Ike himself. Though by now they've probably got him completely isolated."

General Patch's serious face lit up when he smiled. "I'll keep that in mind, George," he said.

The General introduced me, took a sip of his drink, put it down on the table, hard.

"Look, Sandy," he said, "I'd rather be shot than spend the evening sitting around this Anglican bordello. How about it, Codman?"

"What about a show?"

"Anything worth seeing?"

"Yes. The Lunts in *There Shall Be No Night.*"

"The Lunts are always good," General Patch observed expectantly.

"Never saw them," General Patton said. "What's the play about?"

"The Russian invasion of Finland. Really about war in general. Bob Sherwood's best, I think."

"Is he that O.W.I. individual I saw in Casablanca?"

"Yes."

"You're sure it's good?"

"Yes, sir. I saw it during the Boston tryout. Twice."

"Are you game, Sandy?"

"Yes, sure."

"All right. Get three seats."

Phone call to Colonel Solbert of Special Services.

"You would pick the one show that is sold out for the entire engagement," he said.

"The General knows he can depend on you, Colonel."

"All right. All right. Call you back."

A few minutes later, "Three in the fourth row center in your name at the box office. Curtain goes up at seventeen-thirty."

"Funny hour to be going to the theater," the General said, looking at his watch. "Tell that corporal to produce some sandwiches and Mims to have the car here at seventeen-twenty."

With the faint hope of preserving the two Generals' incognito, I phoned the theater and arranged to have them smuggled in through a fire exit. By the time we got there the show had started and they slipped unnoticed into their seats. Alfred was in the midst of the broadcasting scene. Remember? Even before he had finished and Lynn had said, "You are wonderful, darling," both Generals were completely engrossed. What a play it is! And what acting! Not until the entrance of the German consul, however, did I realize that since you and I saw it, the locale has been transferred — for obvious reasons — from Finland to Greece and the Nazis substituted for the Russians. The changes in the text are surprisingly few and the play's total impact is, if anything, more shattering. You remember in the next to the last scene when Alfred, learning that his son has been killed in action, prepares to accompany the other doomed occupants of the schoolhouse on their final combat mission. Halfway through his valedictory he is interrupted by off-stage gunfire. Last night the sound-effects man might just as well have taken the evening off. With perfect timing a buzz bomb crashed through the roof of what must have been a fairly nearby building. The theater shook and bits of plaster sifted down over actors and audience alike. Alfred never batted an eye.

"The Germans are only a short distance away," he said, going right on with the lines of the play, "so please permit me to finish." Throughout the auditorium not a cough, not a shuffle of feet. A profound hush unbroken until the scene's end and Alfred's exit as he rips off the Red Cross arm band. And then applause such as you have never heard, surpassed only when the final slow curtain came down on Lynn and the old uncle in the family sitting room waiting with shotguns across their knees for the Germans to come. For the next ten minutes there was a standing ovation, the like of which I would never have thought possible in an English theater.

Backstage Lynn and Alfred were quite surprised when we irrupted into their dressing room. I may say their first question was to ask after you. Their suggestion that we all adjourn to their apartment at the Savoy was accepted with alacrity and Mims got us there in record time.

"How did you arrange for that appropriate bombardment?" the General asked Alfred, who was passing the drinks around.

"You know, the same thing happened in Birmingham," Alfred said. "Remember, Lynnie?"

"Yes, I remember," Lynn said. "The audience loved it."

"Curiously enough," Alfred continued, "if one is on stage it is not at all disturbing."

"True," Lynn said. "It doesn't seem to have anything to do with one-self, merely with the character in the play."

"That's interesting," the General said. "I have made a profound study of the fear emotion, and what you say confirms a theory of my own."

As the evening progressed, both Generals warmed to their own subject matter. For an hour, two hours, three hours, they regaled the Lunts with tales of the Far East, of Africa, of Sicily. Something General Patch said made Lynn ask, "What exactly, General Patch, are you fighting for?"

"Why, what all of us are fighting for — to resist aggression, to defend our country, to preserve our way of life."

"And you, General Patton?"

"Sandy is talking through his hat," the General said. He raised his glass to Lynn, the familiar *enfant-terrible* gleam in his eye. "I, dear lady, have been fighting all my life and hope to continue indefinitely to do so for the simple reason that I love fighting."

Of course, both Lynn and Alfred were entranced.

February 7, 1944. So much has happened since I wrote to you last and all of it good — yet as usual I can only retail the froth — though pretty fine froth at that.

Last week Rod Tower and Joe Larocque came in and dined with me at my temporary apartment and we had a lovely evening. Rod seems very chipper and I was really awfully glad to see him. He had to go back to work, but Joe spent the night. He has a swell job, was in great form, and even with a two-day beard looked wonderful. Next evening dropped in on Lynn and Alfred, who were quite pleasantly surprised. It *did* seem like old times, and we laughed and wept over Alice and Alec.*

* Alice Duer Miller and Alexander Woollcott had recently died.

After that to supper at Marian Hall's, where were Julian Allen and, believe it or not, Adele Astaire. She hasn't changed at all as far as I can see nor has her language. I almost forgot to say that Bill Donovan was there too. It was fun seeing all those people, but now the real work begins and will continue indefinitely. Was glad to find that I remembered practically the entire score of *Funny Face,* though Adele was better than I on *The Band Wagon.* However, with no disloyalty to George Gershwin, my favorite song this year is that one of Vernon Duke's that Evelyn Hoey used to warble — "April in Paris."

February 22, 1944. The nicest birthday present today was three letters from you. You *did* see Campanole. I am so glad. *Confused!* Of course he's confused — that's his great charm. If he weren't confused he wouldn't be nearly as much fun.

Bunny? Yes, I miss him more than I can say, but perhaps before too long we will be reunited. As I wrote to him yesterday, we have done quite a tour together in both wars and I do so hope we can make the *grande rentrée* arm in arm, so to speak.

In re "the unbearable flatness of life for all returning soldiers," I think on the contrary, much much on the contrary. For the young, the heedless, the unhappily married, the congenital misfits — sure — but for any and all with the slightest semblance of roots or human relationships or habits, return to civilized living will be sheer heaven. One of the many ironies of this war is the perverse fortitude of the Boche engendered by his own obscene way of life. He knows he is licked now. The odds have more than evened up and if he had any sense he would throw in the sponge now as he did in 1918. But he won't for the simple reason that his upbringing and indoctrination have effectively removed from the peaceful way of life all desirability. For what, indeed, does postwar Germany hold for the young Boche? Himself void of the simplest humanities, what does the prospect of the homeland invite? Why *should* he want to go back to Germany? Would you? *So* we, who, with a few exceptions, e.g. the boss, don't really much *enjoy* war, will be obliged by the Boches' carefully cultivated inadaptability to peace to fight to the finish — and it *must* be to the finish *this* time. Not only the Boches — and then the little yellow men — but also the cumulative desire to go home. The last will require more character than the first two put together. I *know*.

February 23, 1944. More letters from you today.

Think of Gus being a private in the Army. It's all pretty remarkable. Am writing to him in New Mexico. Isn't that one of the places we went through coming back from Hollywood?

Went to a Red Cross tea this afternoon. Very pleasant, very county — wholesome girls with the clean, crisp quality of green lettuce, as Alec once remarked. Their collective sense of humor, however, is somewhat different from our own. While I was standing in the dense crowd talking to Lady Something-or-other, a slight gesticulation with which I was trying to emphasize a point dashed a full cup of tea out of the hand of nearby somebody else — down the back and over the derrière of one of our naval commanders — a four-striper. That *he* didn't think it funny was not surprising, particularly as his uniform was brand new and the cup very full — loaded beyond the normal ration allowance with sugar and cream — but after it was all over and I had wiped him off and apologized and he had moved sourly away I *did* think the girls might have cracked a smile. They *didn't* — at least not until after I had explained to them how screamingly funny it was and even then they seemed only half convinced.

March 8, 1944. Pleasant evening in town last night. On the way home stopped in to say hello to Alfred and Lynn. The preliminary dialogue went like this:

Desk clerk on phone: "A Colonel Codman to see you."

Lynn's voice, very firm: "Tell him we are not at home."

I grabbed the phone. "How do you mean, not at home? This is Charley Codman."

Lynn: *"Darling,* why didn't they say so? Come right up," etc.

Then after a while: "But who is this Colonel Katzman they said was downstairs?"

It invariably goes like that — none of our old friends of that *monde* can accept the idea of me as a *militaire* — I don't know that *I* can.

Very pleasant gathering. The Greek ambassador, Lady Sibyl Colfax, Mr. and Mrs. Hamish Hamilton — publisher friend of Alfred's and Cass's and Louis Bromfield's. Oh, I almost forgot, also present was Bob Sherwood, as lean as life and twice as tall. He said he's formally asked for me three times and been turned down three times. I'd never even *heard* about it.

March 15, 1944. I *can* say, I guess, that I am living in a pleasant country house, Peover Hall, Knutsford, with all the people I know and like, sharing a room with Charley Odom, and that we are working like hell and that the future should be, to say the least, interesting. We occasionally see some of the local people at Red Cross Club openings or Sunday lunch or now and then here at the house for movies. Last night, for instance, we had a showing of *Madame Curie* and one or two guests came in, including an American girl friend of Edgar and Hope Scott's who had seen them recently. A nice Philadelphia girl married to a Lieutenant Bromley Davenport.

Yes, I think you would like General Patton, although about three quarters of the time you would probably be holding your ears, which would be a pity, too, because the amazing flow of language is studded with almost continuous gems. A real and literal *enfant terrible — enfant* (see *High Wind in Jamaica*) in his candor, intuitiveness, shrewdness, and unawareness; *terrible* in the intensity of his convictions, his self-discipline, and all the Spartan virtues. And a marvelous Thespian gift and sense of humor — the latter, of course, not to be depended upon. Yes, fate so far has been and is being good.

Last night Bunny dined with the boss and me. It is certainly grand to have him with us again.

Went to see Lord Edgerton* this morning. A wonderful place — like a set for *The Earl of Chicago*. Having got lost in the miles of driveway coming in from one direction, I asked him on leaving whether I couldn't go out the other direction.

* The local great landowner.

144

"You might try it," he said. "Personally I haven't used it for some years, seventeen to be exact — don't fancy the view. However, it's probably passable, though my friends tell me it is in sad need of repair."

His friends are quite right.

March 22, 1944. No news today but I thought you would enjoy the following dialogue.

Scene: the mess.

Characters: our household of eight, plus Campanole (who is back) and Paul Harkins (his father used to be the dramatic critic of the *Boston Record*), a very good guy.

A great deal of kidding of Campy about the girls — he is supposed to be Casanova incarnate — quite heated stuff about the relative merits of the *femmes* of Casa, Palermo, Naples, et al. Towards the end of dinner it was going pretty strong when in a momentary pause Harkins, who hadn't contributed much — and he's no prig, either — pushed his plate away, leaned back, and said:

"Well, speaking for myself, I have yet to see in all of Morocco, Algeria, Tunisia, Egypt, Sicily, Italy, or what have you a single girl who is one tenth as attractive as my wife."

Silence, then the boss put down his coffee cup.

"Harkins," he said quietly — he's wonderful at the quick switcheroo — "that was a very fine thing to say. And I have *no* doubt it is true — of all of us."

March 24, 1944. No, I don't regret any of the requests that have been made for me so far. I guess it is on the cards that I should continue with the boss. He seems to want me, and that being the case, I ought to see quite a lot of country, and familiar country at that. My job is the same, but there will be more and more to do. Yesterday he said he had started to recommend me for promotion to a full colonelcy but found that this could not be done without relieving me from my present job. I said — and meant it — that for the coming party there is nothing I would like so much as to remain with him. So that is that.

Here in the country the day-to-day life is not very different from that at the palace, except busier. Same cast, both as to principals and extras, including our faithful cooks and waiters.

Breakfast 7 to 7:30 — orange juice, cereal, eggs, *tea.*

Lunch — soup, one entree, dessert.

Dinner — soup, roast, dessert.

I have a nice room, shared with Charley Odom, open fireplace burning the old-fashioned cannel coal.

This evening a bunch of us are going to a soirée at the Leicester-Warrens', parents of Lady Leese, wife of Sir Oliver Leese, Commander of the British Eighth Army. It's a lovely house and ought to be quite pleasant, especially as Bunny, Charley O., and I will act as sort of ushers.

March 25, 1944. Well, this seems like old times, jaunting along over the haze with the boss in a nice new plane. Just a local flight, but very pleasant after the many long, cold motor rides of the past few weeks.

The party last night at the Leicester-Warrens' was a great success. After it was over and we had come home to our hall the boss sat up with Charley Odom and me for a couple of additional hours — his Alpine lamp is in our room, which makes it all very cozy — and we had a post-mortem worthy of 53 Pinckney Street. Gosh, I wish you had been there. I have seldom laughed longer or harder. The boss going over his dialogue with an enormous Amazon:

"When I first came to the north country I found myself on my back most of the time," she said.

"Have you many children?" the boss asked.

"No, no, you don't understand," she said. "The hunting field — fences — tossed frequently — always lit on me back. What."

"Quite," the boss said.

A lot more.

Also about how the boss, on the night before we sailed from America, went to see General Pershing — he was his aide in the last war.

"General," he said, "I can't tell you where I'm going, but I couldn't go without coming to ask you for your blessing."

"You shall have it," General Pershing said. "Kneel down."

What he said will only appear posthumously, but it was very fine stuff.

I don't know if I am getting this over to you, but to me the straight *moyen-âge* quality which permeates every thought and action of the boss is terrifically exhilarating and we all *so* need it at this point.

April 10, 1944. Jimmy Cagney, who was to give a show in the afternoon, came to lunch. Very quiet and reserved and, like Bob Hope and all the others, played straight man for the boss. A nice, likable guy, actually a little reminiscent of Georgie Cohan.

In the afternoon it rained and then cleared up. Went over to Sir Robert Burrough's for tea. He has two daughters — one who hunts, one who wears a monocle — and a South African daughter-in-law. It was all a little like Tolland and rather cozy and pleasant, particularly as none of them are too keen about anything. Even the hunting girl doesn't insist that you jump on that horse which is so quiet with the children. I brought them all back to the hall for dinner and for the movies — it was supposed to be one of Cagney's but turned out to be Joan Crawford — and then motored them all back again by the light of a sultry bomber moon. Well, that's about all — it is six o'clock and nice and sunny and I'm going to take a walk with Bunny.

L O N D O N

May 12, 1944. From that apartment in town where the boss and I are spending a day or two, here are some random thoughts regarding my old branch of the service. No, I honestly don't think I have any regrets whatsoever in that direction. In the first place, one way or another, I have already as it is had more time in the air in this war than in the last — not combat, of course, but then it wouldn't have been combat flying in the Air Corps and somehow I think there would have been something just a trifle *gênant* about being a nonflying, or at least noncombatant, aviator. And don't get me wrong. I have the warmest sort of feeling for all my old friends in the Air Corps and they all seem to be more than genial as far as I am concerned. If I have a real justification for being mixed up with this war it is chiefly in terms of the things you and I have been doing since the last war (our travels in France) and it is a satisfaction to feel that those qualifications have been put to some use — immediately after the original landing, on and off over the intermediate period, again now, and pretty soon more so, I imagine. Finally, there is this point — flying *was* the new game, the novel feature. In this war the novelty (in the present form, anyway; basically, of course, it is age-old) is the amphibious landing — and while, as you know, I like my comforts as well as the next person, there is a certain special kick in wading ashore in unlikely places, particularly in the company of a personality who I for one am convinced is a great — and a necessary — man.

May 27, 1944. Writing you in an easy-riding plane, jaunting home to Peover Hall in the cool of a lovely summer evening, after a lovely, lovely day — a day with the Air boys.

This morning at a very interesting conference before a large and very interesting map, someone suddenly pounded me on the back and hissed in a low voice, "You're looking well," and it was Joe, whom I was particularly delighted to see as I hadn't seen him for a long time. He nudged me again and said:

"Look who I've brought with me."

Sure enough that cigar-store-Indian face and wonderful laugh — Colonel Ralph Stearley.* So you needn't write Mildred to find out where he is. Has a swell job, looks wonderfully — *very* put out when I told him he had been reported sick.

At lunch — I of course had lunch with him — he gave me all the gossip about the old section.

This afternoon a number of visits to outfits that seemed, oh, so natural. Except mechanically, things haven't changed very much since the last war. The same sort of leafy dells, the same sort of nervous anxiety before the briefing — the briefing itself a great improvement here, I must say. The warming up, the take-off — a beautiful sight that — the rendezvous, and off to the target. I would have given a million dollars to have had you at that briefing, and seen your face when they

---

* Major General Ralph Stearley, USAF (Ret.).

flashed the picture of that particular target (Berlin) on the screen. I think you would have died with pleasure.

June 6, 1944. D Day. I can just *see* you listening to the radio announcement that we have just been listening to and what it will mean to you. By one of those coincidences of which the world is so full there arrived just before the broadcast a letter from St. Jean. I know you will keep it for me as it evokes so much of the essence of those fearsome days of 1940.

Yesterday I took a long walk with Bunny, who had just got news of the death of his father. Here, too, many memories of the old days came back with great clarity and little sense of lapsing time between. Time and space and strange entities.

June 8, 1944. I can still visualize you listening in on all the rushing events of the last two days and can imagine your thoughts as all those good old familiar names crowd into the teeming air. There is nothing I can write you about at the moment except the visit to our place of a big shot whose aide, when I went up to him to give the high sign, turned out to be Charley MacArthur. While he and his boss were in talking to my boss, word came that a strange female was lurking around some fairly secret precincts. Investigated and found it was Charley's driver, a Yugoslavian WAC.

Charley's departure in the best tradition. "How is Theodora?" "Fine." "What do you hear from Helen . . . etc. Well, so long, look me up at Claridge's." He dashes out to his waiting boss, the Yugoslavian WAC throws her into second, Charley waves out of the window, his hat flashing with glinting stars. In the general excitement he had taken my boss's cap.

June 14, 1944. In following all the events of the last week I can practically feel you looking over my shoulder. If I don't answer in detail it is because there is practically nothing I can write about at the present time except to say that we are all pretty busy and watching and waiting.

You are quite right. This is the main event and all of us now are in something much bigger than any individual.

June 26, 1944. Well, here I am again on that very comfortable train in a lovely stateroom watching the late evening landscape slide by the window. Have covered a lot of ground today with the boss and General Bradley and it's all been pretty interesting.* At dinner we worked on the boss's boss to try to get Lebel attached to us and I think it may work out.

Spent a good part of the day riding with his British aide, who is a great friend of Jock Balfour's. The world does seem to get smaller and smaller each day.

I am glad you are going to see Arch Alexander. Give him my very, very best. He did a swellissimee and I can think of no one with whom I have been thrown in this war whom I like and respect more than I do him. Both he and Jean are lovely people and I envy you seeing them, and now to sleep to the clackety clack of those railroad rhythm blues.

July 4, 1944. If I could only explain it to you — which I can't — you would at once realize that this job combines *all* the elements in a way no other that I know of does.

What do I *think* about things, you ask. Well, that's a tall order, but I can tell you the essentials anyway. I think that what has been accomplished since a year ago last November, when we scrambled ashore at Fedala with 75's whistling around in rather unfriendly fashion, to the present moment is a rather remarkable performance, and to have been even a tiny part of it, and still be, is satisfying. I think I am very lucky to have been where I have been and am and where I will be.

For me it has been so far a *bonne guerre.*

Yesterday I found myself at lunch next to a sympathetic Commandant. One thing led to another and such is the plethora of coincidences in this strange war that it was almost without astonishment that I learned that he was the owner of that old Voisin in which I took my first plane ride in 1915. And here we are again working the *rentrée* together.

---

* This trip was taken in General Lee's private car to inspect many divisions, including the French 2d Armored Division (Leclerc).

CHAPTER VIII

France

(July–August, 1944)

The movement of Headquarters, Third Army and General Patton to the Continent was top secret. Interception of German radio messages gave definite proof that Hitler thought the original landing was a feint and that the main invasion would be made between the Somme and the Seine rivers and that General Patton, due to his great success in the amphibious landings in North Africa and in Sicily, would be in command of this main effort. The G-2 Section of Allied Headquarters had aided and abetted this belief by Hitler. In fact, so successful were they that many German divisions were held in reserve by Hitler in order to meet this phantom attack.

July 6, 1944. Shortly after the morning briefing at Braemar House, Salisbury, our final headquarters in England, we drove to the nearby airstrip. Al Stiller and I checked with Meeks on the bedding rolls and personal effects. General Patton, followed by Willie,* briskly mounted the steps of his C-47. Climbing aboard a few moments later, we found Willie already curled up and asleep in the General's peep, which, with wheels blocked, was lashed aft. The General himself was in his accustomed forward seat securing his safety belt.

"We'll pick up our air cover before hitting the Channel," the pilot said. The General nodded.

---

* The General's bull terrier.

"O.K. to start, sir?"

"Go ahead," the General said.

The engines turned over, coughed, settled to a normal hum. Down the runway, gathering speed. An imperceptible lift. Airborne. Plenty of room to spare. The General looked at his watch. "Ten-twenty-five," he said. "Exactly a year ago to the minute we cast off from Algiers on the *Monrovia* for Sicily."

"This time I doubt if we get our feet as wet," Al said.

"I know," the General said gloomily. "A hell of a way to make an amphibious landing."

Since D day the possibility that the war might end suddenly had preyed on the General's mind. He had been edgy, restive. Now he was silent, almost despondent.

We passed over some scattered clouds. Ahead the coast line. Over the Channel at ten thousand feet the ocean surface seen through a light haze appeared an unreal gray-green blur. From above and to the right two of our escorts swooped past and under with a wing-waggle salute. Over a cloud bank, like a solid snowdrift in the sunlight. The sea again, sparkling. Suddenly, and at an unexpected angle, the coast line of the Cotentin Peninsula, and, directly below, the familiar squat pavilion of the French Line at the end of its now sadly crumpled pier. The General's head was pressed to the window. "Cherbourg," he said. "Not too badly bashed up, I should say."

Now we were following the coast and the wavy white line of breakers. Soon the landing beaches came into view, an appalling spectacle of chaos and destruction. Half-submerged ships and landing craft of all kinds at crazy angles. Uprooted beach obstacles, shattered pillboxes, piles and piles of supplies, from which, like columns of ants, long lines of miniature trucks moved slowly up over the grassy dunes and inland.

With a wide curve seaward we came in for a landing on the narrow airstrip behind Omaha Beach. As we taxied up to the end of the strip Chet Hanson, General Bradley's aide, came running out to hand-wave our pilot in. Once more the General looked at his watch. "Eleven-twenty-five," he said. "From Norfolk to Casablanca it took us eighteen days. From Algiers to Gela, Sicily, five days. And now France in one hour." He sighed. "Well, come on. Let's see if there is still a war going on."

The distance to General Bradley's headquarters in a partially wooded field south of Isigny was only a few miles, but what with the endless two-way stream of trucks, weapon carriers, half-tracks, and peeps, we arrived an hour late for lunch. The General spent the afternoon conferring with General Bradley and General Hodges and later with Lightning Joe Collins, Commander of the VII Corps. Having got Al and me fixed up with a tent next to theirs, Chet and Lou Briggs (who had gone to meet us at Utah Beach, in case we had been forced to land there) brought us up to date. Due to the proximity and intensity of the Corps artillery barrage, the briefing took some time. It was past midnight when we crawled into our bedding rolls. "I don't believe," Al yawned, "the General need worry about missing his war."

July 7, 1944. Morning session with General Bradley and his staff, for which Monty and his Chief of Staff, General de Guingand, drove over from Bayeux.

"They put in several hours," the boss said later, "explaining why they had not yet taken Caen, their D-day objective."

After lunch the General bade them farewell and we drove off in the direction of Carentan to find our first C.P. in France. It took some finding, as General Gay and an advance party had taken pains to locate it in a thoroughly secluded apple orchard whose only approach was a narrow grass-covered lane in the *bocage* country southeast of the small town of Bricquebec near the village of Nehou (near St. Sauveur) in the center of the Cotentin Peninsula and less than ten miles behind First Army's front lines.

The ground was hard and dry, the tents nestling beneath the conveniently spaced apple trees invisible from the air.

The General was pleased with the setup. But he is not going to be happy until Third Army becomes operational and the divisions now attached to First Army, together with other units to arrive from England, come under his full control and command.

July 12, 1944. This morning, your first letter since we left England, and very welcome it is. What, you ask, is a typical day. One rises with the sun from one's wet sleeping bag, wrings the dew out of one's uniform, shaves with a helmet full of cold water and a small hand mirror swinging from the nearby apple tree — we are still in the orchard. Breakfast in the General's mess tent with the Old Man, Generals Gaffey and Gay, Harkins, Odom, and the other aides. With luck a quick visit to the latrine in the woods before accompanying the General to morning briefing. The latrine, incidentally, is something the General can take or leave.

"I guess I'm made like a horse," he says. "Can go anytime. Very convenient."

The briefing is held in a sizable wall tent. Big situation map. Folding camp chairs. The assembled staff members rise as the General enters with aides and Willie. He takes his seat, under which Willie curls up in a ball and goes to sleep. Each section chief — G-1, G-2, G-3, et al. — goes before the map and gives a snappy résumé of yesterday's activities and the picture as of this morning. Sometimes the General asks a question or two, or makes a short statement; sometimes not.

During the briefing, Mims and another driver have brought the General's and a spare peep to the tent entrance. The briefing over, the General steps into his peep, Al and I take our places, and we are off. If the General is to visit corps or division headquarters (the usual objectives) Al or I, or both, will have previously checked with Colonel Brent Wallace, Chief of Liaison Section, and marked on our maps the ever-changing position of each corps or division to be visited. By the time one gets there, it has often moved. Al and I more or less alternate riding with the General. The other follows, or leads, in the second peep, whose function is to serve as protection and a spare in case of tire trouble or breakdown. Both peeps are equipped with machine guns. Leading can be rather hectic — the General likes to drive fast — and map reading in a fifty- or sixty-mile breeze while trying to identify road signs — often removed, misplaced, or reversed by the departed enemy — is not always easy. Several times we have got him hopelessly lost. He is quite good-natured about it.

In the last few days we have visited all the divisions of VIII and XV Corps and numerous abandoned German rocket-launching sites — including a gigantic project on which, up until D day, several thousand slave laborers had been working. Nobody here seems to understand its exact purpose or function. "Obviously intended for a go at London," the British tell you. "More likely New York," say our engineers. Take your choice.

We usually get back to the orchard in time for supper and Willie's play hour. He likes to be swung around in the air while attached, with bulldog tenacity, to the end of an apple branch. After supper the General retires to his trailer to write up his diary, and Al and I creep back into those sleeping bags.

July 14, 1944. Bastille Day. This morning the General went with the engineering officer to look over Utah Beach, so I got hold of Bunny and we took a peep ride through some of the neighboring towns. In the main *place* of Bricquebec — there was some sort of fair going on — we stopped to look around. A crowd collected around our peep. Two little girls, aged perhaps five and seven respectively, came up and solemnly handed each of us a small bouquet. We thanked them, reciprocating with two small pieces of chocolate, which, with dignity, even a certain reserve, they accepted. I realized afterwards that this exchange of amenities constituted, for me at least, first contact of any kind with French civilians since landing in Normandy. Such is the self-containment of the U. S. Army.

A few minutes later — we were still conversing with the local citizenry — the smaller of the two little girls, blond with very round blue eyes, popped up again beside the peep and held out an expectant hand. Bunny and I were both reaching for our chocolate bars when the elder sister, a darker and sterner edition, pushed her way through the crowd, seized the more volatile member of the family by the arm. *"Enfin,"* she said, marching her off, *"faut pas exagérer, hein?"* In contrast to the insistent "cigarette, chewing gum" refrain of North Africa, Sicily, and the Middle East, a refreshing expression of French *mesure*.

July 15, 1944. Late yesterday afternoon, I went with the General to the funeral of General Theodore Roosevelt, who had died in his sleep the night before. The service was up quite near the front. As the casket was being lowered, the reverberations of our antiaircraft opening up on a German photographic plane re-echoed through the wooded cemetery.

"Roosevelt would have liked that," the General said on the drive home. "A great leader and a very brave man. Bad luck that he was not killed in action."

July 16, 1944. This morning the General inspected the German defenses around Cherbourg and immediately ordered a detailed study thereof. "We'll undoubtedly be running into the same kind of setup in Brittany and other places," he said.

On getting back, there was a message to the effect that Harvey Bundy* and his boss, Mr. Stimson, would arrive by air tomorrow morning.

July 17, 1944. Quite a busy day. Immediately after breakfast we drove to the airfield outside Cherbourg to meet Mr. Stimson and his party. Delayed by fog, their plane was an hour and a half late. General Bradley, who was also supposed to meet the Secretary, was even later. However, after their arrival, there still remained time for a visit to the beaches and an alfresco lunch at First Army Headquarters. "The Sec," as Harvey calls him, was in fine fettle and seemed impressed by what he saw, particularly the beaches. For visiting firemen they are sure-fire.

July 30, 1944. Two more funerals. That of General Lesley McNair (Chief of the Army Ground Forces), who was top-secretly visiting the front lines and instantly killed by a "short" from one of our own bombers. The death of Paddy Flint (Colonel Harry A. Flint, Commanding Officer of the 39th Infantry Regiment), shot through the head

* Harvey H. Bundy was Special Secretary to the Secretary of War, Mr. Stimson.

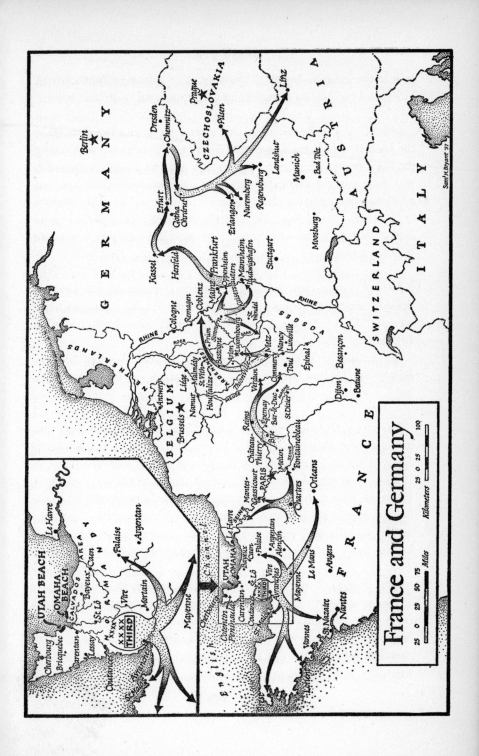

France and Germany

Sam H. Bryant '57

leading an attack, was a blow to the General, who liked and admired him deeply. "I hope I die as well and as painlessly," he said.

Day before yesterday the signal for which the General has been itching came through. As of August 1, Third Army will be fully operational and General Bradley has adopted practically all of General Patton's plan. Four days ago First Army started its push on Saint-Lô. For the last three days, the General, if not Third Army as such, has himself been operational in a big way.

Have been on the go early and late. The Old Man is now really taking charge. What with visiting all the units, marching in ranks with an Infantry regiment on its way into the lines, flying in L-5's up and down the front at low altitude, the last few days have been busy ones. They are likely to become even busier. Today we are breaking camp and tomorrow the headquarters will move up to another orchard southeast of Coutances.

August 8, 1944. What a week. Have been riding postilion with the General throughout practically every daylight hour. By the time you receive this, you will doubtless know that on August 1, Third Army exploded out of the Cotentin Peninsula through the Avranches corridor and since then has been going in every direction at once. The Old Man has been like one possessed, rushing back and forth up and down that incredible bottleneck, where for days and nights the spearheading Armored divisions, followed by motorized Infantry, have been moving bumper to bumper. More marching in ranks, the General occasionally darting out to haul an officer out of a ditch in which he has taken refuge from a German plane, or excoriating another for taping over the insignia on his helmet. "Inexcusable," he yells. "Do you want to give your men the idea that the enemy is dangerous?" Pushing, pulling, exhorting, cajoling, raising merry hell, he is having the time of his life. Our headquarters moves daily, in a series of one-night stands, and we are for the moment located in a tree-covered gully near Avranches.

A few days ago, in Avranches itself, we were blocked by a hopeless snarl of trucks. The General leaped from the peep, sprang into the abandoned umbrella-covered police box in the center of the square, and for an hour and a half directed traffic. Believe me, those trucks got going fast, and the amazed expressions on the faces of their drivers as recognition dawned were something.

We have been bombed, strafed, mortared, and shelled. The General thrives on it. Yesterday on the way back to our headquarters we were speeding along through choking dust under a high blue heaven criss-crossed with the vapor contrails of our tactical planes. It was a bad stretch of road from which our bulldozers had recently pushed to either side of the reeking mass of smashed half-tracks, supply trucks, ambulances, and blackened German corpses. Encompassing with a sweep of his arm the rubbled farms and bordering fields scarred with grass fires, smoldering ruins, and the swollen carcasses of stiff-legged cattle, the General half turned in his seat. "Just look at that, Codman," he shouted. "Could anything be more magnificent?" As we passed a clump of bushes, one of our concealed batteries let go with a shattering salvo. The General cupped both hands. I leaned forward to catch his words. "Compared to war, all other forms of human endeavor shrink to insignificance." His voice shook with emotion. "God, how I love it!"

And here, I believe, in the unabashed enthusiasm, more, the passionate ardor for every aspect and manifestation of his chosen medium, lies the key to General Patton's success. The A.D.C. of an Army Commander is afforded the opportunity of observing the personal approaches and techniques of scores of other commanders from battalion to the summit. I am quite ready to believe that there may be other E.T.O. Commanders who equal our own in mere technical proficiency. I have seen or heard of none, however, who can even remotely compare with General Patton in respect to his uncanny gift for sweeping men into doing things which they do not believe they are capable of doing, which they do not really want to do, which, in fact, they would not do, unless directly exposed to the personality, the genius — call it what you will — of this unique soldier who not only knows his extraordinary job, but loves it. Here in France, as in Sicily, an entire army, from corps commander to rifleman, is galvanized into action by the dynamism of one man. Even his military superiors find themselves irresistibly, if reluctantly, drawn into his magnetic field, and what was originally planned in the rarefied atmosphere of higher headquarters as the securing of a modest bridgehead bids fair to develop into a race across the Continent. Rash? Far from it. The General knows exactly what he is doing, and if at times the higher staffs turn green around the gills when across their astonished situation maps flash the prongs of seemingly unprotected spearheads launched deep into enemy territory, it is only because they have yet properly to gauge the man's resourcefulness. As for his subordinates, more than one corps and division commander, in the course of a whirlwind visit from the Old Man, has felt a sinking in the pit of his stomach on finding himself and his command catapulted into outer space, but all of them have learned that he never lets them down. They know that if the unexpected happens, he will find a solution, and what is more, he will be up front to see that the solution is applied.

Three times in the last few days, in as many tents and wooded fields, the same dialogue with minor variations:

Division commander: "But my flanks, General?"

The General: "You have nothing to worry about. If anything develops — and it won't — our tactical Air will know before you do, and will clobber it. That will give me plenty of time to pull something out of the hat." A pat on the shoulder. "Get going now. Let the enemy worry about his flanks. I'll see you up there in a couple of days."

And he does, too. Evening before last, at supper, the General, looking up from a report which a messenger from Operations had just delivered, said sharply:

"Tomorrow morning have my peep and an armored car ready. Immediately after the briefing we'll go up and take a look at the Sixth Armored."

Al led off in the armored car and I rode with the General in his peep. For the next three hours we pursued the 6th Armored up the Brest peninsula. Soon we were well ahead of our own Infantry and I found myself sympathizing with the division commander's concern in regard to his flanks and rear. At more and more frequent intervals we ran into groups of F.F.I.'s (French partisans) who were having a field day mopping up the German detachments scattered in the wake of our Armored drive. Full of good will and Calvados, they regaled the General with glowing tales of their own prowess, together with contradictory reports as to whether or not the woods immediately ahead were still full of Boches.

For the record, the French irregulars have given very real and valuable assistance, not only in mopping-up operations, but in sabotage, bridge-blowing, and ceaseless harassment of the retreating Germans. Around noon finally, and without incident, we caught up with a combat team of the 6th and eventually located General Grow,* whom the General complimented on his progress thus far.

"Keep going," the General said as we left. "There is nothing to stop you between here and Brest."

Cross-country to the 83d Division to confer with General Macon on tomorrow morning's attack on Saint-Malo. Home via VIII Corps Headquarters near Saint-James.

In the last letter I failed to mention the landing of Leclerc's 2d Division Blindée. You would have loved it. On the way home from some errand or other, I ran into them unexpectedly as they humped their way up over the dunes from the beach. Naturally I turned my peep around and rode along with their leading column. In the first small village, only a handful of people, two or three old men, half a dozen women, some children. From their point of view, nothing unusual about a column of presumably American tanks rumbling through the *place*. Nothing, that is, until through the hatch of the leading tank popped an unmistakably Gallic head encased in a woman's silk-stocking skullcap. Singling out a hefty citizeness with two children and a pronounced mustache, the tanker leaned precariously in her direction. *"Dis, donc, ma mignonne, on t'emmène à Paname, hein?"*

The lady's jaw dropped almost to her ample bosom and the eyes of the other villagers bulged as they caught sight of the small tricolor flag painted on the tank's side. By the time they came to, the leading tank of the first French fighting unit to land upon the soil of occupied

---

* Major General Robert Grow, commanding the 6th Armored Division, one of the most dependable in the Third Army.

France was well out of town. The next village was a larger one. Had some intuitive grapevine been at work? I don't know. But thronging the *place* were at least fifty people, their arms loaded with flowers, fruit, bottles, jugs of cider, loaves of bread.

The column entered the *place* at a good clip. In no time at all the excited villagers, laden with the produce of Normandy, were swarming up, over, and into the receptive tanks. Why no one was killed in the rush, I shall never know. Three towns later, the 2d Blindée looked more like a parade of floats in the flower carnival at Nice than an armored division on its way into the lines. Perhaps in *les fruits, les fleurs,* the *paysans* of Calvados have hit upon a particularly effective form of camouflage, or maybe they know instinctively, and better than we do, how to boost Gallic morale — as, indeed, why not? In any event, within twenty-four hours XV Corps reported that the "French 2d" was happily engaged in killing Germans with a gusto and efficiency which warmed the General's heart.

"When we visit them tomorrow," he said, "remind me to take along a bagful of Bronze Stars."

August 15, 1944. Our present C.P. is just north of Le Mans. On the way, the General visited the twelfth-century Château de Fougères.

At the end of yesterday's briefing the General addressed the staff.

"In the last two weeks Third Army has advanced farther and faster than any other army in history. In the weeks to come it is my intention to advance farther and faster still."

After that we took off in two L-5's — over very fluid territory, I may say — to visit XV Corps, where the General apprised General Haislip of the plan to launch XV, XX, and XII Corps on Dreux, Chartres, and Orleans respectively.

"If I say so myself," the General said, "it is a hell of a good plan, and wholly mine."

General Haislip agreed.

You will probably be hearing a good deal about the Falaise pocket, within whose confines, if the General had been allowed to carry out his plan, the entire German Seventh Army could have been and should have been destroyed. To close the narrow gap between Falaise and Argentan, the General had thrown together a provisional corps comprised of the 2d French Armored and two Infantry divisions, the 80th and 90th. Led by General Gaffey, the provisional corps had actually reached a point less than ten miles from Falaise, into which advance elements of Canadian Armor and Infantry were already filtering, when Army Group cracked down with a halt order. The General is beside himself, but to no avail. The Ninth Air Force is having a field day slaughtering the fleeing Germans, but many, far too many, are slipping through the unclosed gap. It looks from here as though higher headquarters will have some tall explaining to do.

Two announcements on the radio today: General Patch and Seventh Army landed this morning in the south of France. Later: General Patton is now in command of Third Army.

"The first *I've* heard of it," the General said.

August 16, 1944. Today the General and Al and I made a cross-country run to Chartres. General Walker met us at the bridge, where we waited until the firing had abated a little. Here and there the town itself was scarred, but the cathedral stood there as of old, calm, serene, timeless. The stained glass, removed and stored away early in the war, had been temporarily replaced by ordinary greenish panes.

August 17, 1944. Colonel Griffith, XX Corps G-3, was killed today by a sniper, and Charley Odom was hit while driving through the same stretch of woods through which we had passed with the General only a short time before. Charley was lucky. The bullet was deflected by a rib and he says he should be O.K. in a few days.

August 19, 1944. Last evening the General got word that his old friend and World War I instructor at the Staff School at Langres, General Koechlin-Schwartz, was living in retirement at Vannes, up towards the end of the Brest peninsula.

"Codman," he said, "take a plane, take two planes. I don't care how you do it, but bring my old friend back here to me."

This morning at crack of dawn my flight of two L-5's took off from the nearby airstrip. The first hour and a half backtracking over the familiar green and brown checkerboards of the Sarthe and Mayenne was lovely, but with the unrolling of the Brittany landscape the weather began to foul up. Clouds, gray and black ones. Rain. Bumpy as hell. Can't see the other plane. About fifty more miles to go. To land or not to land. Let's try to get through. After a while it clears a little. Ahead a sizable town and an airdrome. Vannes? Hope so. Yes. Good landing. No one around. Vannes, eight kilometers. Start off on foot. Hitchhike a ride in farmer's truck — one of the old charcoal burners. Nice reception in town. Cheers — flowers, even.

"Where lives the General K.-S.?" Willing guides. A nice old house. A nice old *bretonne. "Monsieur le général* is in his *bureau."* A nice old man in tweeds and felt slippers. At the mention of my General's name he jumped up, raising his arms to heaven. "I knew it," he cried. "As soon as I learned of those mad columns forging their separate ways up the peninsula, I knew that once again my friend Patton was amongst us. Only he would have the audacity. Where is he? I will go anywhere to rejoin him."

"Perfect, *mon général.* I have two planes at the airport."

"Planes!" His face fell. "In this weather? You will stay to lunch and I will consult my wife."

"Are there any American units in Vannes?"

"No."

"Never mind, I'll be back in an hour with transportation for the airport."

Visit to the new *sous-préfet,* recently of the *maquis.*

"I got tired of hiding in an attic waiting for the Vichy incumbent to leave," he said, "so with the help of a few friends, I threw him out and moved in. Transportation? Difficult. Plenty of cars, but no *essence."*

"You need *essence, monsieur le préfet;* I need a car — to transport a General, one of your Generals. Perhaps something can be worked out."

Leaving for North Africa. Major and Mrs. Codman.

Charley and Bunny

General Noguès at an Army inspection at Rabat.
C.R.C. squinting in the background.

President Roosevelt decorates General Mark Clark while
General Eisenhower looks on. The Anfa Conference, 1943.

Landing in Sicily. General Patton and C.R.C. going over the side.

C.R.C., General Montgomery and General Patton in Sicily

Captain Al Stiller, General Gay, General Patton and
C.R.C. at a Red Cross show in Sicily

C.R.C., General Patton and Sergeant Mims, in their peep.
Normandy, 1943.

Willie, the General and Lady Leese, wife of General Sir
Oliver Leese, Commander of British Eighth Army in Italy,
at Knutsford

General Patton decorating C. R. C.
with the Legion of Merit

General Eisenhower leads the way into the salt
mine. General Bradley, C. R. C. and General
Patton in the background.

General George S. Patton, Jr. V–E Day in Germany.

Willie and the foot lockers addressed to Charles Codman
in Boston

The *sous-préfet* leaned back and closed his eyes. "There is, of course, the Packard of Monsieur Chose, but if I requisition it he will not be happy."

"If Monsieur Chose will drive us to the airport he can fill his tank from one of our planes. Wouldn't that make him happy?"

"Yes, that should make him very happy," the *sous-préfet* said, "particularly if he could take along and fill those empty cans which you see there in the corner."

During my absence, General Koechlin-Schwartz had ascended to *his* attic and from a long-locked trunk unearthed his World War I uniform of horizon blue. Standing at the foot of his stairs resplendent in full regalia complete with oak-leaf-bordered kepi, he seemed to have dropped twenty years as he took my salute. Lunch was a huge success. I was able to give Madame and the General news of their daughter in Rabat. With each succulent course and frequent exclamations as to the smallness of the world, we kept turning up mutual friends — the de Limurs, close neighbors, the Hottinguers, the de Luzes, and quite a few others. After lunch, aglow with well-being and an excellent Châteauneuf-du-Pape, General Koechlin-Schwartz and I leaned back in comfort against the cracked upholstery of Monsieur Chose's 1918 Packard. Monsieur Chose himself was at the wheel. From the radiator flew a large Tricolor.

What with the scarcity of private autos, the billowing flag, the horizon-blue uniform, our progress through Vannes snowballed into quite a show, and the old General was kept busy acknowledging salutes and bowing right and left to his cheering public.

"I have never had such a success," he said. "Probably never will again, except possibly at my funeral."

It is now midnight. In General Patton's blacked-out trailer, the two old friends are still fighting two wars. Our own tent has sprung a new leak. Al is snoring happily, and I am finishing this letter by the waning rays of a captured German flashlight.

August 20, 1944. The day following General Koechlin-Schwartz's visit, our C.P. moved to a densely wooded area near the village of Brou northwest of Châteaudun. Here, for one reason or another, we had quite a few more visitors. First, Mr. Patterson and General Somervell, for whom I interpreted at the Anfa Conference in Casablanca. Both very genial.

On August 23, a curious delegation headed by a Mr. Nordling, brother of the Swedish consul in Paris, and a Monsieur de Saint-Phalle, of the Paris Committee of National Liberation, arrived at our woodland headquarters, having managed to get through both the German lines and our own. According to their story, the French underground in Paris had jumped the gun, taken over virtually half the city, and effected a temporary cease-fire with General von Choltitz, the German Commander of *"Gross-Paris"* — the Boches can make even Paris sound ugly. The truce, at best precarious, was in danger of being disrupted at any moment by the Communist element of the partisan movement, in which case von Choltitz, though personally inclined to play ball, would be forced to carry out Hitler's order for the destruction of the city. Thus, they argued, it was essential that regular troops be sent to Paris *at once* to receive von Choltitz's surrender.

Since the matter obviously involved political implications, the General wisely passed the buck and the delegation on to General Bradley, who, with SHAEF's approval, lost no time in turning loose* General Leclerc and the 2d Blindée.

Hardly had the delegation left when a familiar figure came swinging up the path — General Juin, full of *élan* and compliments. In the General's trailer he really laid it on.

"Your epic sweep across France, magnificent, magnificent," he said. "For your daring there is only one word, Napoleonic."

The General was delighted. He was also much interested in Juin's conviction that the best place to attack the Siegfried Line is straight through the Nancy corridor. This — from a connoisseur of the terrain — coincides exactly with the General's own plan to jump the Seine south of Paris and make a direct strike on the Metz-Nancy-Épinal line.

---

* "Turning loose" meant giving full authority and orders to Leclerc to make a dash into Paris.

"It is so obvious and such a sure bet," the General said, "I have no doubt higher headquarters will turn it down."

August 24, 1944. By this time you will have heard the big, big news. Yesterday afternoon the French 2d Armored and the U. S. 4th Infantry Divisions entered Paris. "The Germans surrendered the city to the U. S. Third Army," the B.B.C. announced — not wholly accurately, since a few days previously the French 2d and the 4th had been attached to First Army, but at least poetic justice.

The other piece of news, announced with gusto by our friend Commandant Lebel, now attached to General Bradley's headquarters: "Marseilles has been invested by General de Lattre." With a wink at me, he added, "As an old African, you will not be surprised to hear that the capture of the second city of France was actually effected by General Guillaume and his *goumiers*."

PARIS

August 27, 1944. What a day — a completely satisfactory, profoundly moving, and yet an agonizing day, the first two for obvious reasons, the last for the equally obvious reason that every minute, every second it was inadmissible that you shouldn't have been there. Had hoped to ride in with Leclerc, but that didn't quite work out, so this morning at breakfast I frankly asked the General if Bunny and I could take a peep and run up to see — among other things — whether Bunny's office was still functioning. The General, mildly surprised that anyone should prefer a trip to Paris to the impending active river-crossing, said, "Sure — if you want to — only don't get yourselves shot — and don't forget to come back tonight."

Well, my sweetie, it was all perfectly simple — and, like most events to which one has long looked forward, perfectly natural.

After breakfast I went over to Bunny's tent and said, "Get your gun. We're going up to see whether they are still cashing checks at your bank." His face was a study. Armed with an order, To Whom It May Concern:

DRIVE

27 August 1944

To Whom It May Concern:

Lt. Colonel C. R. Codman, 0448161, and Lt. Colonel B. S. Carter, 0885628, both of Third Army Headquarters, are authorized to make a reconnaissance of PARIS.

By command of Lieutenant General PATTON:

/s/ *Paul D. Harkins*
/t/ PAUL D. HARKINS
Colonel, G.S.C.
Deputy Chief of Staff

we mounted Bunny's peep and set off cross-country to the Fontainebleau–Paris road. A lovely sunny day, hot with a slight haze. Familiar road signs: Corbeil and the Seine, Paris, 30 kms.; Juvisy, Paris, 19 kms.

On the otherwise empty road, more and more unlikely vehicles. Old omnibuses, carts loaded with household furniture, refugees sitting on top. Like 1940, only this time going the right way. Joinville-le-Pont, only eleven kilometers to go. A *sergent de ville* in cape and full regalia plants himself in the middle of the road and waves us down. We stop. *"Vous allez en ville?"* he asks. "Yes." "Can you take me?" "Get in, get in."

We bounce along, the policeman's cape flying in the breeze. "What have you been doing?" we ask. "On strike," he says. "Hiding out *en civile,* but today, *je reprends mon service."* Cobblestones. Closed-down cafés. People in the streets. Lots of waving.

Porte d'Italie. We're in. Everything quiet, no traffic, a few cyclists, a good many pedestrians. We stop to ask about bridges and things. A crowd collects. Handshaking, kissing, back-slapping. You can imagine. *"Ça fait plaisir,"* the policeman said. On down the Boulevard Raspail. It all seems so natural. Rue du Bac, over the river — and there we are, in the most beautiful *place* in the world. A little nicked here and there, but *so* beautiful, so unchanged. Rue de Rivoli. Barricades and burned tanks. Rue de Castiglione. An interesting sight *du côté de chez Swann, le pharmacien.* A tank rammed into its entrance. Place Vendôme. You can picture Bunny's reception at the bank. A lot of telephoning. *"Est-ce que le Baron d'Hottinguer est là?"* *"Monsieur le Baron est mort dans son lit, il y a un an."* *"Ah, pardon, je regrette."* Madeleine de Pourtales — very excited — arrange to see her in the afternoon. Lunchtime. Bunny and I stroll across to the Ritz. I doubt whether the Boches' sheets have been washed yet. Nevertheless, business as usual. The concierge is telephoning the Bristol to see if they can accommodate some clients. An old dowager is asking for *deux places* at the Marigny — where what do you suppose is playing? — *Là Haut.*

First familiar face. At a big table, surrounded by newsmen, Gloria Braggiotti's husband, Emlen Etting, and Polly Peabody. Yes, I knew you'd like that. Bunny and I join them for a while and then get a table *à deux* where we, in turn, are joined by David Bruce and Lester Armour. "Ah, there you are," David said. "Now I *know* everything is normal." He proceeded to give a good account of the previous day — and night. Remind me about that. A rather bad meal — a bottle of only fair Meursault — all beautifully served. Same atmosphere. Same regulars. Practically everyone except Howard. As a matter of fact, I asked Frank, the barman, whether Monsieur Sturges had been in, and he said, "Not yet, but we expect him."

Off again. We find our peep and driver the center of an enthusiastic crowd. It takes quite a while to extricate him and it and ourselves. Over to the Invalides to see the 2d Blindée. What a party *they* had coming in. A bunch of the boys who had no place to sleep went up to Madame Hélène's, where naturally they were greeted with cries of joy, popping of corks, and an invitation to take over the whole place, *gratuitement.* That was fine and they moved in bag and baggage. Later in the day they went off to conclude some unfinished business. On their return they found to their consternation that the F.F.I.'s had also paid a visit and shaved all the little heads of all the little inmates — including the *sous-maîtresse,* on whose dome they stenciled a neat black swastika. "Did you stay just the same?" I asked. *"Ah, ça, non, alors. À la campagne un régime d'oeufs à la coq, ça va encore, mais à Paname, depuis le temps qu'on attend, on a bien le droit de s'offrir une poule — avec plumes."*

We were just about to leave Leclerc's boys, when I happened to ask who their American Air liaison officer was and where. I'd heard a rumor. *"Ah, oui, en effet,* Lieutenant Colonel Rod Tower." *Coup de téléphone. "C'est le colonel Tower à l'appareil? Ne quittez pas; on vous parle." "Allô. Ici le colonel Carter et le colonel Codman de la classe de quinze de l'Université de Harvard."*

You could hear the thud as he fell off his chair. "For Christ's sake, where are you? Right, Claridge's in a quarter of an hour." A suite at Claridge's. Champagne. Perrier Jouet '29. Rod's account of coming in with the French. He *was* along. He and André de Limur and Ernest Hemingway. Rod at his best, imitating the French tankers, the welcoming populace, Boche tanks, machine guns, sound effects, everything. Held up by fire at the Porte X. Bullets whizzing. Hemingway: "Compared to Spain, this is nothing. Just a bunch of crap. Come on, let's go," etc., etc.

In the *"centre,"* he depicts the crowd going wild. Champagne on every street corner. Then put-put-put-put, machine-gun fire. Into a doorway with glass and drinking companion. Put-put stops. Out again. More clinking of glasses and on to another *quartier*.

"Makes me thirsty to tell it." Rod pressed the bell. More champagne.

Enter two episodic characters. A Belgian Commandant, friend of Rod. His wife, a sun-ripened South American lady. By this time we were reminiscing about World War I.

"Impossible," the ripe lady purred. "You were babies."

"Twenty-year-old babies. But thanks just the same."

"You must give me the recipe."

"Superfluous, madame, in your case."

Phone call for the Belgian Commandant. "Must leave at once," he said. Exit Commandant and sun-ripened wife.

Rod is now bathing and Bunny telephoning. I go out on the balcony — almost across from where we watched the procession for the King of England — remember? What a city. You just can't faze it. No traffic to speak of, except a few cyclists, but both sidewalks crowded with *promeneurs,* strolling at that inimitable leisurely pace, everyone calm and collected and quite *content.* The tables in front of Fouquet's crowded to overflowing. Most of the men without hats, most of the girls in short cotton-print dresses — and prettier than I remember them. I suppose they don't eat so much. An old dame with red hair urging on her Pekingese. No success. Try another tree. So calm. Yet one shot from a rooftop and the crowd will scatter like leaves.

Random thought: Paris *is* Clarence Day's cat world.

Well, it's time to go over to the Travelers' Club and *that,* you may be sure, hasn't changed either. The same old-timers saying the same old things. General de Chambrun glad-handing all American arrivals. "I *must see* my old friend Patton at once. Magnificent, his campaign. Do tell him to get in touch with me here."

Out of nowhere a bouncing apparition, André de Limur. Embraces. "How is Ethel?" "How is Theodora?" More champagne. Pommery, I regret to say. André very typical. "I'm not *entirely* happy in my present job," he says. "Sleeping in tents and eating out of mess kits is all very well, *but.*"

Time to go up to the d'Harambures — prearranged by Bunny. Out to the peep. It's *gone!* A passer-by: "Ah, yes, there was a little accident in the next street. The F.F.I. have borrowed your peep to tow one of their trucks." Around the corner we find our peep being hitched up to an enormous van bristling with armed F.F.I.'s. Big crowd. A lot of argument. Someone brings champagne and we talk them out of it.

A turn around by our old hostelry (the Berkeley). It still has a Boche sign on it and the terrace restaurant is closed. I haven't the heart to go in. I simply *won't* go in there until you and I make our *rentrée together.* Up the Champs Élysées. We make the driver take it slow. His name — the driver's — is Shoulder. It is his first trip to Paris. He is fascinated — as well he may be. He'll never see it just like this again. No one will. Every ten or twenty yards we are obliged to stop and take bows. The Arc de Triomphe. The *biggest* Tricolor you've ever seen. Fills the entire space. We circle it. Visions of that morning in 1940 when we saw the Ambulance Section off to Abbéville.

Avenue Victor Hugo. Quieter here. Fewer people. Might be 1939 or 1929. The d'Harambures. They all rush out into the street. Bunny gets an ovation. In. More champagne. Clicquot this time. Old Madame Vagliano, other Vaglianos, *potins*. "How is Julian?" etc., etc. Time for everyone to go on to the Mouchys', where Madeleine de Pourtales is to meet us. Another acclamation. Jean, her husband, there — back from being a prisoner in Germany.

The entire group radiate a happiness which is wonderful to see and share. Four long years. Each and every day of those four years, at the same hour, all the members have met to exchange information and "keep up each other's morale," as Ethel Merman used to sing.

Time to go. Must be out of the city before dark. They all come out into the street. To hell with the snipers. Shoulder, as always, surrounded by an admiring crowd. A very pretty girl is attaching a tiny American flag to his windshield. She is half sitting on the longitudinal bar of her bicycle. And now she produces an equally tiny French flag and crosses it over the other. Most *unréglementaire*. "Please explain to her," Shoulder says, "that after the war I am coming to live in France — permanently."

"How will your wife like that?" I said.

"She'll like it — or lump it," he said.

We drove slowly through those serene *quartiers* to Bunny's apartment. The old concierge and two friends and a policeman were having a *petit verre*. It was a lovely meeting. "Monsieur Carter, Monsieur Carter." They kept touching him to make sure he was real. One more call. His father's house. Much the same scene. Then the husband of the concierge said, *"Et comment va monsieur votre père?"* And Bunny had to tell them.

And now the shadows lengthen and the evening comes. Past the Grand Palais. Over the bridge. You know what the river looks like at that hour! And the *quartiers* beyond, and how one hates to leave. Just as we hated to leave on June 6, 1940. Just as one *always* hates to leave. I suppose I'll be back from time to time, but I'm not much interested in that. Not until you and I come back together.

The return ride was neither short nor long, but timeless. The road a darkening ribbon running through fertile fields under a mother-of-pearl sky.

And now we are once again in our neck of the woods and soon we shall be on from here and you will be reading of some very, *very* familiar names. Meantime I never missed you so much.

CHAPTER IX

On the Rampage Again

(August–September, 1944)

General Patton felt that this was the time to make an all-out effort by using highly mobile units, widely separated, moving in every direction. He was convinced that we could create such confusion in the German rear that they, having practically no communications, would find themselves in a state of chaos. Such a state would undoubtedly be helped by the French rumors.

Time and time again he told his staff and commanders: "Now is the moment. They are ours for the taking. If we delay, the price will be written in blood."

His hopes, his aspirations, his dreams were doomed by higher headquarters. This to him was a period of absolute frustration. He knew we could go to the Rhine. One unit reached and spent the night in Metz, a fortified city. A portion of the 3d Cavalry Regiment pushed into Germany, but all of this to no avail. The Third Army was halted and these units pulled back, and later came the bloody battle for Metz — the terrible losses of American manhood at the Moselle and the Sauer.

August 30, 1944. Third Army is on the rampage again. We have taken Château-Thierry, Châlons, and Reims. While the General got a green light, with certain reservations, for his strike east, he is much disturbed by a sudden reduction in our gas supply, due, he believes, to the priority given by SHAEF to Monty's northern drive. On getting back this evening to our new C.P., he discovered that XII Corps instead of pushing on to Commercy, as directed, had halted at Saint-Dizier.

"Why?" he demanded sharply.

"Gas for the tanks estimated to be in insufficient supply," General Gaffey said.

The Old Man nearly went through the roof of Operations. "Send the following order to General Eddy at once," he barked. "Continue until gas is exhausted, then proceed on foot."

He was still fuming when he reached his trailer. "In World War One, not far from here, I drained three quarters of my tanks to keep the other quarter going," he said. "Eddy can do it now."

As things are likely to continue active, with little chance of writing letters, I'll improve the shining hour by reporting on Ogden.*

While our C.P. was still near Fontainebleau, one of our divisions appeared on the map to be close to Brie-Comte-Robert, so I asked the General if I could take a run up there to get news of Ogden, regarding whom the family has heard little or nothing since the German occupation.

"Sure," the General said, adding as usual, "Don't get yourself shot."

It was not a long run by peep, but for the last ten kilometers, the abnormal emptiness of the road suggested considerable fluidity. Whether the division had gone through or bypassed the area there was no way of knowing. Arrived at the entrance to Grégy without incident. The big grilled gates were open, the lodge empty. The grounds seemed in fair condition, and from where the avenue curves up through the woods, the deer could be seen skipping cheerfully around the park.

Except for a couple of cracked window panes, the château itself looked intact. I rang the bell. Daisy (Ogden's cook) answered. She was quite surprised to see me. Madeleine, the Alsatian chambermaid, was on the stairs, her arms full of crumpled sheets and pillowcases.

"How is Cousin Ogden?" I asked.

* Ogden Codman, the author's elderly cousin, a widower of eighty-five, long-time resident of Château Grégy, Brie-Comte-Robert.

"He is all right," Daisy said. "The Germans left this morning. That is their linen which Madeleine is sending to the wash. They stole most of the mattresses and both cars. Your soldiers came up from the direction of the river, charged across the lawn, and kept right on."

"Where is he? In the sitting room?"

"No, in bed."

"In bed? At two in the afternoon?"

"Yes."

Ogden, pink and serene, was sitting up in bed, reading. His old-fashioned nightshirt was of peacock green silk and the matching nightcap had a jaunty tassel.

"Why, Charley," he said, carefully putting the book face down at the open pages, "this is a pleasant surprise. I didn't know you were in France. What are you doing here?"

"I'm in the Army."

"And how, may I ask, do you happen to be in the Army?"

"Well, there is a war going on and I thought —"

"Yes, yes," he said, "and a very annoying war it is too. For the last year there have been nine German officers and three women staying in the house. I believe they have only just left."

"What did you do about them?"

"What did *I do* about them? Nothing. I merely went to bed."

"Have you been in bed for a year?"

"Oh, no. I get up from time to time to go to the bathroom or fetch a book. I've done a lot of reading. Are you familiar with Orsoni's *The Eighteenth Century Palazzo?*" He stroked the open book. "Excellent. I recommend it to you."

"What are you going to do now, Cousin Ogden?"

"Stay in bed," he said cheerfully. "It is the only sensible place to be during a war."

"And after the war?"

"Well, after the war I suppose I shall get up."

"How did your German guests behave?"

"I did not see them, but as far as I know they gave no trouble. That is, until this morning when some kind of soldiers — yours, perhaps —

appeared in the field beyond the road and the Germans rushed out
and began shooting."

"What did you do?"

"I rang for Daisy and told her to go down and tell them that I
would *not* have them shooting cannons on my front lawn, and to stop
it *at once*."

"And they stopped?"

"Naturally."

"Then what?"

"They returned to the house. There was a lot of gabbling in the hall
and Daisy tells me that a few minutes later they all jumped into a truck
and went away."

"That's good. I can't stay long, Cousin Ogden; tell me, are you
really all right?"

"Quite all right, and very glad to see you. By the way, how is your
boy? What, he's in the Army too? Goodness, I'd no idea he was so
grown up. Will he be coming to France?"

"I expect so."

"Good. He must come out for a week end. In fact, he can make
Grégy his headquarters and come and go as he likes."

"I'll tell him."

"Have you been to Hamburg yet?"

"Not yet."

"That's a pity. You must go to Hamburg. We have a cousin there.
What *is* her name now — married to a lawyer chap. She'll be delighted
to see you." A pause. "Come to think of it, whom did you marry?" he
asked. "A Duer, wasn't it? Yes, yes, of course. Joe Larocque's daughter.
I used to see a lot of Joe in New York in the old days. He had some fine
first editions of the Restoration period." He picked up the volume of
Orsoni. "Do remember me to him when you see him."

"I'll do that."

I went downstairs to find out from Daisy how things were really
going. In the hall, Ogden's neighbor, Monsieur Pontauson. Do you
remember him? Very small, very thin, hops like a bird. Right out of
Caillavet et de Flers.

"*Ah, cher ami,* what a joy. At last a member of the family. As a neighbor and old friend I do what I can, but I am not, *hélas,* a member of the family. I trust that they are all in good health, the family. After the war I must once again visit your great and admirable country."

We adjourned down the hall to the salon, where, for the next half hour, Monsieur Pontauson regaled me with stories of his triumphs at Alliance Française meetings from Boston to Los Angeles.

"About Ogden," I said. "Is he able to manage all right?"

"Ah," he said, raising his arms ceilingward, "such courage. Of course, I come every day. I do what I can. But it is hard, very hard. The Germans, relatively correct. But the *Italians* — you knew that the Leopolda* has been occupied by the Italian Air Force. They are infinitely worse than the Germans, with even less respect for nice things."

The household, he confirmed, was running along without too much difficulty, since, besides Daisy and Madeleine, there remained Oscar, the chauffeur, and the couple at the lodge.

"Time for me to shove off," I said. "I'll go up with you and say good-by to Ogden."

To pass through the hall, Monsieur Pontauson drew from an inside pocket of his *veston* a pale blue silk scarf which he wrapped carefully around his throat.

"You are very imprudent not to wear your overcoat in these freezing corridors," he said disapprovingly.

Upstairs, sitting by the bed, Madeleine was doing Ogden's nails.

"How beautiful," Monsieur Pontauson whispered. "The hands of a prelate."

"I should have left sooner," Ogden said. "After eighty, the obvious advantages of Europe over those of America no longer matter. Besides, for an elderly person, Europe with its wars is far too uncivilized."

"How true," Monsieur Pontauson said, "how very true."

"Well, good-by, Cousin Ogden. See you in America after the war," I said.

---

* Ogden Codman's villa on the Riviera.

"Yes, yes, of course," he said. "Meantime, don't forget to look up our cousin in Hamburg. What *is* her name?"

August 31, 1944. The Old Man is off for the day with General Bradley. I commandeered a peep and set out from our woodland dell (near Châlons) in the direction of Épernay to do a couple of errands. Business concluded, it seemed justifiable to make a slight extracurricular detour, the same that you and I made in 1940 on our last motor trip from Paris. This time the sun is shining warmly on the ripening grapes and there are no roadblocks guarding the bridge to Ay. The town itself is somnolent. Very few people in the narrow streets. The brass plaque, Maison Bollinger. The familiar high wall. The gate. The bell. When I pulled it, after a slight hesitation — so much may have happened — it gave off the same rippling sound. A pause. The gate door opens and there holding the handle as if frozen to it is Lily. For a moment she went quite white. *"Pas possible,"* she said. Then we embraced.

With Jacques's picture looking down at us from the mantelpiece, we sat before the same fireplace, Lily on one side, Monsieur de Rocheprise — yes, he has aged a good deal — on the other. For a while we didn't talk much. "You remember, the evening you came we were burning our papers," she said.

"Yes, I remember."

She spoke of Jacques, of his failing health, of his death — calmly, almost serenely. A brave girl. Practically singlehanded she has been running the entire business and quite evidently doing a superb job. When the German gauleiter for Champagne arrived — Rocheprise volunteered this — she refused to taste her wines with him — an unheard-of affront which cost her heavy extra taxes. On the other hand, when forced by requisition to deliver, she did not, as many others did, substitute inferior wines.

"I could not do that to the Bollinger name," she said. "Thus we had the sad honor of being drunk by Goering and his gang."

I am writing Walworth* about my visit, but in case the letter mis-

---

* Walworth Pierce, President, S. S. Pierce Company of Boston.

carries, here are a few *potins* which you might relay, together with my very best to him and to Vassar. Bob de Vogüé is still a prisoner. Perrier Jouet is now being run by M. Budin, Mazzuchi having transferred to Mumm's, replacing Robinet, who is through. Mumm himself came back, of course, from Germany and took over during the occupation. Last week he departed hastily whence he came, and Mazzuchi is now trying to unscramble the Franco-German ownership.

Throughout Champagne the Germans have got away with a lot of wine, but when the dust settles, my guess is that most of the established firms will soon be able to furnish from a half to three quarters of their normal U.S. quotas.

Now as to vintages:

1937 — Good. Lily's is excellent.
1938, 1939, 1940 — Might as well forget them.
1941 — Not much good in general.
1942 — Some, e.g. Mumm, claim it is pretty good. I rather doubt it.
1943 — Good, but few houses had enough bottles. Lily a fortunate exception.
1944 — This autumn the yield will be small — almost half the vines were frozen — and the quality probably poor, since, with the *vendange* only three weeks off, it is now clouding up and the forecast is for rain, rain, rain.

It seems very flat doing this without you. Next one, God willing, we'll do together.

Before leaving, I walked across the yard with Lily to the herb garden — near the cellar entrance where Jacques bumped his head, remember, when he went down to fetch us up that memorable bottle of his 1915 — as she wants to send you some verveine leaves to make an infusion for old times' sake. You will find these wrapped in the enclosed note from Lily "For Theodora."

September 16, 1944. Back in my leaky tent in the wet woods after a couple of very, very busy weeks climaxed by a plane trip to England and back. The General is perpetual motion personified, pleading, cajoling, threatening, in his efforts to persuade SHAEF to keep the ball rolling. And the ball *is* rolling, rolling through territory whose every city and town bears a nostalgic name. Commercy, Ligny-en-Barois, Bar-le-Duc, Verdun, Toul. Yesterday — you have seen the news by now — Nancy fell.

"This is where we came in," the General said when the flash came through. He has a great deal of sentiment about World War I. About ten days ago, on one of those far-forward peep excursions, we found ourselves near the railroad station of Conflans mixed in with elements of the 7th Armored, which had been halted by mortar and machine-gun fire. It wasn't a very healthy spot, but the General, after giving everyone hell and getting the boys started again, insisted on going out into the railroad yards to see where I had been shot down* and take a look at the famous roundhouse which we had "destroyed," but which, after twenty-six years and a lot more bombing, is still there in all its original pristine beauty. Humiliating! After viewing it for a few moments in silence, the General cleared his throat. "A very durable structure," he said.

A few days later, on the way to XII Corps via Toul, Vannes, and Essey, he showed Al and me where *he* had been wounded, and the wall behind which he had lain while directing a tank attack.

On the way home I asked, "While you were lying behind that wall, General, if someone had predicted that twenty-six years later you would be passing through this same spot on your way to the Rhine at the head of an army of three hundred thousand, what would you have said?"

"I would have said, 'An intelligent and far-sighted prediction, because that is exactly what I mean to do.'"

Lily's weather forecaster was certainly right about the rain, which daily increases the difficulties of operating a canvas headquarters. Paperwork blows away through a suddenly raised tent flap, water drips on the carbon copies — in triplicate — intertent messengers bog down in waist-deep mud. The General himself is getting fed up, and the next C.P. is likely to have a roof over it — if we can find one intact. Today it cleared and we took a run up to the 4th Armored, where we

* In World War I.

found General Wood sitting in front of his hillside tent following the progress of a tank battle on the opposite slope.

"It is refreshing to find a divisional C.P. operating at close range like this," the General said.

On returning to our own secluded dell we found Bing Crosby and Dinah Shore waiting to see the General, and, better still, Harry Murray,* who is on some mysterious mission or other. As usual, he was on the run, and as usual full of steam and stimulation.

Bing and Dinah seemed a trifle subdued. To cheer them up I took their picture with the General. It probably won't come out. My photography, as you know, seldom does.

It was now time for the General's weekly press conference, for which the correspondents were gathered in the P.R.O. tent. The Crosby-Shore combo had left to do an early show somewhere up the line, but I have noticed that theater people seem to have a lingering effect on the General, that of inciting him — quite unconsciously — to outperform them. As host to galaxies of stars at Palermo, he consistently topped Bob Hope and successively reduced Jack Benny and Al Jolson to straight-men roles. Now as he strode into the tent, mounted the rostrum, seized the pointer, and turned to the map, you could feel an invisible curtain go up.

His opener was a snappy bit on Com-Z, followed by a masterly résumé of the shortcomings of S.O.S. As the laughs died down, he turned his attention to Monty.

"Yesterday," he said, "the Field Marshal ordered SHAEF to have Third Army go on the defensive, stand in place, and prepare to guard his right flank. The Field Marshal then announced that he will, after regrouping, make what he describes as a lightning dagger-thrust at the heart of Germany. 'They will be off their guard,' the Field Marshal predicts, 'and I shall pop out at them like an angry rabbit.'"

At this point I was called away to take a phone call from XII Corps. When I got back, the correspondents were trooping out of the P.R.O. tent. I didn't hear the General's final word, but the I.N.S. man was still weak with laughter.

* Dr. Henry A. Murray, Associate Professor in Clinical Psychology at Harvard.

"Enjoy it?" I said.

"Enjoy it?" he said. "Listen, buddy, that guy in there, all by himself, without benefit of high-priced writers, music, or scenery — that guy is EIGHT-EIGHTY ENTERTAINMENT."

In this war, one never knows in the morning where one will spend the night. A few days ago one of our heavy bombers which had been pounding Conflans up to the very day we took the town was brought down by enemy A.A. The crew bailed out, landed safely, and made their way to the Conflans railroad station. On hearing of it the General hurried over and decorated all nine of them on the spot. For some time after the ceremony he hung around chatting with them.

"You've done a swell job," he said, "though I can't see that you made any more impression on that durable roundhouse than Codman here did. By the way," he added, "where are you based?"

"At X in the north of England," the bomber pilot said.

"I know," the General said, "not far from Knutsford. How are you going to get back there?"

"We don't know exactly."

"Codman," the General said, "see if that brand-new shiny C-47 General Spaatz promised to present me with has arrived. If so, take it and fly these men back to X. And while you're there, go over to Knutsford and get my heavy coat and rubber boots out of the trunk I left with the Stockbridges. On the way back you might stop off in London and see if my new uniform is ready."

The C-47 *had* arrived and it was brand new and shiny. Furthermore, it was equipped with upholstered seats, pilot, copilot, and, believe it or not, a Red Cross hostess called Caroline Stevens, who comes from San Francisco and knows Bill Crocker.

The bomber boys were to meet me at the plane in half an hour. However, there was a slight delay. En route to the airstrips three of their number were arrested by a thoroughly indoctrinated Third Army M.P. The charge: "Failing to wear helmets, liners, and neckties."

It took some time and the tearing up of considerable paperwork to spring them.

The flight to England was smooth and pleasant. Enjoyable, too, was the picture of an active U.S. bomber crew returning from a mission ensconced in luxurious easy chairs while the trim stewardess plied them with tea, sandwiches, and frequent bulletins.

"We are now passing over the well-known bathing resort of Étretat," she would say. "Note the steep *falaises* and the picturesque fishing boats with their nets spread out to dry on the shingle beach. Our altitude is three thousand feet. The outside temperature is fifty-four. Thank you."

The boys loved it. They also, one and all, had got a real bang out of the General. "What a guy!" they kept saying. The tail gunner, and youngest member of the crew, had been rather silent. "Gee," he said during a pause, "I never thought I'd get to meet him. It was worth being shot down for."

"You're so right," the others chorused.

After-dark landing in England. Too late to call up respectable English friends in Knutsford. Or is it? The Leicester-Warrens. My promise that in the unlikely event of a return trip to Knutsford I would call at any hour of day or night. Will do. "Get me Tabley House, please." Mrs. Leicester-Warren on the line. "You must come *at once*. Cuthbert will be thrilled." Borrow a car from the bomber boys and off to Knutsford. Forgetful of that left-hand-side-of-the-road business. A couple of near misses. The lodge gate, the long avenue with its rhododendrons, the great blacked-out house, the old butler, the wide staircase, the Romneys and Lawrences looking down from the walls, the Leicester-Warrens, bless them.

Late supper in the smaller upstairs drawing room. Scrambled eggs, pheasant, and a bottle of Gevrey-Chambertin. Local news. News from across the Channel. Above all, they wanted to hear about the General, whose course they had plotted as best they could with pins on a small-scale map of France.

"And now you must get a good night's sleep," they said.

Up the stairs, candlestick in hand. A large shadowy room. A vast four-poster. And *then*, mark you well, three — repeat, three — FIRSTS since leaving England: (1) my first bath, (2) my first bed, (3) my first pajamas — Cuthbert's.

The sun was filtering through the heavy curtains when the butler woke me with that salubrious prerising tea tray. I couldn't imagine where I was. Another bath. An English breakfast, kippers, porridge, eggs and bacon — the works.

Grateful, reluctant leave-taking. Motored over in my borrowed car to the Stockbridges. Naturally, they had left the previous day on a two weeks' vacation, taking all keys with them, so the retrieving of the General's coat and boots involved the hiring of a locksmith and the breaking open of all the General's trunks. As to be expected, they were in the last one.

London. A phone call to Gertie Legendre. "Come and dine," she said. "Bruce and Effie Hopper are here."

The house she has leased from an English lady is buried at the bottom of a maze of mews and is hard to find even by daylight. The driver of the motor-pool car, a British WAAC, said she had not done much driving in London. I gave her Gertie's address on a slip of paper, which she glanced at without comment. It is quite a long run from the airport, but she made it without lights and without missing a turn.

"You didn't seem to have much trouble finding it," I said, signing the transportation slip.

"Why should I?" she said. "It's my house."

Five thousand feet up in that shiny new C-47. The Channel less crowded than last July. The Seine, winding between bridgeless abutments. Paris from the air particularly inviting. I'd forgotten how green is the roof of the Madeleine, how white the Sacré Coeur. Soon Châlons and a sea of ripening grapes.

"Do you want to take over?" the pilot said.

"Sure," I said.

He moved out of his seat, stood up. Yawned. Now we were moving steadily over even more familiar territory. Tail wind. Must not overshoot. Verdun, Douaumont, Étain — our first bomb target of World

War I. Conflans, the roundhouse, and the well-remembered field nearby.

"*You'd* better take over," I said to the pilot. "I've only landed here once before, and it wasn't a very good landing either."

"When was that?"

"Almost an hour and twenty-six years ago."

"Jesus," he said, grabbing for the controls. "If I'd known that I certainly wouldn't have chosen today to fly with *you*."

September 25, 1944. Three letters from you today, and such wonderful letters. It is uncanny the way you have pinpointed just where our divisions are and what they have been doing. Am glad you are not working for the other side.

Yes, it is strange to be back in places so familiar, strange, and somehow rather sad, because all these ancient towns and villages, whose houses, inhabitants, chickens, and manure piles look and sound and smell exactly as they did a quarter of a century ago, seem to exist only to be pushed around. 1870, 1914, 1940.

"*Pourvu qu'après ça ils nous foutent la paix.*" The sigh of more than one octogenarian with three-time memories seems a reasonable enough prayer.

Day before yesterday, Al and I accompanied the General on a really forward look. The regiment to be visited was stretched along the line of the Moselle all the way from Metz to Thionville. At one point, where our troops were paper thin, it became evident that we were getting into fairly fluid territory. Mims slowed down.

"Keep going," the General said. Another ten minutes and it was clear that we were well out in front of everything.

"Stop here," the General said, adjusting his field glasses, with which he swept the ominously quiet slopes just ahead. "I feel rather like Marshal Ney," he continued impassively. "I don't remember what battle, but at a critical moment Napoleon, riding cross-country, comes upon the Marshal wandering about by himself with a rifle over his shoulder.

" 'Is your rear guard adequate?' the Emperor asks.

" 'Quite adequate,' Ney replies. '*I* am the rear guard.' "

Well, nothing happened. For the General, a disappointment.

Why, might you ask, does he do it? The answer is not wholly simple. Despite his natural audacity, General Patton is both canny and conservative. Ninety per cent of the personal risks he takes are carefully calculated for their exemplary effect on his command, *all* of his command, from G.I. to divisional and corps commander. Classic examples have been his D-day performances on the beaches of Fedala and Gela. Among the *djebels* of Tunisia and the hills of Sicily there were many others, all of them spectacular, all of them successful, all of them legitimate means to an end.

Increase in the size of his successive commands and the weight of his responsibilities has, I think, been matched by some, though hardly a proportional degree of prudence. In France he has been, on the whole, content with the ordinary occupational risks incidental to daily visits to the front line by peep, i.e. road accident, sniping, strafing, bombing, and return flights to Army Headquarters — often at twilight, sometimes after dark — in small unarmed liaison planes, his theory being that the Commander should always be seen going to the front, never coming away from it.

What of the relatively infrequent gamble for gambling's sake — such as the jaunt into no man's land — without apparent purpose or result? Looking back, I believe this type of chance-taking springs from a need, a compulsion on the General's part to compensate for the almost unbearable sense of frustration induced by enforced inaction and passivity.

After the Sicilian campaign and the soldier-slapping incident, the General, believing — and being deliberately allowed by higher headquarters to believe — that not only his career but, worse still, his usefulness as a combat commander were in serious jeopardy, became deeply despondent. During this depressing period, General Keyes, who had a corps in Italy, suggested that he fly over for a visit to the Italian front. General Patton accepted and within twenty-four hours we were winging our way across the Isle of Capri and the Bay of Naples. Within another twenty-four hours both Generals were inspecting a forward O.P. in front of Cassino. General Patton, pleased as punch to be once again within gunshot of an active front — *any* active front — lost no time in climbing over the protecting sandbags and taking pictures of the enemy emplacements on the opposite slope. The German artillery responded with a deadly accurate salvo of 155's which set fire to the O.P. and almost buried the General in mud and dislodged rocks. From the number and proximity of the still-smoking shell splinters, steel-helmet dents, and a providential dud, the General was certainly justified in concluding as we descended from the O.P. that this was his closest call to date.

"It proves that my luck is still in," he said, "that I shall live to fight another day."

I think I wrote you about all this when it happened last January.

I remember wondering, just before the lightning struck — I did not know the General as well then as I do now — whether his seeming rashness on this and other occasions could conceivably be motivated by an unconscious death-wish. My fleeting notion could not have been sillier. Poet, romantic, realist, possessor of unbounded *joie de vivre,* General Patton is the last person on earth to voluntarily forego a single instant of what he conceives to be his destiny. From the age of five — or quite possibly less — all his intellectual, physical, and competitive powers have been focused upon and engrossed by the art-science of warfare, and his manifest intention, his duty, his joy is to squeeze the orange to the last drop. His oft-repeated credo in regard to the professional soldier that the consummation devoutly to be wished is "a quick and painless death inflicted by the last bullet of the last battle" is no mere figure of speech. He means every word of it, and the *key* word is "last." The *last* bullet, not the next to the last. If he has anything to say about it, he will be in there pitching to the bitter end.

The trouble is there are times when he is not sure just how much he *will* have to say about it. This is one of those times. In less than two months his army has chased the enemy through Normandy, Brittany, along the Loire, north and south of Paris, across the Seine, the Marne, the Meuse, and the Moselle, through the fated Ligne Maginot, over the German border, and into the vaunted Siegfried Line. Nantes, Rennes, Le Mans, Angers, Orleans, Rheims, Nancy reclaimed, and now our forward elements within the ancient fortress city of Metz. Over two hundred thousand of the enemy killed, wounded, or captured. Our own casualties for the same period were less than fifty thousand.

The Germans are on the run. There is nothing in front of us. Again, and again, and again, the General exhorts, pleads with Army Group and SHAEF. Now is the time to deliver the *coup de grâce*. Delay, and they will reform, reorganize, and counter. They are expert at doing just that. If for political reasons, out of consideration for the sensibilities of a gallant but less mobile Ally, higher headquarters, remote in its ivory tower hundreds of miles behind the lines, procrastinates, then indeed we shall have a battle on our hands, then indeed American and Allied blood will flow, freely, needlessly.

These are some of the corroding thoughts to which the General finds an antidote in an occasional roll of the dice with fate. In all probability he will be held in leash. If so, there will be savage and costly reprisal. Then, as usual, General Patton will be called in to save the critical day.

"After that," he says, "I shall move heaven and earth to be sent to the Orient, where we of Third Army, together with Admiral Nimitz, will finish off the Japanese."

P.S.

September 25, 1944. Two messages today: (1) a wire from General Marshall to General Patton asking the latter to look up the former's World War I landlady, a Madame Jouatte, at Gondrecourt; (2) a restraining order from Army Group putting Third Army on the defensive until further notice.

CHAPTER X

Slowdown

(September–October, 1944)

On 23 September 1944 General Bradley attended a meeting at Supreme Headquarters called by General Eisenhower. Present were General Eisenhower, Admiral Ramsay, Air Marshal Leigh-Mallory, General Devers, General Spaatz, General Lee, and all Army Group Commanders except Field Marshal Montgomery, who did not appear. He sent his Chief of Staff. Pursuant to instructions received at this meeting, General Bradley placed the Third Army definitely on the defensive. In turn, on 25 September, General Patton issued a letter of instruction to corps commanders. This order depicted General Patton's concept of fighting. He clearly recognized (a) that morale is the most important item in battle; (b) that once you stop the forward impetus, it is most difficult to get it moving again; and (c) that the enemy must not know your intentions.

September 27, 1944. Yesterday, the General, Colonel Campanole, and I took another of those trips into the past. In Gondrecourt we found that Madame Jouatte had long since moved away.

"That being the case, let's see if we can locate some old friends of our own," the General said. "Drive to Chaumont, to the Hotel de France."

The Hotel de France, in the center of the town, is one of Chaumont's smaller and older hostelries. Unstarred by Michelin, its table d'hôte **is** nevertheless better than average. Dependable too, no disturbing innovations.

"Same menu," the General said. "The identical meal I had here in the autumn of 1917 with General Pershing, Harbord, and Jacques de Chambrun."

"Not bad," Campy said, "not at all bad."

"You must have been here during the last war," the General said to the *patron*.

"No, that was my father. He died seven years ago."

"Do you know if Mademoiselle Chose still lives in Chaumont?" Campy asked, a far-away look in his eye.

"Mademoiselle Chose?" The *patron* shook his head. *"Connais pas."*

"That is always the way it goes," the General said.

As we were leaving, the local gendarme came in. "Tell me," Campy said, hope still springing, "do you by any chance know a certain Mademoiselle Chose?"

"Why, yes." The gendarme's tone was surprised.

"You do!" Campy was all eagerness. "Where does she live?"

The gendarme looked at Campy with a sympathetic, if speculative, eye, hesitated, then cleared his throat. "I think that if the Colonel wishes to preserve his illusions he will do well not to insist."

"Come on, Nick," the General said, climbing into the peep. "What he is trying to tell you is that now she is too old even for you."

A stop at General Pershing's former headquarters to see General Patton's old office. Then on through Langres to the village of Bourg, the site of his 1918 tank brigade headquarters.

At the edge of the small square a grizzled old boy in sabots was pitchforking manure into a cart.

"Stop," the General said. The peep drew up alongside the manure pile.

"Surely you were here during the last war," the General said.

The old man leaned on his pitchfork and for a moment or two surveyed the General. Then his eye lit up.

"But certainly, Colonel Patton," he said. "I remember you well."

Almost immediately a crowd gathered. Shouldering his pitchfork, the manure shoveler took the lead, and we rode down the main street escorted by virtually the entire population of Bourg.

"This is more like it," the General said. Old landmarks and memories. His office, his billet in the château of Madame de Vaux.

"It takes one back," the General sighed, not unhappily. And he liked it when, as we left, old Pitchfork saluted and said, "You must come and see us again, Colonel Patton."

Home via Neufchâteau and a slight detour through the woods above Amanty to view the wheat field from which in 1918 the first American bombers of World War I took off for that roundhouse at Conflans. The General got quite worked up about it. Even insisted on getting out and taking pictures. *Au fond,* he is a most kindly and considerate person.

September 29, 1944. Visitors. General Eisenhower and General Bradley came to lunch, to meet and talk to all the corps and division commanders. Eisenhower's assurances that Third Army would eventually receive adequate supplies and resume a major role were encouraging. Our boss was at his best, making sure that the "Supreme Commander" — he never calls him Ike in public — got all the limelight, at the same time seizing the opportunity to get him apart in order to press his own theses — in particular his conviction that the Germans will try to capitalize on our slowdown by an attempt to recapture Nancy.

October 6, 1944. Old Home Week in Nancy. Third Army Headquarters will move into the French barracks on the Rue du Sergent Blandan and I have been putting in a busy day with the *préfet's* requisitioning officer looking for a suitable house for the General. Combed the entire city from south to north without finding anything that would fit the bill.

From the suburb of Maxéville the road, curving up the pleasantly wooded high ground above the brewery, skirts a high, impenetrable stone wall.

"What's in there?" I asked. "It looks interesting."

"No, no, it's not interesting." The *préfet's* man was very positive.

"And anyhow, it is occupied, as are all the houses in this neighborhood."

"Hold everything," I said.

By getting up on the car roof it was easy to straddle the wall. A nicely kept park, a pond, and through the trees an attractive two-story house with a tower at one end. I dropped over the other side of the wall and made for the house. A flock of geese waddling up the lawn from the pond. On the terrace a handsome baby carriage. As I approached the front door, there appeared, around the conservatory, a lady in white with dark hair, no hat, and two small girls, each holding one of her hands. I introduced myself.

"I am Madame Paul-Cavallier," she said. "My daughter Guillaine, my daughter Brigitte. We love very much the Americans. Do give yourself the trouble to enter." She had bright brown eyes, a rather aquiline nose, an amusing mouth, and a very strange accent. The sizable salon off the conservatory was sunny and cheerful. Right up the General's alley, I thought.

"What can we do to make pleasant your stay in Nancy?" She clung insistently to her halting English.

"Well, the fact is, I am looking for a house."

"A house?"

"Yes, a house for immediate occupancy by an important visitor to Nancy." An inventorial look at the furniture and curtains. "Perhaps you can help me."

Her face clouded. You could see she was doing some fast thinking.

"*This* house," she now broke into incisive French, "would of course be entirely impractical for your purposes. On the other hand, I have just thought of another house, quite near here, larger, more convenient, its entrance gives on the Rue Auxonne. It would be perfect."

"Whom does it belong to?"

A pause, then deadpan, "My mother-in-law."

"What would your mother-in-law do?"

"My mother-in-law, all of us love the Americans. I feel sure she can be persuaded to go to her house in the Landes. I will speak to my husband."

On returning to the car I found the *préfet's* man biting his nails. "Everything is arranged," I said, "and everyone is happy." He seemed quite surprised.

Back in Étain. At supper the General was depressed. Our attack on Fort Driant has bogged down. He hates to withdraw but has about made up his mind that further attempts to take it at this time are not worth the price. General Marshall arrives tomorrow.

October 7, 1944. Last week we moved the C.P. — thank God — to Étain, where the General and his immediate household now occupy a small residence on the main street. Its grounds include a wooded area in the back of the property. There we have set up the General's trailer, in which he still sleeps, and his latrine, since the plumbing in the house does not work. So far his only concession to "going soft" is to come up to the house for meals. As for Al, George Murnane, Charley Odom, and myself, we have gone as soft as possible.

Our first visitor was Prince Felix of Luxembourg, consort of S.A. la Grande Duchesse Charlotte, ruler of said Grand Duchy. The Duchess is still in London, where she has remained since the hurried departure of the royal couple in May, 1940. The Prince wears British battle dress and is officially an English Brigadier. Since the Avranches breakthrough he has visited our headquarters several times, hoping — and with sound logic — that ours will be the first Allied troops to enter his capital. The General has become very fond of him, and for that matter he is a great favorite with all the staff. Back in the Le Mans period, when things were uncomfortably fluid, Prince Felix wanted to visit the 2d Blindée and I was elected to take him up to their C.P. Yes, you've guessed it. I got him and myself thoroughly lost. We had left our peep nestled in some shrubbery and were wandering around a dense and ominously silent forest, Tommy guns at the ready, when, to my unbounded relief, a couple of local F.F.I.'s appeared from nowhere — as they have a way of doing — and set us on the right track.

"I am very sorry, sir," I said as the peep got rolling once more.

"Quite all right," Prince Felix said. He is a big good-natured man, and no one has ever seen him ruffled. "I enjoy a walk in the woods before lunch. I admit," he added, "to be captured at this stage of the game by the Germans might prove awkward. My wife would be furious."

And now at Étain, the General, from whom this episode had been carefully concealed, was saying, "Your country awaits you, sir."

"Thanks to you, sir," the Prince said.

"First we will have lunch. Then Codman will escort you to your capital. In style," the General added. "Now that we are out of the woods I have a limousine."

Propitious departure. Guard of honor, a platoon of M.P.'s. Handshakes. Salutes. The General's everyday salute is about as snappy as they come, but for special occasions he always seems able to step it up even more. As the cortège moved off in the direction of Longwy and the Luxembourg frontier, he gave it the works.

The afternoon was mild and sunny — for once — the Prince, as always, relaxed and affable. In the towns through which we passed, our column — scout car ahead, the General's limousine next, followed by an ancient British saloon coupé piled high with the royal luggage, and, bringing up the rear, a peepful of M.P.'s — attracted a certain amount of attention. Even on the open road the occasional detachments we passed gazed curiously at our heterogeneous procession.

We were winding through a bit of grazing country whose farms and outbuildings bore marks of recent artillery fire. "I had the honor of accompanying one of your divisions through here," the Prince said. "There was some stiff fighting."

Then as we skirted a pasture full of placidly munching cows, he broke into French. *"Tiens,"* he said, *"les mêmes vaches. Animal étonnant, la vache. On tire des coups de fusil de tous les côtés, les obus sifflent, les types tombent, et ça continue à mâcher, à brouter, avec ce parfait calme. La vache est difficilement déconcertée."* ("Well, well," he said, "the same cows. Astounding animal, the cow. On all sides, rifle shots, whistling shells, men dropping, and the cow continues chewing, grazing, with that perfect composure. A cow is not easily disconcerted.")

"American cows are higher strung, less contented," I said.

"*Ah, vraiment?*" he said. "Very interesting. That may account for the superiority of our European cheeses."

We are still discussing the qualities of the cow when, on the out-skirts of a small town, we flashed by a sentry in exotic headgear who came smartly to attention. The Prince peered out at the approaching buildings — he is slightly nearsighted — and said, "This must be Pétange. Perhaps I should prepare to greet our subjects."

I lowered the right-hand window. The Prince sat forward on the edge of his seat. To each individual and occasional small group who stared curiously from the narrow sidewalk, he bowed and waved graciously. The audience response was somewhat negative. Suspended across the main square, a sizable banner, black, yellow, and red. On catching sight of it, Prince Felix hastily raised the window and sat back against the quilted upholstery.

"Wrong flag," he said. "Belgian! I'd forgotten that their frontier curves south at this point."

At the next town, Mims signaled the scout car to slow down. This time there was no question about it. It was Pétange all right. The flags were red, white, and blue. The bystanders, on recognizing their Prince, cheered wildly. The real ovation, however, came as we clattered over the bridge and through the neatly paved streets of his capital, the minia-ture city of Luxembourg, which so closely resembles the second-act set of all the old Shubert musicals.

At the palace, it took a little time to get the doors open so we could drive in. "*On n'attendait pas Votre Altesse jusqu'à la semaine pro-chaine,*" a flustered major-domo kept saying as he fumbled with the huge lock.

"Did the Germans do much damage?" the Prince asked.

"On the whole they were quite correct," the major-domo said.

The ground-floor hall was in semidarkness and all the furniture shrouded in dust cloths. A half dozen buxom maids on their knees bus-ily waxing the parquet floor. As the Prince made his way past them to the grand staircase, each would rise, smile, drop a curtsy, and resume her waxing. In the big reception room on the second floor, the Prince here and there raised the corner of a drop cloth to view, with a certain resignation, the ponderous furniture beneath.

"I had rather hoped," he sighed, "that the Boches would take all of these. However, my wife will be happy and that is all that matters."

"Good-by, sir, and good luck," I said.

"Thanks so much," he said. He really has a very nice smile. "When we are a little more settled you must come and see us."

October 10, 1944. Early 6 A.M. start with the General. Made General Eddy's headquarters in Nancy in time for breakfast with General Marshall, who had arrived to visit the front. A full day. A long drive to the C.P. of 6th Armored, where General Gerow had convened General Wood and also General Paul, commanding the recently arrived Yankee Division. After that, a visit to the 35th Division and a fire-direction center, which General Marshall seemed to find interesting. On the way back, enemy artillery let go with a succession of salvos which followed the line of our vehicles with considerable accuracy. Fortunately, each salvo was a couple of hundred yards over, so there was no harm done. Considering the amount of high brass involved, the General's surmise that there had been a leak seems reasonable. However, General Marshall appeared delighted with his day; in fact, our boss says he has never seen him in better humor.

October 14, 1944. Am writing this aboard the General's C-47 — under difficulties, as we are flying under the clouds at low altitude and it is bumpy as hell — on the way back from Liège, where a royal reception was held at First Army Headquarters in honor of General Bradley, who was made a K.C.B. Generals Eisenhower, Hodges, Simpson, Collins, and Gerow were all there. King George arrived just before lunch — pleasant, rather shy. After chatting with one and all — the reputed impediment in his speech is unnoticeable — he simply handed General Bradley the box containing the insignia and we all went in to lunch.

We are now comfortably installed in the house — or rather houses

—of Madame Paul-Cavallier's mother-in-law. The General, General Gaffey, and General Gay are in the big house. Al and I, and, of course, Charley Odom, George Murnane, and General Gaffey's aides, Wysong and Taylor — the latter had a close call a couple of weeks ago — are in the nearby guesthouse. Taylor's close call consisted in stopping a shell splinter during the bombardment, up at a 35th Division O.P., which very nearly obliterated three Generals — Eddy, Gaffey, and Gerow. He — and they — are lucky indeed to be alive.

Am grateful to know that the long drawers are on their way, since the daily peep trips to the front get longer, wetter, and colder. This is in no way a complaint, since now we at least have a warm, dry place to come back to, whereas the unfortunate combat soldiers up front are really taking it on the chin, and I'm afraid that for them there is worse to come.

October 17, 1944. Day before yesterday, a letter from Marrakech from Pierre Lyautey asking for a report on the house — now a museum — of his uncle, the late Maréchal Lyautey, which is at Thorey, not too far from here. As his uncle's executor and beneficiary, he is naturally anxious to know whether the house and the Maréchal's unique library and Moroccan souvenirs are intact. I showed the letter to the General and he said, "Go to it."

Before climbing the Paul-Cavallier wall, I had visited, among others, a certain Monsieur Salin, an archeologist, who was reported to have a promising house, and had learned that he had been a great friend of the Maréchal. Having left him with his roof over his head I was now able, with a clear conscience, to call him up and ask whether he would take me — or rather, be taken by me — out to Thorey to see what was what. He accepted with alacrity.

It is touching to share with a civilized Frenchman his excitement over his first automobile ride in four years. Moreover, Monsieur Salin was just as anxious as I was to learn how the Maréchal's house had fared. At Thorey, a tiny village, we located the guardian, Monsieur Colin, a wonderful character, the *ancien zouave en civile* to the life.

"Ils ont touché?" Monsieur Salin was breathless with suspense.

"*Vous allez voir,*" Monsieur Colin said.

Once inside, it was clear that all was well. As a monument to a genius the house is perfection. Neither large nor elaborate, every room is exactly as the Maréchal left it, breathing Morocco and France, simplicity and greatness. The famous *salle africaine* at the top of the house is surprisingly small, but everything in it is — as one would expect — a gem of its kind, and entering it you embark on a personally conducted tour of the masterpieces of Rabat, Fez, Marrakech, and the whole Moroccan *bled*. You would particularly like, I think, the enormous wax *cierges* of Moulay Idriss, the holy of holies, presented by the Sultan to the Maréchal during a severe illness. Upon his recovery the Maréchal called on the Sultan to thank him. "You must come to Moulay Idriss," the Sultan said, "and thank, not me, but Allah for curing you." No infidel, as you know, has ever entered the sacred precincts. The Maréchal was enormously pleased — *and* tempted. Monsieur Salin imitates him perfectly, the sudden change of pace, the brusque shake of the head. "No," the Maréchal said to the Sultan, "I know and you know that I am a close enough friend to justify my going, but nevertheless I will not go. I shall have successors, and I do not wish to create a precedent."

A coony old boy.

It was time to go and we were about to leave. "But Monsieur Salin," the old guardian said, "surely you remember that before a visitor was permitted to leave, Monsieur le Maréchal always opened the blinds of the west window."

"*Ah, oui, je revois le geste.*" Monsieur Salin stepped quickly to the window and threw open the shutters. Across the fields beyond the town the afternoon sun bathed the slopes of the hills of Lorraine.

"*Là voilà*" — the ringing tones were those of the Maréchal — "*la Colline Inspirée. Écoutez bien et vous l'entendrez respirer l'âme de la Lorraine.*"

P.S. Additional folklore: On the way home, passing through Vézelise* we were delayed for a few moments near the town hall by a congestion of ox carts.

* A town officially known — owing to its location in a sort of natural bowl — as "*le pot de chambre de Lorraine.*"

"Monsieur Salin," I said, "you who are an archeologist must surely be familiar with the replica of the famous *pot de chambre*. Is it not situated here somewhere in the *place?*"

"It is so long since I have been to Vézelise," he said, a little shame-facedly. "Let us ask a citizen." The first citizen to pass within hailing distance was a reserved-looking young girl in black carrying a prayer book. Monsieur Salin lowered the window, leaned out, raised his hat.

"*Pardon, mademoiselle,*" he said diffidently, "would you have the kindness to indicate to us the statuette of the famous little, er, excuse the word, the little *pot de chambre.*"

Taken off guard and with color slightly heightened by injured civic pride, the young lady of the prayer book pointed back to a niche in the municipal façade we had inadvertently passed. "*Mais, enfin, monsieur,*" she said, "*vous y tournez le dos.*"

October 21, 1944. General Spaatz and Julian Allen here last night. Also General Patton's nephew, Freddy Ayer, for whom, since the General was tied up with General Spaatz, I gave a party at Walter's on the Place Stanislas. If I say so myself, it was quite a good party — Julian, Bunny, Gaspar Bacon, Monsieur et Madame Paul-Cavallier, and Marlene Dietrich, who is entertaining the troops around Nancy. The champagne was next to flat, Clicquot '21, but still good, and everyone got remarkably fluent in three languages. During the first part of dinner, a couple of M.P.'s kept coming in and announcing — very respectfully — that "someone's jeep was blocking the entrance to the prefecture and could they move it," or "were there any military present under the grade of Field Officer; if so, they must be off the streets by ten." After a while I caught on. They just wanted to have a look at Dietrich, so I posted them outside in the corridor — we have a private dining room *au premier* — where they could see her through the door. She was being quite interesting on the subject of the alleged collaboration of Arletty, Guitry, and Chevalier — the last "cleared" by the Syndicat des Artistes on the grounds that he sang only once and without pay at Stalag 2A — when word was sent up that a group of French journalists wanted an interview. She said No, so I went down and appealed to their chivalry, pointing out that any publicity might endanger her life. Why? Because, confidentially, she had, before leaving Germany, turned down Hitler's advances. He was still out to get her. Nancy is full of German agents. They wouldn't want to have her kidnaped, would they? Well, no, they supposed not.

When I got back she was by a coincidence expounding to Gaspar the thesis that had Hitler not become an embittered vegetarian there would have been no war.

"Why was he an embittered vegetarian?" Gaspar asked.

"Because of his thwarted love life," Marlene smoldered. "Unfortunately for the world, the first girl laughed — a nifty title, by the way, for something or other."

This morning, accompanied the General and General Spaatz to the 4th Armored to see a demonstration of ducks' feet — homemade extensions attached to the tracks of the tanks, enabling them to weather the fearsome mud and wet terrain which is making life miserable for the combat troops. The boss always gets a great lift out of General Spaatz's visits. They talk the same language and have great respect each for the other. They also enjoy kidding one another — a superfluous observation, since the esteem in which General officers hold one another is always in direct proportion to the asperity of their verbal exchanges, whereas politeness among professional officers of whatever rank is invariably the outward and visible symbol of cordial dislike.

After breakfast, prior to leaving for the front, the General's eye was attracted as though by magnets to General Spaatz's well-pressed slacks and low shoes.

"Tooey, the well-dressed airman," the General crowed. "It is just as well you are occasionally given the opportunity to get out and see how the other nine tenths live."

General Spaatz, whose metabolism is geared to the later rather than the earlier morning hours, let it go.

From General Wood's headquarters, General Patton went on with Al to inspect three regiments of the 26th Division, and I drove back to Nancy with General Spaatz. He, too, gets a kick out of finding himself back in this part of the world, and seems to enjoy reminiscing about the old days at Issoudun.

In contrast to the confusion of the Tunisian and Sicilian campaigns, the correlation of Air and Ground efforts throughout the campaign in France has been a howling success. Our own Nineteenth Tactical Air Force, commanded by General O. P. Weyland, has been a tower of strength. Besides protecting the Army's flanks while we ran wild from Brittany to the Loire, Weyland's boys have dumped tons of napalm and skip-bombed the hell out of forward objectives and enemy tanks. During the hopeless flying weather of the last weeks they have performed prodigies of valor over and upon the fortresses and big gun emplacements of Metz.

"You heard how they knocked out that long-range railroad gun by skip-bombing and sealing off both ends of the tunnel from which it has been operating?" I said.

"Yes," General Spaatz said. "Opie is a good boy."

It was just about two years ago that I said good-by to you and climbed with Bunny into that taxi which whirled us off to Fort Meyer and thence to Norfolk, Virginia, on the first stage of this somewhat checkered travelogue. If anyone had told me then that I would be assisting at the 1944 *vendange* on the Côte d'Or — and without you — I'd have been incredulous. Yet that is precisely what I have been doing.

General Spaatz had left and that evening at dinner the General was unusually silent. When the General is silent it is just as well not to break in on his train of thought. Even Willie knows that. Sitting up on his chair by the sideboard, he kept quiet.

At length the General pushed away his plate. "That village we went through this morning, the one where the mayor was addressing the townspeople — all fifteen of 'em — from the top of that rubble pile, what's its name? Buissoncourt?"

"Yes, sir," the Chief of Staff said.

"I'm not sure about the mayor," he continued, "but that identical pile of rubble was there in 1917, twenty-seven years ago."

"The Germans bashed that intersection yesterday," the Chief of Staff said. "One-fifties. You would think that by now anyone would know enough not to build houses in the vicinity of a crossroad."

The General crumbled a slice of toast on the tablecloth and with a flick of thumb and middle finger lobbed a piece in the direction of the sideboard. Willie did not have to move. His jaws just opened and snapped shut.

"No, the French never change," the General said. "That is why they are indestructible."

The mess sergeant passed the meat. The General took sparingly of it. His nervous, agile fingers toyed with another piece of toast, but Willie, sensing his owner's mounting restiveness, knew there was nothing in it for him.

With a sudden motion, the General brushed away the littering of toast, picked up a spoon, bent it double, tossed it aside. "How long, O Lord, how long?" His eyes flashed dangerously. "We roll across France in less time than it takes Monty to say "Regroup" and here we are stuck in the mud of Lorraine. Why? Because somewhere up the line some so-and-so who never heard a shot fired in anger or missed a meal believes in higher priorities for pianos and ping-pong sets than for ammunition and gas."

The mess sergeant refilled the General's glass with chlorinated water.

The General eyed it wryly. "Is this the best the vineyards around here can do?" he said.

"This is beer country, General," I put in.

"True," the General said, "and by now every unbombed brewery from Maxéville to Charmes is undoubtedly occupied by Com-Z or the Service of Supply. Too bad we didn't take Dijon," he mused. "I could do with a good Burgundy. That reminds me" — the tone was crisp — "Hap, find out where Seventh Army is and send someone up there tomorrow with a request for that fat engineer who was with us in Sicily. No, never mind, I'll write Patch myself. You, Codman, be ready early in the morning. Take my command car; I'll be using the quarter-ton."

The field set in the next room rang. George Murnane went in to take the call. In a moment he returned. "General Bradley for General Patton," he said.

The General arose. Willie slid down from his chair and pattered along at the General's heels.

"Hello, Brad, this is George. What does SHAEF want now?"

3 P.M. the following afternoon. Mission accomplished. But hold on. Hadn't the General said he could do with a good Burgundy? "We'll go back a different way, Sergeant," I said. "Bear left."

"Boulevard Sévigné?" he asked.

"Yes. Been here before?"

"Six weeks," he said, "during World War One."

Changeless Dijon. As we clattered over the pavement of the Boulevard Sévigné down the incline to the Gare Dijon-Ville, under the railroad bridge, along the tram line past the canal, it all looked much as it had in the spring of 1940 when you and I last visited it. Only now it was autumn and the slopes to the right of Route Nationale 74 were golden indeed.

Gevrey-Chambertin, Vougeot, Flagey-Échezeaux. The signposts read like the Burgundy section of Nicolas's wine list.

Right turn.

With the silhouette of a 1913 Maxwell, the weight and speed of a medium-sized steamroller, and a transmission whose song might be likened to the relentless grinding of boulders on the reef of Norman's Woe, the command car of World War II surpasses all other vehicles of the U. S. Army in majesty and discomfort. As we roared and coughed up the rocky road, the *vendangeurs* among the nearest rows of vines turned with astonishment from their picking. A man waved his hat. A girl held up a purple bunch of grapes and waved that. Someone started shouting. Others took it up. You could tell only from their open mouths. No sound could possibly compete with the scream of the command car's low gear. The sergeant was saying something. Rounding the last curve, we chugged into the empty *place* and slowed down.

"What were you saying, Sergeant?"

"I was just thinking that Seventh Army must be popular around here," he said, "or maybe they just haven't got this far yet."

"Maybe. Round the church," I pointed, "and into that lane."

"O.K."

"Next right. And don't knock down the wall."

We made it, and came to a halt in the middle of the courtyard of the Domaine of the Romanée-Conti. The door of the office opened and there was Madame Clin, her spectacles glinting in the sunlight. The thing about Madame Clin is that nothing ever catches her off balance. She looked at the command car and its occupants, first through her spectacles, then over her spectacles. Having taken everything in, she advanced neither slowly nor rapidly across the yard. "Well," she said, "for a good surprise this is a good surprise."

Monsieur de Villaine? Well. Monsieur Clin? Not so well. And the Germans, how did they treat you? The Germans are pigs. Unfortunately, the local gauleiter knew his Burgundies only too well. Fortunately, however, his eyesight was imperfect.

Somehow I could not bring myself to ask about the '37's. At length Madame Clin drew from the folds of her dress the familiar key. "Come," she said.

The sergeant and I followed her down the stone steps into the cellar. With candle held high she proceeded on past the rows of casks. "The forty-threes," she said. "Later we will taste them, but now —"

The cellar ended in a wall of seemingly solid masonry; against its damp surface the last barrel snuggled closely. "If you will just move it, please," Madame Clin said.

A full cask of Burgundy is a hefty proposition. The sergeant spit on his hands and grasped the further rim. "Gently," Madame Clin murmured.

In response to the sergeant's trial tug the big cask upended with disconcerting ease. "Empty," he said, regaining his balance.

In that portion of the wall against which its side had lain, a number of stone blocks had been removed. Bending down, Madame Clin thrust the candle through the irregular black hole. "See," she said.

The yellow rays penetrating the gloom revealed the damply gleaming masonry of the end wall, the real end wall, and, stretching off into the darkness, a double line of neatly stacked bottles.

Madame Clin reached in and withdrew one, wiped off with her apron the heavier layers of caked dust and mold, set the bottle together with three glasses on the upended cask, and reached into her pocket for her corkscrew. The long straight cork came out with a resounding pop. Madame Clin smelled it, then poured the wine into each of our extended glasses and her own. For a while no one said anything. As hands cupped around the glasses warmed the wine, the pungent aroma of great Burgundy coursed through inhaling nostrils. "To your health," Madame Clin said.

"To yours."

With the musical clink of thin crystal, the three glasses touched. We drank. Sergeant Hawley was the first to speak. "Some *pinard!*" he said. "What's it called?"

"Romanée-Conti 1937," Madame Clin said. And for once she really smiled.

After saying good-by and extricating the sergeant and the command car from a mound of children we rolled off down the road to Beaune. The *côtes* are really glorious. Symphony of bronze, browns, Indian reds. Even up our way I have seldom seen better.

Right turn at Aloxe and up through the vineyard to Château Grancey. Wagons full of purple grapes backed up to the *cuverie,* and there, sure enough, supervising the unloading, Louis-Noël Latour, and Jean, and the sister who looks like them, and all the children.

Big ovation. The first question, from everyone: "Madame Codman, she's not with you? It isn't possible."

Down cellar. Dégustation. The sergeant too, and, of course, all the children. By the time we came up, it was dark and I murmured something about the Hotel de la Poste. They would not hear of it. Maman is coming out from Beaune, you must stay here. But my driver. Naturally, he, too, will stay.

"And how," I asked, "is Monsieur Latour, your father?"

There was a momentary silence.

"How could you know," Louis-Noël said. "My father died two years ago."

It was a shock, and I know how badly you, too, will feel about it.

Later, Louis-Noël told me it was cancer of the stomach. Luckily, it did not take long.

Dinner at Grancey. So reminiscent. God, how I missed you. How everybody there missed you. Maman's arrival. She has not changed a bit. *"Madame, c'est plus fort que moi, je vous embrasse."* She was very cute and kept asking and asking about you. More than most, the French know from sad experience what it means to be separated from those one loves.

Dinner was so like old times that it hurt. As the Corton, white and red, took hold they all began talking at once, arguing, kidding in the manner that only a united French family can argue and kid. Missing was the patient, indulgent eye of Monsieur Latour, *père,* surveying with pride, affection — albeit a certain remoteness — his effervescent off-spring, but I noted that already Louis-Noël's own manner had undergone a subtle change. With the assumption of his father's position he had taken on stature and there were moments during the evening when his resemblance to the departed patriarch was startling. Monsieur Latour, Sr., is a difficult man to replace, but I am confident that Louis-Noël will be more than equal to his rightful role.

After dinner, politics and war, of how in 1940 the Germans burst into the room where we were sitting brandishing revolvers. "If any man, woman, or child in your town so much as raises a finger against our soldiers, you will be shot, all of you, without ceremony," they said.

"Quoi qu'il y avait des gens assez louches dans la région," Madame Latour commented, *"personne n'a bougé — heureusement."* Which, after all, is a point of view.

And so to bed, and a sleep as deep and enveloping as the bottomless mattress of the guest room's sturdy four-poster.

Awakened by the *femme de chambre* bearing a pitcher of very hot water. From the window the vineyards in the early morning light, a sea of shimmering gold. Franco-American breakfast with the entire family, *croissants,* butter — and *what* butter — and, from the K rations which the sergeant broke out, good American coffee.

To the Latour office in Beaune, the entire family packed into the command car. An hour or so in the office discussing this and that. All our 1937 reservations are intact and will be shipped as soon as the French Government and ours have ironed out the technicalities. Next week they are expecting the visits of le Commandant Knight, Monsieur Raymond Baudouin, and Monsieur Schoonmaker — so you can see everything will soon be back to normal. Midmorning. Having loaded up with a reasonable amount of good Aloxe-Corton for the mess, and for special occasions some Charlemagne '34, together with a few precious bottles of Corton Grancey '29. Good-bys.

A run down the line to see the Marquis d'Angerville. As usual he was in his sky-blue overalls and black sabots supervising the boys in the *cuverie,* his watchful eye on the alert for the slightest deviation from *les coutumes loyaux et constants.* His first words: "How is Madame Codman?" His second: "Last week we heard her on the Boston short-wave radio." He was quite steamed up about that. Rather vague about the subject of your talk but emphatic about its being *plein d'élan.* To get a rise, I said I had been glad to hear that he had not lost too much of his wine to the Boches. Instant flare-up. *"C'est des intéressés qui vous ont dit ça,"* he snapped. "The Germans requisitioned forty per cent of all my wine." As a matter of fact, that is about the average, but he is a marvelous little gamecock, and I know of no one who can make himself madder quicker — except, of course, the General.

With a case of his Volnay Champans '34 lashed to the spare-tire bracket, I struck out for Puligny. Monsieur Colin-Bouley was — so his Madame informed me — out in the vineyards. Pointing the command car up the little road which winds past the crucifix — remember? — we ground up the incline and amongst the sacred vines of the Grand Montrachet of the Marquis de Laguiche. There sure enough was Monsieur Colin-Bouley surrounded by a platoon of busy *vendangeuses.* Sensation. The *vendange* itself came to a complete halt as the grape pickers crowded around the command car. They sat in it and on it, crawled under it, patted it, then individually and collectively they said what every man, woman, and child in France invariably says when confronted with U. S. Army vehicles: *"C'est bien pratique ces petites voitures là."* Yes, our '33 Montrachet is safe and well. Also that of Berry Brothers, and I will so advise our friend Rudd.

Back along Route Nationale 74, direction Dijon. Only two more stops. First, Nuits-Saint-Georges and the perennial Monsieur Camille Rodier, he too unchanged by the vicissitudes of war. "We envisage an early reunion of the Chevaliers du Tastevin, at the Château du Clos Vougeot — you know, of course, that we have bought it. I trust that you, and Madame Codman, our first American lady member — I do hope her ankle has completely recovered — will attend. Also, we are expecting General Eisenhower and Monsieur Bob Hope. Monsieur Williamme Bullittee called last week. *Naturellement je lui ai fait des prix d'ami, comme à vous-même."*

Arrived back in Nancy to find a letter from Walworth announcing the death of his, and our, good old friend Alfred de Luze. Their fathers were friends, so were their grandfathers. Three generations of Pierces and de Luzes. Good friends, good wines, never a written contract, simply mutual trust and confidence. Speaks well for both Boston and Bordeaux.

Bordeaux—when will it be liberated? I shall try to get word from both of us to Francis—he will feel dreadfully about his father—but am not too hopeful of getting through. What a fine old boy he was. And very fond of you. *"Madame,"* he used to say, *"j'ai l'impression que vous êtes très volontaire."* How right he was, and is.

I don't suppose this letter will get to you on or before your birthday, but in any event many happy returns, mine in particular, I hope, before next October 31.

October 28, 1944. Last week, at the house of the mother-in-law of Madame Paul-Cavallier, things were rather hectic for a while. A long day of visiting the divisions. Everybody tired. Early to bed. Three in the morning. A terrific crash. Another. Both close. Shattering of glass. Into our clothes, fast, Al, George, and the others. Over to the General's house on the run. Quite a few of the windows blown out. The General himself emerging from the front door as we got there.

"Must be two-eighties," he said. "Near miss on Gaffey's room."

Over our garden wall, flames were shooting up from a small three-story residence immediately across the narrow street.

"Come on," the General said.

One of the shells, maybe both, had demolished the front of the house. What was left of the second-story flooring was hanging like a curtain over the smashed-up furniture and debris of the ground floor. The top floor was on fire. Under the debris, someone groaning. Two occupants of the house who had managed to get out and several neighbors were milling around in the littered sidewalk when we got there. One of them was tugging on what seemed to be a man's leg sticking out of the rubble. The General dove in first and we all began removing brick and hunks of mortar. Another leg appeared. The General grabbed it. "Pull," he said. The groans rose to a howl. "Wait," the General said. Relinquishing the leg, he dug feverishly into the debris. Another leg, the leg of a table. "Here is the trouble," the General said as he jerked it free. "He's stuck under his own dining-room table. Easy now," he said to the Frenchman on the other leg. "We don't want to pull his head off."

The groans continued. *"T'en fait pas, mon vieux."* His neighbor had recognized his co-rescuer. *"Le fameux général Patton lui-même est en train de te décaler. Ça n'va pas barder."* ("Don't worry, old boy. The great General Patton himself is unearthing you. It won't take long.")

Another terrific crash as a third shell landed in the middle of the road, showering us with stones and plaster. "They seem to have us zeroed in," the General said. "There you are," he added, as the stunned and disheveled inmate was dusted off and helped to his feet. "Should be all right — except for a stiff neck."

Miraculously enough no one was badly hurt. Walking back to the house, the General paused to view the nicked cornice over General Gaffey's window. "Close enough," he said. "And I don't mind saying I have seldom been more scared."

CHAPTER XI

Metz and the Saar

(November–December, 1944)

The general plan was for Montgomery's armies, the First American and the Third American Armies to make an attack all along the front on or about 10 November. On 2 November, General Bradley came to Headquarters, Third Army and stated that the British would not be ready to jump off in time for the offensive — in fact, would not be ready before the first of December; that the American First Army could not attack until they were reinforced by divisions which were then with the British Army. He wished to know General Patton's desires. General Patton said, "I will attack alone with or without Air support." General Bradley said, "The date of the attack and the hour will be up to you," and left. General Patton's staff remembered that it would soon be two years to the hour and date since Patton's first attack in this war was made off the coast of Casablanca and unquestionably due to sentiment, the attack was set for 8 November at 0500. At that hour, the largest concentration of artillery probably heard during the war started. It consisted of 158 battalions opening fire at 0500 on 8 November 1944. Thirty minutes later seven Infantry divisions and three Armor divisions advanced through the attack. Later a German General who had been captured (Blumentritt) was asked if the Germans

*were surprised by the day of the attack. He quickly replied,
"No, not one bit. We knew Patton would commemorate his
first battle of this war."*

November 7, 1944. Tomorrow Third Army once more attacks.* It
has been a tough week. The weather awful. The Moselle has been rising, not by inches but by feet, and acres of surrounding countryside are
under water. One of the corps commanders and a division commander
came to see the General early this evening to ask for a postponement.
The General listened carefully.

"You feel that under present conditions you cannot undertake the attack as planned?" he asked.

"That is correct, sir," they said.

"Would you care to make recommendations as to your successors?"
he said quietly.

Changing his tone, he drew them over to the map. "This is what we
are going to do," he said. For half an hour, into the drained reservoirs
of their self-confidence he poured and pumped the elixir of his own
vitality.

"And now," he said smiling, "go back to your headquarters, have a
big drink, and get some sleep."

"Don't worry, General," they said, "the attack will go on."

"You're goddam right it will," the General said.

The General arose, looked at his watch. "Ten-thirty P.M.," he said.
"Exactly two years ago we were on the cruiser *Augusta* approaching
the Moroccan coast. It was blowing hard and the question of a postponement came up. Tonight it is raining even harder than it was blowing then."

At the foot of the stairs he paused. "I think," he said, "that today has
been the longest day of my life. There is nothing I can do now but
pray." Then seizing the banister rail, he went up to his room, briskly.

* For this campaign, Third Army was composed as follows: XX Corps; 10th Armored;
95th, 90th Infantry and XII Corps; 4th and 6th Armored Divisions; 80th, 83d, 35th,
26th, and 5th Infantry Divisions.

November 8, 1944. Shortly after 5 A.M. our artillery barrage commenced. It was long and loud. The house shook and through the curtains of the front windows the sky gleamed and surged with multiple flashes. Shortly before eight o'clock General Bradley telephoned.

"Are you attacking, George?" he asked.

"Yes, Brad," the General said. "Can't you hear our guns?"

"Without Air support?" General Bradley sounded incredulous.

"If it clears, our Air will get going during the day," the General said.

"Fine," General Bradley said. "Hold the line, Ike wants to speak to you."

"George, this is Ike. I expect great things of you. Carry the ball all the way."

"Thanks, General, I will," General Patton said.

After a hasty breakfast, the General, Al, and I took off for a forward O.P. of XII Corps overlooking the river. The rain had lightened to a mere drizzle as we rattled eastward, and by the time we reached the O.P. the weather, for the first time in days, looked promising. Unfortunately, the crossings were so obscured by our own smokescreens that little could be observed. Around ten o'clock, however, the sun appeared, and with it a glorious sight — our fighter bombers, hundreds and hundreds of them, streaking like shining arrows against a sky now interlaced with crisscross vapor contrails and the smoke spirals of our planes' markers.

"I'm almost sorry for those German bastards." The General's eyes shone.

Whirlwind visits to the C.P.'s of three Infantry divisions and the 4th Armored. All along the line the news is good.

By late afternoon General Eddy signaled that virtually all our units are on their objectives. Now the rain has started again.

This evening at supper, the General, for the first time in days, was relaxed and talkative. His insistence in going ahead despite the advice of his best and most trusted leaders was paying off.

"I have always maintained," he said, "that there are more tired division commanders than there are tired divisions."

November 9, 1944. More of the same. Another great Air show, this time augmented by the Eighth Air Force, whose bombers battered the forts surrounding Metz.

Flood conditions are bad and many of the bridges are out. Crossing the river at Pont-à-Mousson the General's peep got stuck in the mud on the far side. We had to be pulled out by a truck.

This evening at dinner a very pleasant group of guests — General Spaatz, Jimmie Doolittle, Ted Curtis, Julian Allen, and Bruce Hopper. The General voiced a glowing tribute to the Air effort, not only in terms of the present attack but throughout the whole campaign. Compared to the earlier cat-and-dog relationship between air and ground forces, Overlord * and the battle of France have indeed proved a honeymoon.

"Individual personality plays a much greater part in warfare than most people realize," the General said. "Frankly" — he turned to Spaatz — "I look upon yesterday's bomber missions as so many expressions of your personal friendship, and that of Jimmie Doolittle, for me."

"Right you are, Georgie," they chorused. "You're the kind of Ground Force Commander we like to help out."

Bruce, whose civilian status allows him considerable leeway, has developed quite a talent for tossing into the arena controversial morsels for the high brass to chew on.

"Speaking of the Ground Forces," he said, "why is it that our Infantry is the most unpopular and least effective of the various branches of our service?" They all kicked this around for a while and it was the General who eventually came up with the "gadget theory." "The American soldier is primarily gadget minded," he said. "Give him a tank, an airplane, a cannon, or even a truck, and he takes an immediate interest in the gadget, and because he does, he masters it, and because he masters it, he becomes, in terms of that gadget, the best damn soldier in the world. If in addition he can ride in or on the gadget he is completely happy. Unfortunately, the infantryman has no gadget other than the M-1 rifle. The M-1 rifle properly used is a marvelous weapon of

* Code name for Normandy invasion.

destruction, but it has not enough moving parts to interest the gadget-minded American soldier. Moreover, he can't ride on it or in it and he hates walking. Hence the U. S. Infantry is at a grave disadvantage as against the gadget branches, such as the Artillery, the Engineers — even Ordnance, the S.O.S., and the Air Force. It will be the duty of future Commanders to develop a gadget which will interest the U.S. infantryman."

"How about motorized roller skates?" General Spaatz said.

"Speaking of Commanders," Bruce said again, "I noticed a few days ago our Supreme Commander referred to a certain Allied leader as the greatest Commander in all military history."

General Patton started to take a deep breath, but someone else got there first. "I have given that remark careful thought," he said, pulling on his cigar. "In reply I would say that it is my considered opinion that said leader is the lousiest Commander in all recorded history, both military and civilian."

You can see that a good time was had by all.

November 15, 1944. Speaking of gadgets, which I did in my last letter, the General has a new one, the "auto-rail" formerly used by Goering. It is a diesel-powered railway car which Colonel Muller dug up in a marshaling yard near Paris and which clatters along the right of way at disconcerting speed. With the divisions moving forward in fanlike pattern, the daily visits by peep present a distance problem which is partly solved by auto-railing to the nearest railroad point and using divisional peeps from there on.

Day before yesterday marked our maiden voyage. The auto-rail got us to Thionville in record time. From there we peeped across a tread-way bridge under a smokescreen to visit General Van Fleet, who took us to the battlefield where the day before he had repelled a severe German counterattack following the 90th Division's spectacular crossing of the Moselle. The General was both impressed and delighted.

"Never in my life have I seen so many dead Germans all at once," he said.

It was dark and rainy when we regained the auto-rail and got under way. The railroad sergeant had prepared a light supper for the General, Paul Harkins, Al, and me, but the violent lurchings of Herr Goering's chariot made eating difficult, and after scalding both knees with coffee, and almost putting Paul's eye out with a forkful of cold salmon, I gave it up and went forward to the control room.

In the obscurity of the curtained-off compartment, Pétard, the French "chauffeur," and Corporal Hart, one of our railroad boys from Texas, crouch over the dimly lit dials. Pétard, a beret capping his bullet head and a limp cigarette stuck to the corner of his lower lip, manipulates the controls. He speaks no English. Hart, tall, lean, cadaverous, does not know a word of French. They understand one another perfectly. And why not? Every small boy of whatever nationality has always aspired to the career of either candy-store operator or locomotive engineer. For Pétard and Hart communication in terms of a sort of innate railroad Esperanto presented no difficulties whatever.

Really raining now. To the constant honking of the raucous siren and the crazy cadence of the windshield wiper, the unleashed autorail hurtles against solid black waves of lashing water. An amber signal light flashes past.

"Easy, easy." Palms down, Hart's hands rise and fall as if addressing an imaginary keyboard. "The Pompey bridge should be just ahead."

"Pourvu qu'il est encore là." Like all Frenchmen, Pétard is something of a pessimist.

It *is* still there, and we crackle across it like a drummer performing a run on an out-of-tune xylophone.

"O.K." Hart shrugs.

"Hoquet," Pétard echoes.

A deep reverberating roar. For a moment the rain ceases. Swoosh. There it is again.

"Le tunnel," Pétard says.

"Yeah, the tunnel. I'm glad that is still there, too." Hart looks at his watch.

The rain has turned to snow. The windshield wiper creaks, bucks, heaves mightily, jams.

"Merde," Pétard explodes. "How you say, 'sheet'?"

"No, no, not 'sheet.'" Hart is quite cross. "I told you before: ess, aitch, eye, tee — as in mess kit. Now try it again."

"*Ça va, ça va. T'en fais pas.*" Pétard moves the control lever up another notch. "*Et puis*, SHEET, *alors.*"

Visibility zero. Pétard opens the small side door, inches out in front of the windshield, makes a couple of passes at it with his glove. A swirl of snow as he backs in again.

"*Hoquet.*"

"O.K."

I return to the main compartment to get warm and write this letter. The General is dozing. So are Paul and Al. We are slowing down a bit now. Signal lights, streaks of red, blue, amber. A sustained lurch as we hit a crossover, the wheels screaming like those of a New England milk wagon on a subzero morning. The long, low line of the Nancy train shed. The General wakes up. "Has Mims been alerted?" "Yes, sir."

We slide to a stop. The air brakes heave a post-arrival sigh. Out. Place Thiers, and Mims with the peep. Slippery cobbles. Cours Léopold. Rue Auxerre. Home.

"*Hoquet.*"

November 16, 1944. Yesterday General Eisenhower and Jimmy Gault* arrived for lunch. Both in excellent form and most genial. In the afternoon we all went up to XII Corps so that General Eisenhower could inspect detachments of the 35th and 26th Divisions.

Every Commander has his own inspection technique. General Eisenhower's approach to combat troops is now fairly standardized. The unit to be inspected opens ranks and the Supreme Commander walks, neither fast nor slowly, up one line and down the other. The photographers make sure they get an effective background of mud, and, if possible, ruins, blasted trees, etc. Every dozen yards or so General Eisenhower stops to speak to an individual soldier. The dialogue, with only minor variations, goes like this:

Supreme Commander: "What do you do in civil life, soldier?"

* Colonel James Gault, British P.A. (Personal Assistant to General Eisenhower).

Soldier: "I'm a farmer, sir."

S.C.: "Fine, fine, so am I. What do you raise?"

Soldier: "Corn" (or wheat, or whatever).

S.C.: "Fine. How many bushels do you get to the acre?"

Soldier: "Oh, in a good year, maybe umpty bushels."

S.C. (thunderstruck): "You do? Well" (smiles broadly) "all I can say is that after the war is over, *I'll* be coming to *you* for a job." (Brisk again.) "Meantime, do me a favor, will you, soldier? Go in and get this war finished up, *fast* — so I can go fishing."

Dinner at the General's house in Nancy went swimmingly. General Eisenhower seemed pleased with Third Army's progress in the envelopment of Metz and its strike to the Siegfried Line, and our General made considerable headway in selling him on a more liberal policy in re battlefield promotions and decorations. Around eleven, General Patton accompanied General Eisenhower and Jimmy Gault to the Grand Hotel, where they were spending the night in that rather gloomy suite you and I had on our last visit here. It has a fireplace, you may remember, which has not been used since the hotel was built. General Patton and Jimmy decided to build a fire and in their enthusiasm set the chimney on fire. The service at the Grand Hotel is just as indifferent as ever, and we had to get in our own engineers to put out the conflagration. It was all very jolly and the two Generals sat up and talked until after 2 A.M.

This morning, inspection of Quartermaster and Ordnance installations in and about Nancy. After lunch, our General said his good-bys and went to his office, and I guided General Eisenhower and Jimmy to the outskirts of town and put them on the road to Paris. Tomorrow, Walter Lippmann, whom I shall be glad to see again.

November 23, 1944. Thanksgiving Day. Metz has fallen to XX Corps, or at least there no longer is any organized resistance within the city. This morning there was a guard of honor with ruffles and flourishes to celebrate General Eddy's capture of Nancy in September, and now that of Metz by General Walker. It is the first time in over four hundred years that the Fortress City has been taken by assault.

Followed, a genial Thanksgiving lunch and in the afternoon a visit from General Giraud, who, as former Military Governor of Metz, wanted to present his congratulations, which he did, in very flattering terms. We are also expecting General Bonesteel — almost as good a name for a General as Ironsides — who is supposed to be General Eisenhower's hatchet man, and the day after, Averell Harriman, whom I have not seen since the Anfa Conference.

To answer the questions in your last letter: (1) have not received the heavy drawers and socks but they will probably arrive any day now. Hope so, as the peeping gets progressively colder and wetter. (2) Yes, I answered Neysa's letter about Cole's leg two weeks ago, but hear that some of our mail got sunk at about that time. (3) Why do I say "peep" instead of "jeep"? Have put the question, as follows, up to Al, who knows more about vehicles than the Chief of Ordnance.

Me: "Al, what is the correct name for the vehicle we have been riding in all over North Africa, Sicily, England, and France?"

Al: "The quarter-ton."

Me: "I see. What is a jeep?"

Al: "No such thing as a jeep. That's just civilian talk for *any* Army vehicle. Means nothing."

Me: "I see. What is a peep?"

Al (reluctantly): "Well, you might say it's permissible to refer to the quarter-ton as a peep — the General does — but I prefer to call it by its right name, which is the quarter-ton."

So there you are, right from the horse's mouth.

December 1, 1944. Just back from a mission to the headquarters of General Devers and that of First French Army.

Sixth Army Group Headquarters seems to be permanently established in great comfort at Vittel. Having transacted my business, immediately got in touch with Archie Alexander, who is with Harry Parkman's Civil Government Section. Arranged, at his kind suggestion, to spend the night at his quarters. Dined with Cabot Lodge, whom I ran into in the lobby of the vast palace which houses the Devers headquarters. He is head of the Liaison Section and his main job, I gathered, consists in keeping General de Lattre de Tassigny, Commanding First French Army, both happy and in order, a tricky assignment for which no one could be more pre-eminently qualified than Cabot. His chief assistants are Chan Bigelow and the son of the Aga Khan, who occupy with him the attractive villa at which we dined. All three in excellent form. Through his father, Aly Khan is able to slip in and out of Switzerland with the greatest of ease and has promised that on his next trip to Geneva he will get me some Patek Philippe wrist watches, one for you and a couple for the General. Said next trip, Cabot predicted, should take place any day now, since Aly's local heart throb of the moment is beginning to act up a bit.

Long talk with Archie before going to bed. I got a great lift from seeing him and hearing of you at first hand. Am glad you are seeing Jean. I can think of no couple for whom I have greater admiration and affection.

Up betimes to make an early start for Besançon and thence to the headquarters of First French Army at Montbéliard. Winding up through the foothills of the Vosges brought back memories of the old Section Three days, the Model-T Ford (American Field Service, World War I). So did the detachments of French *fantassins* swinging along at that unmistakable short rapid gait so incongruous with the present Americanized uniforms in which they are not in the least disguised. You would get quite a thrill, I know, in seeing this French Army — '14 variety, not '40 — bowling along over its own home grounds. Four hundred miles from the Mediterranean to the Vosges in three weeks. Then an inevitable slowdown. Now a fresh start again. General de Lattre, from all accounts, must be quite a man. The combative spirit, the legendary temper, the dramatic flair, the *bons mots*. Like General Patton, his credo is offense, offense, offense. Occasionally he gives a bit of it to his superiors.

First French Army Headquarters is Montbéliard's rather modest hotel, which they have taken over in its entirety. The first person I ran into was Bill Bullitt, all done up in the uniform of a French Commandant. He is head of de Lattre's Liaison Section and his assistant turns out to be none other than my old friend Fernand Auberjonois

of the Moroccan landing and Rabat days. We were swapping gossip
at the foot of the hotel stairs when from the mezzanine landing there
came a sudden scuffling of feet and clicking of heels. On either side
of a double door giving on the landing a giant *sénégalais*. With a
flourish each placed to his potent lips a gleaming trumpet. The hotel
was still re-echoing with clarion sound as the double doors flew open
and a trim, decisive figure swept through and descended the stairs.
Under the jaunty set of the kepi a hawklike nose, bright roving eyes.
Under the left arm a swagger stick, in the right hand a pair of spotless
yellow gloves. In the lobby he stopped and chatted for a moment with
the assembled group.

"Ah, you are with General Patton," he said. *"Quel chef formidable."*

Supper that evening at the hotel mess was so like all the French
popotes of old. Conversation, rapid, general, and vehement — leavened,
incidentally, by three striking WAACs, *les demoiselles* Troisier, Le
Sieur, et Charles-Roux, who constitute the distaff section of the General's brain trust. Its head, who arrived shortly before we sat down, is
— who do you suppose? — Monsieur — I mean Capitaine — Tron. I
told him I had had the pleasure of attending his daughter's christening
in Algiers, and he told me that both she and Madame Tron are now
in Paris, which is nice to know.

Elated, as well they may be, by the way the First French Army is
forging ahead, all members of the staff are obviously very much under
the spell of Monsieur le Général de Lattre de Tassigny.

"Il est impayable, le général," the most decorative of the WAACs
effervesced. "Did you hear his *mot* yesterday? 'That I should be referred to as Théâtre de Marigny, *ça va encore,*' he said, 'but to be
dubbed the Two of Clubs I find exaggerated. Why the Two of Clubs?
*Parce qu'on prétend q'en ma personne la France a joué sa dernière
carte?'* "

Before going to bed, walked home with Auberjonois in the cool of
the evening — and I may say the Vosges air bites shrewdly.

"This must be quite an entertaining headquarters," I said.

"It is," he said. "The only out is that one seldom gets any sleep. The

General is a nocturnal. By midnight he will be back in his office, and around two or three in the morning we will all be summoned to a conference of some kind."

"Like Lyautey."

We talked of Morocco and of Fernand's billet with the old *contrôleur* who had helped ransom Vincent Sheean from Abd-el-Krim.

"Here," he said, as we arrived before the door of a tightly shuttered house. "My landlady is an old maid. Very kind. She insisted on knitting me a heavy woolen comforter for my bed."

"Must come in handy these cold nights."

"It does. But each time I draw it up over me I am embarrassed."

"Why?"

"It is a replica, in colors, of a full-size American flag. When it covers me I feel I should lie at attention until the arrival of the burial squad."

December 15, 1944. The weather continues awful. Notwithstanding mud, flood, trench foot, and bitter German resistance and counter-attacks — how right General Patton was about the folly of letting them get their second wind — Third Army is now, as you doubtless know, across the Saar.

Another visit from Generals Spaatz, Doolittle, and Vandenberg to correlate an Air-Ground attack on the Siegfried Line. This will be really big. Watch for it. I can't say more.

Last week we received notice of an impending influx of Congressmen — including Clare Luce.

"See that no drinks are served, and only the simplest food — just sandwiches, preferably stale ones," the General said. "Otherwise, they are sure to go back and say we are living too well and wasting government funds." The lunch went off without untoward incident. The General particularly affable, the Congressmen noticeably gloomy. During the afternoon, however, word came that Representative Luce, on a junket to an Artillery unit, had pulled the lanyards of two of our guns, lobbing a couple of shells on enemy-held Fort Driant. I have seldom seen the General angrier.

A much more rewarding visit was that of Madame la Maréchale Lyautey, who gave us all a marvelous evening — and me a very active day. It came about in this way: Last week I learned quite by accident that she was expected in the Nancy region in connection with activities of the French Red Cross, of which she is a big wheel. I asked the General whether he would like to have her to dinner. He said he certainly would.

Next morning I started bright and early by peep for Thorey, where she was supposedly staying. On the way it began to rain, as usual. Arrived at Thorey in a downpour to learn from Monsieur Colin that Madame la Maréchale had just left — hardly five minutes ago — to visit her niece in Lunéville. Cross-country in the driving rain to Lunéville. Some difficulty in finding the house of the niece. Madame la Maréchale had just left for Nancy, to preside at a meeting of eminent medicos, left hardly five minutes ago. Well, at least I was keeping even. Nancy. Its tram line. Its wet cobbles. The rain still coming down in torrents as I draw up at the given address. Brass name plate: Dispensaire Lyautey. Ring. The *directrice,* big, bustling. Madame la Maréchale has just left, hardly two minutes ago. Gaining. It seems she merely opened the meeting here and rushed off to preside at the big Croix Rouge convention across town. It is now four o'clock. We will telephone her at five when the meeting should be terminated. Meantime, will you not come in and visit our *dispensaire.* With pleasure. Waiting room. Operating room. *Clinique* — for illegitimate children. Finally a large room divided into small curtained booths — *pour les soins intimes.* The *directrice* did full justice to this department. And now that you have seen our modest little installation perhaps you will give us the pleasure of looking in on our graduating class — the class of student nurses. With pleasure. Another large room. Desks, like a schoolroom. A platform. Somehow I am on it with the *directrice* and a number of rather embarrassing life-size charts — in color — depicting "areas of greatest sensibility." A rustling of starched linen skirts as thirty student nurses spring to their feet and stand rigidly at attention. The *directrice* is introducing someone. Me.

Le colonel a bien voulu nous honorer de sa présence. . . . L'Améri-

*que . . . la grande république soeur . . . la France . . . l'Alsace . . .
Lorraine . . . Lafayette, Rochambeau, Codman, nous voilà.*

A few well-chosen words followed by a stroll with the *directrice*
up and down the starched ranks of *infirmières étudiantes*. And you,
mademoiselle, what part of France do you come from? The Charol-
lais? Ah, yes, how often have I admired your beautiful white cattle.
And your specialty? The heart? One can see that you have great
natural aptitude. . . . I almost envy your wounded. . . . And after the
war you must visit *my* country . . . all of you.

After months of observing, with a kind of detached admiration, the
inspection technique of the high brass, am surprised to find that it is
not at all difficult.

It is five o'clock and the *directrice* is telephoning the Croix Rouge.
*"Oui, Madame la Maréchale vient de terminer la séance — à peine
une minute*. She is leaving to pack her trunks, since she is sailing at
dawn for Morocco. Will she come to the telephone? I will find out.
Ne quittez pas."

I grab the phone. *"Qui?"* A young vibrant voice with rising inflec-
tion. "Madame la Maréchale, General Patton asks whether you will do
him the honor of dining with him this evening."

"General Patton? Why, yes, certainly. With pleasure. Where? At
what time?"

"I will come for you anywhere you say, in an hour."

"C'est entendu."

Armed with the address, I returned to our house to report to the
General, alert the mess sergeant, and dry myself out.

Dinner was a great success. For hours she regaled us with souvenirs
of her husband, of Rabat, of Pringe Aage, of the Foreign Legion, of the
Glaoui, and of her nephew Pierre. The General was crazy about her.
I told her of our tea with le Maréchal and about our stay in Fez during
the Riffian uprising.

"Ah, yes," she said, "a delicate moment. At night the dissident tribes
would venture to the very walls of Fez. But the Marshal was fore-
handed, and then too he had brilliant subordinates in that region. At
Fez itself, le général de Chambrun and le capitaine de Lattre de

Tassigny; le colonel Giraud and le capitaine Juin at Taza; and in the middle Atlas, le commandant Guillaume."

"I am proud that they are all my friends," the General said.

"And I," la Maréchale said, "am proud to seize this opportunity of thanking you personally, General Patton, for freeing not only la Lorraine, so dear to my husband and me, but also for liberating our beloved *seconde patrie,* le Maroc."

Tears of emotion were shining in her eyes. Then she smiled broadly.

"I wish, however, that in liberating Morocco you had waited one more day."

"Why?" The General was surprised.

We were in the sitting room now, with chairs drawn up before the fire. Madame la Maréchale took a sip of her liqueur and placed the glass on the table.

"Well, you see, it was this way," she said. "Late in October, 1942, there were rumors that something was afoot. I planned to regain Rabat by way of Oran and engaged passage the first week in November on the *paquebot Ville d'Alger* sailing from Marseilles. In the middle of the night of November seventh, or rather the early morning of the eighth, I was sleeping peacefully in my stateroom when suddenly a series of explosions almost lifted me out of my bunk and I awoke to see what I took to be fireworks streaming past the porthole."

"What did you do?" the General asked.

"I rang for the *femme de chambre* and told her to go up and find out what it was all about. She returned a few minutes later and said, '*Figurez-vous, madame, nous sommes en pleine guerre navale.*'

"Not wishing to be sunk or, worse still, taken prisoner *en chemise de nuit,* I arose, dressed, and mounted to the bridge, where I found the captain had turned the ship about — we were in the entrance of the harbor of Oran — and was putting back to Marseilles. I argued with him for a full hour, insisting that he should continue into Oran, but to no avail. It is one of the few arguments I have ever lost, and with it the pleasure of being in Morocco for your arrival."

"The loss was all mine," the General said.

"You are most gallant," she said rising, "and now I must leave you.

I am sure you have had an active day, and I do not wish to interfere with your repose. Furthermore, I have some letters to write before packing my trunks."

"What time are you leaving Nancy?" the General asked.

"General Catroux is calling at five o'clock in the morning to drive me to Marseilles, where the cruiser which is to take me to Casablanca is waiting."

"I am afraid you will not get very much sleep," the General said.

"Ça n'a pas d'importance," Madame Lyautey said, holding out her hand. "As my husband used to say, after eighty, sleep becomes superfluous."

Among the various visitors we have had, I may have forgotten to mention Governor Lehman, who turned up early this month. The General enjoyed both him and his visit. As he wanted to see the mud and the floods, I took him up to the 4th Armored.

General Wood, you will be interested to hear, is going home on leave, to be replaced by General Gaffey. The latter, as you know, is primarily a combat Commander, and a damn good one. He is delighted to get out into the field again, and furthermore, it will further his chances of getting a corps and promotion. Thus General Gay once more becomes Chief of Staff of Third Army, and thus is General Patton's diplomacy in the face of SHAEF's exigency while we were still in England fully vindicated.

This is a mean campaign. The meanest so far. The way the boys in the front lines are taking the almost intolerable conditions is beyond praise. I need not tell *you* what a joy it has been, and continues to be, to work with the French, and I suppose that *au fond* it is my French Army background which got me this enviable job, but the fact remains that my strongest reaction to World War II is one of cumulative and unbounded admiration for the American effort, its spirit and its execution, its G.I.'s and its officers of all branches. In Africa, Sicily, Italy, England, France, on airstrips, in ordnance depots, hospitals, supply dumps — not to speak of the front lines — you will find groups of Yanks who are not immediately defending their farms and families, who hate war and brutality and filth, but who are doing a job because they feel it is necessary.

Well, that's my thought for today.

P.S. Our long stay in Nancy is coming to an end as we are soon to move to Saint-Avold, a gloomy bilingual town close to the German border. Ran up there a while ago with George Murnane in search of possible quarters for the General. It is going to be a toughie. One of the several depressing features of Saint-Avold is the large number of time bombs left by the departing Germans. Concealed in walls or cellar, each can, and does, completely demolish a house, and each has a delayed fuse good for twenty-one days. The day before our visit, a passable villa which the local authorities had earmarked for the General had gone up with a bang, and as we came to the residential district, which is on a hillside, a blowzy chalet of the gingerbread school of architecture spurted sudden flames and smoke, then with a roar slid into the valley.

"Well," George said, "at least there is another house we won't have to bother to look at."

P.P.S. Yesterday was the culmination of a series of daily whirlwind trips with the General to the decidedly unattractive cities and towns of the Saar. Ugly and grimy in themselves, the fact that in many of them street fighting still continues and that most of the bridges are under fire in no way enhances their beauty. Will be glad when we get the hell out of this neck of the woods.

In the afternoon, visited the 90th Division and the domicile of Herr von Papen. While the General was decorating an engineer in the garden of same, the Germans laid down a noisy but fortunately harmless barrage. The General enjoyed it.

Your letter about the Rector* arrived only a few minutes after I had mailed my letter to you of yesterday. It seems impossible that the Rector should be dead. If one tried to catch his basic quality in a single word, that word, I think, would be aliveness. Aliveness, and a spontaneous single-minded directness of thought and action. Possibly this is an oversimplification, but I am sure there is a common denominator

---

* The Reverend Endicott Peabody, Head Master, Groton School.

which explains the marked similarity of two men of utterly contrasting views, objectives, and vocabulary. It was Bunny, back in Sicily, who first brought it out in the open. The General, in swift and hot indignation over some delinquency, as he believed, on the part of an officer, had been particularly forceful in expressing his displeasure. After the officer's departure in stunned silence — you don't talk back to the General — someone, it must have been General Gay, pointed out that said officer had merely been carrying out a previous conflicting directive which the General had forgotten to rescind. For several minutes the General, standing with slightly bent head, studied the pattern on the rug. Then he straightened up and drew in a deep breath. "Stiller," he said, "go down to that Italian Cavalry depot and get a horse — two horses — you and I are going riding up in the hills. I've been cooped up too long in this goddam office." Sitting down at his desk, he looked up at General Gay. "Hap, have that officer back here at five o'clock. Also, everyone who was present when I bawled him out. I'm going to apologize."

I don't remember all the particulars. It is probably not a very good example of what I am trying to illustrate, but when that evening Bunny said, "Aren't there moments when the General reminds you of the Rector?" the answer was an unequivocal yes. There have been many such moments since. And as long as there exist but two Groties to sit around and talk about the Rector, or two members of any of General Patton's commands to sit around and talk about him, each of these gifted and vital men who have so profoundly affected the lives of so many will remain very, very much alive.

And now I have some melancholy news. Bunny is leaving. Our friend Wild Bill Donovan has made another formal request for him and this time the General is going to regretfully acquiesce. As a matter of fact, everyone concerned has done the right thing. It is an important job — in charge of Bill's Paris headquarters — and no one could do it better, or as well, as Bunny. However, you can imagine how he will be missed here. We have done quite a *bout de chemin* together. However, it's a small world, smaller and smaller, so perhaps our paths will continue to crisscross. I hope so.

CHAPTER XII

Battle of the Bulge

(December, 1944–January, 1945)

In mid-December 1944, just before von Rundstedt's great attack through the Ardennes which produced the so-called Battle of the Bulge, the Allied Forces were lined up, from north to south, as follows: Montgomery's Twenty-first Army Group was on the west bank of the Meuse; Simpson's Ninth Army on the Roer, a few miles across the German border; Hodges's First Army, having captured Aachen and traversed the Hürtgen Forest, extended south to a point east of the city of Luxembourg; Third Army was preparing its own attack on Germany from the Saar. (Ninth, First, and Third U. S. Armies constituted Bradley's Twelfth Army Group.) Devers's Sixth Army Group, consisting of Patch's Seventh Army and de Lattre's First French Army, was on the Rhine from Strasbourg to the Vosges. The brunt of the initial German attack was sustained by First Army's VIII Corps, General Middleton commanding.

The Third Army was engaged in the bitter and disappointing attack against the Siegfried Line and across the Sauer River. On the morning of 16 December, the Army Commander, accompanied by his G-2, his Chief of Staff, and Deputy Chief of Staff, as was customary, attended a special secret briefing at 6:30 A.M. At this briefing, the then Captain Helfers of the G-2 Section told the Army Commander that they had listened to German radio messages in code, which code they could break, and that the concentration of troops near Trier was breaking up and on the move. Colonel Koch, the G-2, stated he thought this was an attack. General Patton immediately said, "We'll have to help the First Army out because they will get it right on the nose," and started his staff making plans for pulling the Third Army out of its eastward attack (across the Sauer), changing directions ninety degrees, moving to Luxembourg, and attacking north. Thus, when he was asked by General Eisenhower three days later when he could make an attack, he told him "on the twenty-second of December." General Eisenhower said, "Don't be fatuous." General Patton said, "Never mind dates." He knew then he would make the attack on the morning of the twenty-first of December.

December 18, 1944. Day before yesterday the General visited both General Eddy and General Haislip. After dinner that evening, General Allen telephoned from Army Group to say they wanted to remove one of our Armored divisions to reinforce VIII Corps, which was attempting to ward off a German attack. The General called General Bradley to protest, but the latter said he could not discuss the matter over the phone.

"I guess they are having trouble up there," the General said. "I thought they would."

At yesterday morning's briefing, it was apparent that the Germans were not only continuing their attack on VIII Corps but moving in additional units in front of our XX Corps.

"One of these is a feint; one is the real thing," the General said. "If they attack us, I'm ready for them, but I'm inclined to think the party will be up north. Eighth Corps has been sitting still — a sure invitation to trouble."

Today has been quite a day and we are now back at Rue Auxerre after a wild night ride from Luxembourg, where the General, together with Maddox, Koch, and Muller, attended a conference called by General Bradley. As usual the General was right. The attack on VIII Corps is no feint.

It is now almost midnight. General Bradley telephoned to direct the General to come to Verdun tomorrow morning, the nineteenth, at 11 A.M. to meet General Eisenhower and the high brass. Something is cooking all right. The General is now summoning the whole Third Army Staff, together with General Weyland's staff, to a meeting in the G-3 office set for 8 A.M. tomorrow.

Christmas, 1944. A Christmas no one around here is likely to forget. The General and General Bradley and some very tired members of their staffs are still celebrating it downstairs in the dining room of our present living quarters, the Hotel Alpha in Luxembourg. Sandwiches, coffee, and a small Christmas tree. Not exactly festive. But everything considered, we are lucky to be here. How long we remain is anyone's guess. Am now in my room, in bed, writing this letter. My last letter, I think, was that of December 18. So much has happened since then, I hardly know where to begin.

In the last week the General has been making History, with a capital. At the special 8 A.M. staff session at Nancy on the nineteenth, the General, in one hour, evolved three possible plans for meeting the critical situation in the Ardennes — assigning code names to each. A few minutes after nine, he and Paul Harkins and I took off by peep for Verdun. Arriving there shortly before eleven, we found assembled at Group Headquarters, General Eisenhower, Air Marshal Tedder, Generals Bradley, Devers, Strong, and assorted SHAEF and Group staff officers. I have seldom seen longer faces. General Strong got up before a situation map and gave a short exposé of the picture. It was grim. When he sat down, General Eisenhower spoke.

"George," he said to General Patton, "I want you to go to Luxembourg and take charge."

"Yes, sir."

"When can you start up there?"

"Now."

"You mean today?"

"I mean as soon as you have finished with me here."

There was a pause.

"When will you be able to attack?" General Eisenhower said.

"The morning of December twenty-second," the General said, "with three divisions."

Less than seventy hours. There was a stir, a shuffling of feet, as those present straightened up in their chairs. In some faces, skepticism. But through the room the current of excitement leaped like a flame. To disengage three divisions actually in combat and launch them over more than a hundred miles of icy roads straight into the heart of a major attack of unprecedented violence presented problems which few Commanders would have undertaken to resolve in that length of time.

And now specific questions were asked. To all of them, the General had specific answers. Within an hour everything had been thrashed out — the divisions to be employed, objectives, new Army boundaries, the amount of our own front in the Saar to be taken over by Sixth Army Group, and other matters — and virtually all of them settled on General Patton's terms.

As the meeting broke up, the General turned to Harkins. "Telephone Gay," he said. "Give him the code number, tell him to get started. Then get back to Nancy yourself as soon as you can. You know what to do."

"Yes, sir."

"Codman, you come with me. Tell Mims we start in five minutes — for Luxembourg."

"Telephone General Walker," he added, "and tell him I will stop and see him in Thionville on the way."

As General Eisenhower was leaving he stopped and pointed to the five stars on his shoulder strap. "Funny thing, George," he said, "every time I get promoted I get attacked."

"Yes," the General said genially, "and every time you get attacked I bail you out."

During the long fast drive, the General was silent. It was late afternoon when we clattered into the main square of Thionville, where General Walker was waiting in his peep to guide us to his headquarters. There the General filled him in on the picture to date and gave him his instructions for the immediate future. It was already dark when the General spoke of pushing on to Luxembourg. General Walker dissuaded him. The road is bad at night. Furthermore, Prince Felix was momentarily expected in Thionville and would have news as to conditions in the city of Luxembourg.

"All right," the General said. "If you will lend me pajamas and a toothbrush I will spend the night and make an early start in the morning."

"Codman," he added, "you had better go back to Nancy and get the household moving. Tell Meeks to pack all my things. You and Stiller and he bring my trailer up to Luxembourg as soon as possible."

In a peep furnished by General Walker I set out for Nancy. For the first ten miles or so we made good time. The next twenty, occupied in dodging the hurtling columns of the 4th Armored speeding north, were hectic in the extreme. Occasionally my driver, to avoid being overrun, would in desperation momentarily flash on his headlights, an unpopular move, greeted each time by bellows and curses from the exasperated tankers, and once by a short but happily inaccurate burst of machine-gun fire. I did not learn until the following day that the Germans had been reported to have infiltrated our rear areas with agents dressed in U.S. uniforms and equipped with captured small arms and peeps.

Next day, December 20, was spent packing and loading, and the following morning, December 21, Al and Sergeant Meeks and I rolled out through the grilled gateway of 10 Rue Auxerre, Nancy, for the last time.

The road was jammed worse than ever with our own vehicles hurrying north, and evening had fallen when we lumbered over the broad bridge into Luxembourg. The quaint little city's appearance was transformed. Gone were the American flags, the welcoming banners, the "English Spoken" signs in the shop windows. Groups of silent, anxious Luxembourgeois thronged the street corners and sidewalks; listening to the enemy artillery only six or seven miles distant and making mental count of our tanks and trucks rumbling through their smooth paved streets, the burning question in their harassed eyes was plain. Too little and too late? Their fears were not unreasonable. All had experienced the German occupation; most had suffered the wrench of separation from loved ones deported to slave labor. Some at this very street crossing may well be thinking of the triumphal German entry and the stain there on the paving stones — a spreading stain, a single shoe lying in the reddened gutter — all that remained of the little old lady wantonly pushed from the sidewalk by a drunken storm trooper directly into the path of the oncoming column of German tanks.

At the Hotel Alpha, where we are sharing billets with members of the Group Staff, there is noticeable tenseness. Papers collected, ready to be destroyed. Personal effects packed. Vehicles gassed up and ready to go. And, boy, are they glad to see us — or at least our units. For once a Third Army shoulder patch appears to be a sight for the sore eyes of higher headquarters.

The General himself is the best of tonics. His mere presence has already begun to dissipate the prevailing miasma of dismay. For the last forty-eight hours he and Sergeant Mims, without benefit of staff, baggage, or even a toothbrush, have been charging up and down the fluid lines visiting corps and division commanders, pushing, pulling, relocating, cannibalizing, galvanizing.* He greeted Al and me with a

---

* At this point, General Patton's command consisted of the following:

    VIII Corps — General Middleton
            101st Airborne Division
            28th Infantry Division (greatly reduced)
            9th Armored Division
            Some French Infantry battalions
    III Corps — General Milliken
            26th Infantry Division
            80th Infantry Division
            4th Armored Division
    XII Corps — General Eddy
            4th Infantry Division
            5th Infantry Division
            10th Armored Division (Combat Command A)
            2d Cavalry Group
    XX Corps — General Walker
            90th Infantry Division
            95th Infantry Division
            6th Armored Division
            35th Infantry Division (to be attached to either XII or VIII Corps)

broad grin. "Mims claims the government is wasting a lot of money hiring staff officers," the General remarked. " 'You and me, General,' he says, 'have been running Third Army all by ourselves for the last two days and doing a better job than they do.' "

Half an hour later at supper, General Bradley was himself commenting on Third Army's spectacular move. "All the credit," the General said, and it was characteristic, "*all* of it, one hundred per cent, goes to Third Army Staff, and in particular to Hap Gay, Maud Muller, Nixon, and Busch."

After supper on his way to his room the General said, "Be ready for an early start tomorrow. We attack with Third Corps at six."

December 22. The attack is on.*

We drove to General Middleton's headquarters at Arlon (Belgium) and a short distance up the road to Bastogne, in which the 101st Airborne is cut off but holding. This key town is now surrounded by five German divisions.

The weather has been no good for flying and the results of this first day are somewhat uncertain. The city of Luxembourg is not yet out of danger.

On the twenty-third the weather improved and our Air did a magnificent job on the enemy. So did the Artillery. Our advances, however, were slight. On the twenty-fourth the Germans counterattacked all along the line. These attacks were contained and we were able to air-drop supplies to the 101st at Bastogne.

Partly for purposes of boosting civilian morale the General attended Christmas Eve services at the Protestant Church in the center of the city, occupying the pew formerly reserved for the Kaiser on his official visits to Luxembourg. The church was packed, hence not quite as cold as it might have been, but frigid nevertheless.

Christmas morning. Cold as hell. Up most of the night with what I hope is not dysentery again, but merely a bad piece of salmon. Al and I accompanied the General on his Christmas calls to Generals

---

* Contact followed by probing attacks was made on the afternoon of December 21, 1944. The main attack by three divisions was made at 0530 on the twenty-second.

Paul of the 26th, McBride of the 80th, Irwin of the 5th, and, of course, General Gaffey and both combat commands of the 4th Armored. Am glad to say they all had easily accessible latrines. While at Combat Command A with General Earnest a couple of German planes strafed the road where we were standing. They must have been very poor shots, as we were not a bad target, yet no one was hit.

Well, that's about all for the moment except to say that (1) there will probably not be much time for letter writing in the foreseeable future, and (2) if anyone at home is inclined to take this attack lightly, you can refer him or her to anyone spending the Christmas holidays in Luxembourg.

January 18, 1945. By now you probably have a fairly clear picture of what is happening, and realize — though many of the home folks apparently do not — what a close call it has been! Over twenty German divisions — two *Panzer* armies — attacked on a forty- to fifty-mile front from Monchau to Echternach. The primary objectives were Liège and Namur. They damn near made them. If they had, we could have kissed good-by to Antwerp and Brussels, and hello to a couple more years of war. It was much too close for comfort. At one point, having chased First Army Headquarters out of Spa — the old Hindenburg headquarters of World War I — the Germans were practically on the Meuse. This is no criticism of First Army. If the Ardennes attack failed, it was due primarily to three factors: (1) the dogged, unbelievable, courageous resistance of those hopelessly outnumbered First Army units in the direct path of the German drive — their heroism gained the necessary, the essential time; (2) the lightning move and subsequent attacks of Third Army on the southern flank of the Bulge; (3) the five-day weather-break, beginning just before Christmas, which enabled our Air, and particularly Opie Weyland's XIX TAC, to go to town on the German units, supply columns, and rear areas in a manner which outdid even their own superb performance of the recent past. In the absence or dilution of any one of these three factors all of us here — if not in remoter and higher places — believe the Allied Armies in Europe would have taken a bad, bad licking. As it is, the casualties and the suffering, not only from the continuous action but from the bitter cold, have been cruel.

The General is indefatigable and I don't think he has missed a day in getting out to see the divisions. The entire countryside is white with hard-packed snow and the cold is terrific. The day after Christmas General Gaffey told the General he thought that Colonel Blanchard's combat command (4th Armored) could break through to Bastogne if authorized then and there to move, and move fast.

"Go to it," the General said. As you know, they did.

The Germans are still counterattacking and the party is by no means over, but they do seem to be slowing up. Al and I drove with the General to Bastogne on December 30. The corridor is still uncomfortably narrow. He got an enthusiastic reception and also very real pleasure out of pinning the D.S.C. on General Tony "Nuts" McAuliffe and Lieutenant Colonel Chappuis.* Incidentally, the General himself received a second oak-leaf cluster for his D.S.M. a day or two before.

New Year's Day. The cold and the counterattacks continue unabated. We are making headway, but the going, like the terrain, is tough.

The last two weeks have been an unremitting grind for all the units, which, in spite of repeated German counterattacks and the stubbornest kind of resistance, have advanced steadily. Yesterday (January 17, 1945), accompanied the General and General Hughes, who is visiting us, to Arlon, where General Patton formally congratulated General Middleton and General Milliken on the successful join-up with First Army, finally accomplished by the capture of Houffalize. First Army, which at the beginning of the Ardennes attack was put under Monty's command, now reverts to General Bradley and the Twelfth Army Group.

From Arlon we then went to 6th Armored, the 26th and the 90th Divisions. The General decorated General Van Fleet, who was damn

---

* Lieutenant Colonel S. A. Chappuis, Commanding Officer, 502d Airborne Infantry.

near killed by mortar fire during the attack. By near I mean that the two men standing on either side of him *were* killed.

For the moment, the pressure on the General, and therefore on all the rest of us, is a little less than it has been. In other words, a normal workday, instead of starting at around 6 A.M. and going late into the night, now occasionally allows for a relatively quiet evening. To afford the General a bit of relaxation, it seemed like a good idea, at the time, to show a movie after supper. Special Services came up with *Laura* starring Clifton Webb. To establish the orchidaceous character of *Laura's* interior-decorator "hero," there is a scene early in the picture in which Clifton is revealed in a bubble bath massaging himself with a long-handled rubber brush, while a valet hands him successive jars of bath salts, unguents, and assorted toiletries. The fact that the General had spent a good part of the day up near Bastogne arranging for the relief of frost-bite cases may have been a contributing factor; anyway, as Clifton stepped out of the bubbles into the valet-held folds of an enormous heated bath towel, the General's voice reverberated in the darkness.

"What wouldn't I give to have that so-and-so up here for just twenty-four hours as a replacement," he said.

Since then we have had no movies.

If you run into Clifton do tell him that the impact of his performance on Third Army was terrific, and in all our minds he will forever be indelibly associated with the Battle of the Bulge.

The acquiring of the house which the General mentioned in his letter to you came about as follows: When we first arrived in Luxembourg, Prince Felix very kindly offered the General *his* house. Too big, too far away from our headquarters — a large institutional building on the edge of town — and no time to think about it anyway. As things stabilized, and it seemed more likely that we would really stay in Luxembourg for a while, the General suggested that I look around for something other than his noisy hotel room opposite the railroad station.

There was a grapevine rumor that Prince Felix himself had an eye on an attractive house overlooking the valley not far from our head-quarters. It belonged to a Madame Brasseur, an elderly lady who also owns the Hotel Brasseur, the Number One hostelry in the center of town, which, incidentally, we had requisitioned in its entirety to billet the staff. In the early afternoon of the day the matter came up, I rang Madame Brasseur's doorbell. A nice old *servante* ushered me into the drawing room, where Madame Brasseur and her daughter were having their after-lunch coffee. Both were charming. Madame faintly reminiscent of Eugénie Leontovich as a *mère noble,* Mademoiselle suggesting, to coin a paradox, a contained, rather shy Judith Anderson.

The house itself is lovely and ideal for the purpose. Not too large, easy to protect, assured privacy. Contents and furnishings perfect, including the kind of glazed wallpaper you and I have been dreaming about all our married life.

"Would you, madame, consider making a beautiful gesture on behalf of the American Army?"

"Why, yes, certainly. We are deeply indebted to you. Furthermore, I like Americans. We in Luxembourg used to dance with the Americans during the last war. Now, alas, I am too old to dance, but I am glad you are occupying my hotel. When would General Patton like to move in here? In the spring when we move to the country? In May? Perhaps even in April if he is in a great hurry?"

"Well, to tell you the truth," I said, "the date we have in mind is tomorrow."

Silence, broken at last by Mademoiselle.

"Impossible," she said.

Madame Brasseur carefully put down her coffee cup. She was pale but perfectly composed.

"Nothing is impossible," she said. "My house will be at General Patton's disposal tomorrow."

By this time I had made up my mind to go back and report that the house was plague-struck, or haunted, or in any event completely uninhabitable.

"Your generous offer will be deeply appreciated," I said. "I shall be back in an hour. Please don't do anything until I return."

Quiet talk with General Gay. He got the picture at once and within thirty seconds came up with the perfect solution. I hurried back to the Brasseur house. Madame and her daughter had lost no time. In the front hall two ancient trunks already packed and strapped. Upstairs you could hear the old *servante* moving from room to room. In the drawing room, Madame Brasseur and her daughter sat waiting, Mademoiselle turning the pages of the book she was not reading, Madame gazing through the window across the valley. Outside on the small grass terrace the gardener was nailing down the covers of two packing cases. The sound of his hammer had the finality of the ax blows in *The Cherry Orchard*.

"Madame Brasseur," I said, "the General would like to extend an invitation to you and Mademoiselle."

"Yes?" Madame Brasseur looked up with a half smile.

"That you should be the guests of himself and Third Army at the Hotel Brasseur. The Royal Suite has been readied and I have a car outside, as well as a truck to take care of your personal effects."

Their faces lit up. "I hope you will accept," I went on. "If you do, it will give great pleasure not only to the General but to all the members of the staff who are living there."

"We accept with pleasure," she said.

Within a quarter of an hour their goods and chattels were on their way across town in an Army truck, and I was handing Madame and Mademoiselle into the General's limousine.

"Ah, I forgot," Madame exclaimed. "Do you mind if I go back a moment?"

In the hall she extricated from the closet a small green watering pot, filled it in the adjoining *cabinet de toilette,* and proceeding from room to room, carefully watered each plant. Back in the car. "Can someone care for them while we are away?" she asked anxiously.

"Have no fear," I said. "It shall be done. I will personally see to it. O.K., Mims. Go ahead."

An exclamation from Mademoiselle Brasseur. "What about the rabbits?" she said. *"En effet; va vite,"* her mother said.

The same hall closet. This time a paper bag of meal and a bunch of carrots. We went into the garden, where she raised the covers of two rabbit hutches. "The little one is still growing and must have more than the big one," she said.

"Have no fear. I will see to it personally."

As we came out again to the car, three or four of our trucks swirled into the driveway. M.P. guards, telephone linesmen, engineers with wire detectors, and expert searchers from Security. Since our experience at Saint-Avold and the present threat of Sturmbannfuehrer Skorzeny's infiltrations, whose alleged mission was to "get" Generals Eisenhower, Bradley, Patton, Hodges, et al., the technique of search and delousing had supposedly been stepped up to a fine art.

"Who are they?" Madame Brasseur said.

I had hoped this wouldn't come up, but the rabbits had dislocated what otherwise would have been perfect timing.

"They must be First Army trucks who have lost their way," I said rather lamely. "O.K., Mims. Go ahead."

In the lobby of the Hotel Brasseur, Paul Harkins had assembled an M.P. guard of honor and a reception committee who escorted our guests to their suite in a manner usually reserved for only the V.V.V.I.P.'s.

That evening the General himself called at the hotel to pay his respects. Madame and Mademoiselle, at the largest of the dining-room tables, completely surrounded by admiring members of the staff, were having the time of their lives.

"If only the orchestra were still here," she said, "we could once again dance with the Americans."

"Have no fear, madame," the General said. "I will see to that personally."

We are all delighted with the house. The General and Willie have Madame Brasseur's room on the second floor overlooking the gorge, and General Gay, the daughter's room in front. The rest of us, Al, George, Charley Odom, and Ed Creed, are on the floor above. Judging from her boudoir-library, which I am occupying, Mademoiselle Brasseur would seem to be a rather independent bachelor girl with a commendable taste in literature, since her shelves are filled almost exclusively with Cocteau, Rémy de Gourmont, Colette, Giraudoux, Proust, and, *en plus,* the plays of Shakespeare in French. Thus when it is too noisy for sleep, which it has been at times, as the Germans have our range with a pair of annoyingly accurate long-distance railway guns, I have been occupying myself trying to imagine the reaction of a French audience to Hamlet's needling of his father's ghost in terms of *"Holà, vieille taupe, pourquoi avance-tu si rapidement sous-sol?"* The elder Pitoeff, you remember, did a passable job with *"Être ou ne pas être, voilà le problème,"* which after all does convey the words if not the music, but I can't help feeling that to successfully convey the bitter essence of "Wormwood, wormwood," by simply murmuring, *"Absinthe, absinthe"* — that's what it says in the French text — would tax the virtuosity even of a Gallic Jack Barrymore liberally fortified with double Pernods.

Thank God, and you, for those wonderful long drawers just arrived. They will be life-savers. Compared to the back seat of a back-seat peep rider in the Ardennes, a polar bear's arse is an oven.

Went into Al's room just now to see if he would like a pair. Al was asleep; and since the Skorzeny scare, he sleeps with his fingers on the special light-action trigger of his 45. I had put on your knitted wool helmet, also just arrived, and for which many thanks — though in passing I might mention that in appearance it is far from *réglementaire,* has in fact something of a Teutonic flavor about it, and damn near got me shot.

CHAPTER XIII

Interlude

(*January–February, 1945*)

January 22, 1945. Last Thursday, General Hughes, who has been staying with us, was supposed to fly back to Paris, but the weather closed in. "Codman," the General said, "take General Hughes to Paris in the limousine."

General Hughes's dry, dead-pan sense of humor makes him excellent company. Moreover, he knows his way around. We had been driving several hours when he looked at his watch. "Any prisoner of war camps around these parts?" he asked.

"Yes, there's a big one about five miles from here."

"Let's stop and inspect it," he said. "I ought to turn in a report on something. Anyway," he added, "it's lunchtime, and it has been my experience that if you are looking for a good meal, the best bet the Army has to offer is a P.O.W. camp. That is all they do, eat, and eat well."

Our entrance into the P.O.W. camp, starred pennants flying in the breeze, caused something of a flurry, and in no time at all the Commandant himself came hurrying out, a plump lieutenant colonel, full of zeal and ingratiation.

"I don't want to put you to any unnecessary trouble, Colonel," General Hughes said, "but the Supreme Commander has asked me to make a report on the P.O.W. camps in this area and I want to be able to tell him I have seen your setup, which I understand is a good one."

"No trouble at all, sir," the Commandant beamed. "Before you make your inspection, sir, won't you join us in the mess hall for lunch?"

"Lunch?" General Hughes's eyebrows rose. "I don't usually bother with lunch. However, I do not want to interfere with your schedule. We'll sit down with you for a moment."

Lunch was excellent and copious. General Hughes took two helpings of everything.

"Fine table you serve here," he said, drawing out a notebook in which he made some rapid jottings. "My compliments."

"We do our best, sir." The Commandant felt things were going nicely.

"And the P.O.W.'s — " General Hughes's eye momentarily lit on the generously upholstered figure of our German prisoner-waiter — "do they get enough to eat?"

"Yes, sir," the Commandant said, still aiming to please. "Their fare is exactly the same as ours right here."

"I see," General Hughes said, making some more notations. "No differentiation at all?"

"No, sir," the Commandant said.

"Well, let's take a look around. That is, if I can manage to get up after this princely repast. We might start with the pantry, kitchen, and storerooms."

With the air of Oscar of the Waldorf, the Commandant led the way through the spacious pantry and kitchen, while General Hughes took note of the rows of prime cuts, piles of fresh vegetables, heaps of golden butter, and countless tins of Army rations, presided over by seemingly autonomous groups of sleek round Germans whose faces shone with well-being and excess calories.

"And now the storerooms," the Commandant said.

"I think I've seen enough," General Hughes said. "Let's adjourn to your office, Colonel."

In the Commandant's office the Colonel drew forward a couple of armchairs, seated himself at his desk, and reached for a box of cigars which he offered around.

"Thanks, I roll my own," General Hughes said, pulling out his pack of cigarettes. Lighting one, he expelled a couple of neat rings, and watched them rise towards the ceiling.

"Colonel," he said after a while, "do you happen to have handy a copy of the rules of the Geneva Convention governing the feeding of prisoners of war?"

For the first time a look of concern flickered across the Colonel's bland countenance. I began to feel almost sorry for him.

"Why, yes, sir, I believe so."

"Will you get it out, please?"

"Yes, sir." As the Colonel fumbled with his desk drawer, you could see concern giving way to acute apprehension.

"Now, Colonel, oblige me by turning to Section Eight, Paragraph Six A, and reading aloud the following eleven paragraphs."

With the reading of the second or third paragraph the natural pink of the Colonel's cheeks began to fade, and with the fourth a sickly green infusion indicated the dawn of full realization. The Colonel had been had. The precise, albeit generous, specifications laid down for the feeding of prisoners would have approximated perhaps a quarter, or at most a third, of their present gargantuan menus.

At reading's end there was silence. Then General Hughes cleared his throat.

"What time is the evening meal at this camp?" he asked.

"Six o'clock, sir," the Colonel said.

"Very well," General Hughes said. "Applicable as of six o'clock this evening, you will see that the eleven paragraphs you have just been reading are put into effect — to the letter. Beginning tomorrow you will forward me daily until further notice a written itemized report in triplicate, setting forth the exact protein, carbohydrate, fat, and caloric content of each and every meal served at this camp."

General Hughes flicked a speck of cigarette ash from his trouser leg and got up.

"Good-by, Colonel," he said, "and thanks for an excellent lunch. I enjoyed it."

Paris. Late afternoon. It developed that General Hughes had a date with General Bedell Smith for dinner. I called up Bunny, who, as luck would have it, was free. After a bath I went over to his office, which is located — where do you suppose? — in the Élysée Bellevue, next to the Berkeley Hotel. At the turn of the century, when my family used to stay there, it was the Hotel Meyerbeer, named after the composer of *Robert le Diable,* and its sidewalk café on the Rond Point embodies my first memory of Paris. I can still remember — at least I can still *say* I remember — sitting there with Pa under the *marronniers* in the cool of the evening, my chin barely above the round marble top of the table, sipping a *grenadine à l'eau.* Of far greater interest to my tender imagination than the neighboring Worth and Poiret models were the panting barefoot cab-runners, padding along behind the tourist's fiacre, from the station clear across the city, on the chance, for a few of those large copper sous, of unloading one's baggage, and to me, if not to my father, the brazen chant of the visor-capped news hawkers — *la Patrie, la Patrie* — struck a more arresting note than the big black headlines announcing an event remote and meaningless — *l'assassinat du président McKinley.*

It may seem strange that here in Paris, more than forty years later, getting a meal at a restaurant presents a major problem. For the American in uniform, who is not supposed to deplete French food stocks and for whom Paris restaurants are therefore off limits, there are several alternatives: any U. S. Army mess, of which there are many; any of the expensive black-market hideaways in the center; a few of the higher-class bordels; and the Ritz, in war as in peace a law unto itself. Somehow none of these fitted our mood of the moment.

"I know a place," Bunny said, "that is, if I can find it again."

"Let's try."

Montmartre, up over the butte, down the other side. Simenon country. After a while the streets got so narrow and the impasses so impassable, we left the car and proceeded on foot.

"I think it's around the next corner," Bunny said. Sure enough, jutting at a weird angle from a tightly shuttered building of forbidding aspect, a battered, dimly illuminated sign — Hotel Superbe. Once inside, it was obvious that all was well. Bright check tablecloths, sawdust on the floor, the aroma of good bourgeois cooking, the hum of well-fed conversation. The *patron,* right out of that Arletty underworld play we saw with Sylvia Thompson. A high-voltage *ser-*

vante, Maria, whom *ces messieurs du milieu* seemed to think highly of, and to be getting nowhere with. A superlative meal. *Soupe aux légumes,* the real thing, served from a tureen compared to which the Durgin-Park china is transparent Sèvres. *Poulet rôti, pommes frites,* again the real thing. A perfect Roblechon and tumblers full of a very passable Algerian red which no one had bothered to label Pommard. *Café. Fine maison.* "Could you ask for anything more?"

Well, we went over practically everything from our first-form year to Luxembourg and decided that if we got through this war we would be content to sit out the next one.

It was past midnight as we slipped down through the Place Pigalle, the cat's-cradle of dark silent streets behind the Opéra, across the Concorde, and up the Champs Élysées. A stop at the Travelers' Club for a nightcap. Empty. No, something stirring in that armchair over in the corner. A cheery hello as the familiar figure scrambles to his feet. Le général de Chambrun still greeting the Americans.

And so to bed, pondering on the irony of being in this city of memories, doing familiar things, in familiar places, with people both familiar and strange, every one of whom ought to be you.

Have you ever seen Paris in a real New England snowstorm? Neither had I until yesterday. Neither, I expect, had any of the Parisians with whom I braved the drifts. In the morning the few desultory flakes spiraling past the hotel window gave little indication of things to come, but the cold grays of the Rue François I suggested per contra the desirability of things sunny, warm, and meridional, which in turn put me in mind of Madame Tron and her telephone number. A good idea, as it turned out.

"Have you heard the news?" she said.

"What news?"

"Coursier is being married — today!"

"No!"

"Yes!"

Coursier, you may remember, was quite a friend of mine at Rabat, where he was very much the social bachelor *mondain.*

"Where and when is the wedding?"

"Les Invalides. Midi tapant."

"I will call for you at eleven-thirty."

By eleven the snow was really coming down. By eleven-thirty even the Mount Washington weather station would have taken notice. Across the great courtyard of the Invalides, ladies in high-heeled shoes and silk stockings, leading children in low-heeled shoes and no stockings, minced their way through three-foot drifts to the chapel, in whose open colonnade stood the bridal party, Coursier, *la mariée,* her parents, and half a dozen little flower girls in summer hats and tulle frocks. When Coursier caught sight of me he almost had a *syncope.*

"You have come," he kept saying. "You have come."

To the consternation of a couple of beadles who were giving him the high sign to advance into the church, Coursier sprang down the steps, dragged me up to his intended and the bridal group, and introduced me — not as an old friend, or an American, or a comrade-in-arms, nothing like that. *"Je vous présente,"* he announced in a loud voice, *"un vieux africain."* It is getting to be quite a club.

And now the senior beadle becomes insistent. "I warn you, monsieur, you are going to miss your wedding." He and his colleague close in on the principals, brush the snow off *la mariée* and the flower girls, and gently herd them through the portals.

Until today at high noon I thought that temperature-wise the back of a peep in the mountains of the Ardennes represented the ultimate zero. I can now testify that compared to the chapel of the Invalides in a blizzard, Luxembourg and Belgium may be likened to provinces of the Côte d'Azur.

The hardy French, inured to every form of acute discomfort, took it in their stride. Not I. Twenty minutes of standing, kneeling, chanting, and I had had enough. Half an hour later, fortified by a couple of hot grogs at a neighboring *bistro,* I returned to the chapel to find everything still going strong. Finally, the bridal couple arose and disappeared backstage — or, rather, to what is known as the *sacristie* — to receive the congratulations of the congregation. Having dutifully gone through the motions, Madame Tron and I and the rest of the *invités* battled our way through shoulder-high snowbanks to the Place des Invalides and the General's car, in which — with nine adults and four children — we proceeded to the apartment of the bride's mother, Quai d'Orsay.

The wedding reception was appropriately gay. More important, it was crowded, which made for a buildup of body heat and a return to circulatory normalcy. I sat at the bride's table and there was much clinking of glasses, speechmaking, cake cutting, and, of course, some happy tears.

Around four in the afternoon, with no signs of the party breaking up and with visions of the General's car being buried for the duration, I made a discreet exit. It was just as well. The snowflakes were coming down faster and larger, and it took two hours of blind driving to reach Grégy, where I was spending the night with Ogden.

And now back once more in Mademoiselle Brasseur's boudoir-library to find two more fine letters from you, a nice one from Lynn, who says the new comedy is a smash hit, a New Year's card from General Leclerc, thanking you and me for our *aimables voeux de Noël,* and a most satisfactory letter from Gus, who has been alerted to stand by for assignment over here. It looks as if Ted Curtis had really gone to town in the matter, and that my suggestion to him and Tooey Spaatz that here was an opportunity for the Air Force to secure the services of at least one Codman in the E.T.O. has borne fruit.

You ask about our transatlantic acquaintance, Comte Y. de Z., and his collaborating activities. At the time of the Normandy landing he was reported, by the French, to have given us twenty-four hours before being pushed into the sea. A few days later he graciously extended our time allowance to a fortnight. At the expiration of said period, he ducked underground, with the *maquis* hopefully on his trail. They failed to catch up with him, and, if the following — overheard at the Coursier wedding reception — is a criterion, he appears to be on his way to a comeback:

Spirited young lady: "If he should now walk into the room, I would cut him dead."

Elderly gentleman: "I know how you feel, my dear. He did appear at Monique's tea last week. It was quite embarrassing. Out of courtesy to my hostess, I felt obliged to bow to him, slightly, but I did *not* shake hands."

Lady of a certain age: "Yes, I was there. Most uncomfortable. Monique being one of my oldest friends, I couldn't very well avoid speaking to him when he kissed my hand. However, I did *not* smile."

"Next time, for Monique's sake, she will presumably smile," someone whispered. "However, until the time after next, she may draw the line at hopping into bed with him."

Under the circumstances, it seems futile for Americans in France to strike attitudes in regard to a strictly domestic problem.

A postscript in re the Brasseur house. I wrote you of how, before we moved in, a small army of engineers and security specialists swarmed over, into, and under the premises taking soundings for time bombs, secret staircases, concealed tunnels, and catacombs. After a full day of rappings, tappings, and probings, Captain Deering, the officer in charge, turned in his formal report. The entire property, he certified, was safe, aboveboard, and innocent of any possible skulduggery either actual or potential.

A few days ago — it was at breakfast time — Madame Brasseur telephoned to ask if she could call at the house, at our convenience, to pick up one or two personal effects which she had forgotten to take along to the hotel.

"Take Mims and the limousine and bring her over," the General said as he and Al left for the morning briefing.

At the hotel, Madame Brasseur was, as usual, surrounded by an admiring group, which included, among others, Captain Deering. As we left I heard him say to his neighbor, "A great little old lady, a square shooter if I ever saw one."

Madame Brasseur must have heard him too. "Tell me," she asked as the car turned into her drive, "what is a square shooter?"

"One who is honest, frank, open, forthright," I said, "incapable of concealment."

"Ah, that is flattering." Madame Brasseur smiled. "He is charming, your Captain Deering."

We were in the hall now. "My eyes are not as good as they were," she said. "Perhaps you would be kind enough to accompany me to the cellar."

Leading the way with a flashlight, I preceded Madame Brasseur down the steep stairs.

"Any particular part of the cellar?" I asked.

"Right here in front of the furnace," Madame Brasseur said. "If you will just take that shovel and scrape away a little of the earth."

A couple of inches below the surface, a wooden cover, with a ring in it. It came up easily, revealing a shallow space, perhaps two by three feet, which housed what appeared to be a sizable water main with a valve of the wheel type.

"Now," Madame Brasseur said, "if you will please pull that valve."

"You mean turn it?"

"No, just lift."

It didn't seem to make much sense. However, grasping the rusty handle, I gave a perfunctory tug. Valve and pipe rose like a balloon from its moorings.

"Papier-mâché," Madame Brasseur said. "Very practical, very realistic."

"Very."

Putting down the cardboard prop, I turned the flashlight's beam into the cavity. A strongbox. Another ring.

"Would you once again be kind enough?" Madame Brasseur said.

Upstairs in the hall she produced a small key and opened the lid of the box. Jewelry cases, larger cases — flat silver, I suppose — and nestling in the center, a handsome silver teapot.

Madame Brasseur drew it carefully out and placed it on the hall table.

"My mother's," she said. "Back and forth from the cellar it has been. In 1870, in 1914, in 1940. Tomorrow at the hotel I am giving a tea party. I hope you will come."

"With pleasure."

"Good. Five o'clock."

She patted the teapot affectionately. "It *is* lovely, isn't it? Do you not think my guests will admire it?"

"I do. Especially Captain Deering."

"I hope so," Madame Brasseur said. "At least, it will prove him to be right, that I am incapable of concealment, and — how do you say it? — a square shooter."

February 2, 1945. Yesterday the General peeped up to two of the most "liberated" towns I have yet seen — Saint-Vith and Houffalize. In both the destruction is appalling. Perhaps the sense of desolation is heightened by the intense cold, the temperature being well below zero — *our* zero, not the sissy Centigrade variety. Thank God for those long drawers. I have on two pairs, two undershirts, fleece-lined boots, fleece-lined leather coat, your wool caterpillar helmet under the regular helmet, yet long before the end of the day, every day, the cold has permeated every aching bone in one's body. How the boys up in line, who have no warm place to come back to, take it, day after day, and week after week, is beyond my comprehension.

The General's every waking hour is concentrated on our next forward move to the Rhine. He and General Bradley see eye to eye on the question. Both are convinced that the Germans have finally shot their bolt and that it is folly to slow down now. The difficulty, as heretofore, is to get the green light from Topside.

This evening, after dinner, a message ordering us to give up two more of our units. The General blew up.

"If they continue to rob us of our troops to save the face of Monty, both Bradley and I will turn in our uniforms." They won't, of course.

February 14, 1945. The General has decided to take a few days' leave, his first break of any kind since last October, and we are sliding towards Paris in Goering's auto-rail. It is about time that he got some relaxation other than that provided by Special Services movies. The last one, incidentally, was a particular disappointment to me, as it must have been, or will be, to you. I refer to *Rhapsody in Blue,* supposedly based on George's life. It was not a happy evening. First of all, five minutes of unusually boresome "credits" — producers, assistant producers, third assistant script editors, fourth assistant make-up men, and dozens of color, sound, wardrobe, and washroom attendants.

"If, after the war, I am appointed Motion Picture Czar — and that is about all I'll be good for —" the General said, "the first thing I shall do is to forbid all movie credits of any kind whatsoever."

From there on in, things got worse and worse. From my point of view there was the genuine pleasure of hearing again "Stairway to Paradise," "Embraceable You," "Delicious," and the rest. "American in Paris" wasn't bad, and Oscar Levant's playing comes closer to George's than anyone else's. Nevertheless, an "evening with Gershwin," without Gershwin, is not my idea of a Gershwin evening. And the casting — awful. All through I kept being embarrassed for Ira and Lee, and for Kay Warburg, and for everyone who loved George. Think of what someone with a trace of imagination, or merely a little memory, could have done with, well, let's say, George at rehearsal, singing and playing for the cast, in the pit, standing in back reacting to audience reaction. Where were Gaxton and Moore? And the Astaires? Would not Fred have obliged? Certainly Adele would. And the girl who always fainted when George played — where was she? And the last tragic days, as they really were. Perhaps that would have been too poignant. But as it is, what have you? Some fair, if badly chosen, recordings embedded in two and one half hours of Hollywood tripe. One can hardly blame the General for his parting shot as he made for the stairs. "Tomorrow," he said, "I'm going to call off all attack plans and go sailing. If that picture represents what the American public wants, I'm *through.*"

Anyway, I for one prefer our own phonograph records and our own memories of George, that large cigar stuck in his mouth, wringing magic from our old cracked Chickering in the early hours of the morning; at least, "You Can't Take That Away from Us."

Your last two letters arrived just as we were leaving, and as usual you have our military situation doped out with almost perfect accuracy. It was wonderful having firsthand news of you from Gaspar and I may say he was deeply impressed by your G-2-ing and G-3-ing of the current picture. The boys who do go back and forth have been on the whole very good about getting in touch with wives and families. Doubtless they realize what a morale booster it is. Speaking of which, I'm glad you saw Walter Lippmann.

The General seems to be waking up from his nap, and I am going over to talk to him. He has been invited to a duck shoot with the high brass at Versailles, which may give me a chance to call on Bunny and look around a little on my own. We shall be staying at the George V, which has been taken over by the Army. More anon.

February 18, 1945. We are back in our auto-rail headed east after a rather hectic stay in Paris. On arriving at the George V, we found that the imaginative Beetle Smith had arranged for the General to attend the Folies Bergère, a prospect which met with no great enthusiasm but which nevertheless proved quite entertaining. After an excellent dinner, a large car wafted us up to the Rue Richer, where, at the Entrée des Artistes, Monsieur Derval, the director, received the General with full red-carpet treatment. The curtain was held until the General had been spirited through the wings packed with a couple of hundred awestruck chorines, through the pass door, and into the royal box. "Star-Spangled Banner," "Marseillaise." Curtain going up. The show — the same one, as far as I can see, which has been playing there under various titles since World War I. After a while I went backstage to confer with Monsieur Derval about the *vin d'honneur* for the General during the intermission. The *figurantes* are thinner and therefore more decorative than they used to be, but backstage conventions remain the same. If you talk to them they rather charmingly cover their breasts with a tambourine, newspaper, or anything handy. If *not* talking or being talked to, they are completely unself-conscious. Before returning to the box I stopped in the wings to watch the big laugh number, a clothing-shop sketch, something like Eddie Cantor's old belt-in-the-back tailor skit, only this one is built around the comedian's difficulties with a zipper fly. You can see the possibilities. Out front, the house in a continuous uproar. All the G-string girls had disappeared — for a quick change of G strings, I suppose — except for one little wide-eyed chick in high-heeled shoes and a couple of sequins. Squeezed between the proscenium and the switchboard, she was drinking it all in, apparently unable to tear herself away.

"How many times have you seen this sketch?" I asked. She wasn't laughing herself, just completely enthralled.

"One hundred and forty-six times," she said. "Every night since the show started."

"You must know it pretty well by now."

"*Oh, vous savez ce n'est pas le sketch,*" she shrugged. "*C'est que j'aime entendre rire les gens.*"

Entr'acte. House lights. The musicians duck off. Once again we file backstage. Again all the little naked girls blink their mascara in awe as the General brushes by. The office of Monsieur Derval. Madame Derval very *digne* in black. Members of the company standing rigidly at attention. Speech by Monsieur Derval, thanking the General for saving France and her cultural heritage. Speech by the General congratulating Monsieur Derval on keeping the bright lights of France's cultural heritage burning throughout all these difficult years. Popping of corks. Clinking of glasses.

Time to return out front. As the General got up, Madame la Directrice arose and in a protective, motherly way placed her hand on his arm. "Please remember, General," she said, "from now on, whenever you are in Paris, should you feel the need of a little repose — *enfin*" — breaking into French — "*du calme — ne vous faites pas prier; venez aux Folies Bergère; ici vous êtes chez vous.*"

The General exclaimed, "Jesus! I am not that old!"

Early next morning the General left for Versailles with General Hughes in order to present his views on the military situation before the start of the shoot. I took my time getting up, a rare luxury, and had a leisurely breakfast in my comfortable room overlooking the Rue François I. Telephoned Bunny, Madame Tron, and Diana, and, as luck would have it, connected with all three. Around one o'clock, I went over to the Ritz. On the way to the bar I happened to look into the dining room. At a corner table, Marlene Dietrich and Ernest Hemingway. High sign. Joined them. Hemingway most genial. Seemingly pleased that both Marlene and I preferred *The Sun Also Rises* to all his other books. "That was when I was still unpopular," he said. There followed a good number on Duff Twisden and Pat and Loeb — if that was his name. "L. wanted to kill me," he said. "I sent word for him to come over to the Rotonde and bring his gun. Waited two hours for him, but he failed to show."

"Speaking of guns," Marlene said, "my driver was shot in the shoulder yesterday. Not far from Strasbourg. Most annoying."

"German sniper?" I asked.

"No, one of our sentries. Very poor memory, my driver, never can remember the password."

After lunch, strolled over to the little bar in the Rue Cambon to call on that spectacular cat with one brown and one china-blue eye — remember? No soap. New management. No cat. Sorry.

Tea with Madame Tron at her ultramodern Passy apartment. Everywhere zebra stripes — floors, walls, furniture, not to speak of the *valet de chambre's veston*. Madame Tron, as always, bubbling with good humor and North African gossip. Quite a funny new hairdo.

Supper on a tray with Diana at the embassy. She is in bed with grippe — and what a bed! Bigger than anything Earl Carroll ever dreamed of. But then everything in the British Embassy is of heroic size. The great carpeted staircase up which the flunky leads one is longer and higher than would seem possible, the number of salons through which one passes and the height of the doors to Diana's room incredible. However, the buildup does not let you down, for there, reclining among fur-covered pillows in the center of the gigantic bed, entirely surrounded by enormous mythical animals carved in its every surface, is Diana, effulgent in Miracle nightgown and headdress, looking perfectly marvelous.

A lot of ground to cover, the whole Algerian chapter, which she proceeds to do in her inimitable way. Paris? Yes. It's fun. Pleasant also to have everything done for you.

"In other words, you don't miss the Berkeley."

"In a way I do," she said. "On the other hand" — mock-earnest, opening wide those bluest of blue eyes — "now that we represent the Empire, Winston says we must have better quarters."

On getting back to the George V, I found that the General and General Hughes had returned from the shoot sooner than expected. Something at the pre-shoot lunch had disagreed with the General and he was in bed with a painful attack of ptomaine poisoning for which, when I arrived, Elliott Cutler was prescribing.

"If you can make him keep perfectly quiet, he should be all right in the morning," Elliott said.

The General has a horror of being laid up — to him illness in any form is a weakness — and keeping him in bed had usually proved no easy matter. This time, however, he was as docile as a lamb. General Hughes and I took turns sitting with him and before long he was sleeping like a baby.

Elliott Cutler was right. It is early Sunday morning, and the General, though still feeling rocky, is already up and dressed. The Concorde is deserted and the Rue de Rivoli gray and empty as the car heads for the Porte de Vincennes and the marshaling yards where our auto-rail is waiting to transport us from the Ziegfeld to the Siegfried Line.

"I was right in bypassing Paris in August," the General said as he lowered himself into his seat. "I should have had sense enough to let it go at that."

CHAPTER XIV

Across the Rhine

(February–March, 1945)

General Patton, as usual, was eager to be moving forward. For months he had eyed the concentration of two German armies in the Palatinate (between the Rhine, the Moselle, and the Sauer). He felt that this campaign would have to be in three phases: (1) drive the small concentration of troops out of the triangle between the Moselle and the Sauer; (2) push forward to the Rhine and to Koblenz; and (3) the final and main objective, the destruction of the German armies in the Palatinate. General Bradley was most reluctant to approve this campaign. He, after consulting with General Eisenhower, as late as 8 March stated that it was foolish to think that an attack with armor could be made across the Moselle and through the Idarwald Mountains.

On 9 March, the Army Commander, after leaving careful plans with his Chief of Staff and having made a code to be used between himself and his Chief of Staff, left for a visit to General Eisenhower's headquarters. That evening, at about 8 P.M., the Commanding General of the XII Corps, General Eddy, called the Chief of Staff on the phone and stated that he had secured a bridge intact across the Moselle. The Chief of Staff called General Patton and told him this and asked for authority to launch the preplanned Palatinate campaign. After consulting with General Eisenhower, General Patton said, "Go ahead." At midnight that night, General Eddy again called the Chief of Staff on the phone and stated that his first report was in error; that they did not have a bridge over the Moselle. The Chief of Staff said that he must be mistaken; that he must have a bridge over it by morning; that the campaign would go ahead; and then he added, "Matt, if you don't do it, I shall be a private!"

The general plan of this campaign, which was most successfully launched by the Third Army, was:

VIII Corps — General Middleton — continue harassing in the area of Koblenz

XII Corps — General Eddy — with five divisions, cross the Moselle; move rapidly in rear of the German troops occupying the Siegfried Line

XX Corps — General Walker — with six divisions, attack from a position twenty to thirty miles south and west of Trier

This attack of the XX Corps was to give the Germans the opinion that it was the main effort. Thus, the movement of divisions to this corps. In fact, however, the main effort was by the XII Corps.

February 20, 1945. The day before leaving for Paris the General took quite a spectacular trip. In the teeth of terrific opposition and fearful weather the 5th Infantry Division had just crossed the Sauer into Germany, a feat comparable to the amazing river crossings of the peerless 90th. Dashing in a peep across a narrow smoke-screened pontoon bridge, under and over which the current is running fast, can be a little nerve-racking, especially under fire. However, it passed off without mishap. Our boys on the other side were quite surprised to see the General, and he in turn, in spite of graphic reports, was astounded by the elaborateness and ingenuity of the German pillboxes. Here an old farmhouse with a false front concealing heavy armor plate and half a dozen machine-gun emplacements. There an innocent-looking barn whose door at a touch swung open to reveal the muzzle of an 88 peering through six feet of reinforced concrete. Both were successfully taken from the rear.

"Now I *know* the Germans are crazy," the General said. "No more crazy, however, than our own directive from on high to maintain an 'active defense,'" he added bitterly. "There are times when I'm sorry the word 'defense' was ever invented. From the Great Wall of China to the Maginot Line, *nothing, anywhere, ever,* has been successfully defended."

I know of no one who would get more of a kick than yourself out of crossing the German border and seeing the bombs and shells falling, for a change, on German houses, German towns, and the German countryside. A satisfactory day.

P.S. I have a feeling that as time goes on, the General's interpretation of the term "active defense" will become more and more personalized.

February 22, 1945. Celebrated Washington's and my birthday by carrying a suitcaseful of Bronze Stars up and down two lines of twenty Army nurses whom the General proceeded to decorate. Thence to 4th Armored for more decorating. Finally, XX Corps, where the General learned to his intense disgust that one of the division commanders had succeeded in losing a bridge train. He was very angry. General Walker even angrier, which is perhaps why General Patton, who has a very high opinion of General Walker, contented himself with saying, "You should have seen that it was in place. So should I. We have all three fallen down on the job."

In parting he added, "General X will lead his division across the river in the first boat, or, if necessary, swim."

Am writing this while waiting at the airstrip for General Bradley, who is coming up to visit the General, presumably for the purpose, as Paul Harkins says, of "getting his batteries charged." As a matter of fact, General Bradley and our General have seen eye to eye on practically every matter of importance. Throughout the entire Ardennes campaign, General Bradley never once interfered and since then has been doing everything in his power to persuade SHAEF to let Third

Army carry the ball. I believe that each has deep respect and considerable affection for the other, and that furthermore, the tactful and understanding manner in which the relative reversal of their command roles has been handled reflects great credit on them both.

And so endeth my fifty-second year, most of which, it seems to me, has been spent in the back seat of a peep.

March 1, 1945. General Walker called after lunch to say that Trier had fallen to the 10th Armored. The inside story of this bootleg operation will, I think, shed interesting light on the General's implementation of "active defense."

March 10, 1945. Yesterday, we flew to Namur for a big get-together at General Bradley's headquarters in the Château de Namur overlooking the Sambre and Meuse. General Juin conferred the Legion of Honor, Grand Officier, on the General, also on Generals Doolittle, Bradley, and Hodges. Other ranks, Commandeur, I think, were awarded to Generals Vandenberg, Simpson, Brereton, and Gerow. A large dinner and a good time were had by all. Between the fish and the roast the General was handed a wire stating that a bridge over the Moselle had been taken intact. On the strength of this message General Bradley then and there O.K.'d Third Army's plan, and General Patton at once left the table to put in a telephone call. On his return, he stopped for a moment to speak to Juin, who had been needling him a bit for allowing Hodges to steal a march via the Remagen Bridge.

"When you get back to Paris," the General said, "don't fail to read your favorite newspaper. Within a day or two you will see who is stealing a march on whom."

The telephone call had been to General Gay giving him the order for the attack on Koblenz.*

March 13, 1945. Last week the General, Colonel Campanole, and I went to a dinner party at the Wendels'. They have a vast château some

---

* This was the launching of the successful Palatinate campaign which culminated in the crossing of the Rhine and the destruction of two German armies.

distance south of here, and I remember Bunny said he used to go there for the shooting. The Ironmaster himself was away, so the honors were done by Madame de Wendel, a wonderful old dragon, *d'origine grecque,* with a rich bass voice. The big sitting room with its heavy furniture is reminiscent of Louis Bromfield's *House of Women* stage set. So are those present: le Comte et la Comtesse de Mitry, he, one of the Wendel managers, she née Wendel; their two daughters, Hélène et Marie-Thérèse, aged sixteen and eleven respectively; the mayor of Metz; a *sénateur* whose name escapes me; *and* Mademoiselle Ségolène de Wendel, dark and decorative, though scarcely in the first bloom of youth.

The General was in a genial mood and throughout the evening obliged the gathering with picturesque and gory incidents of the re-cent campaign. Campy was on Madame's left but devoted most of his time to the somewhat puzzled sixteen-year-old on *his* left.

The dinner, *"un petit dîner de guerre,"* according to our hostess, was superlative and beautifully served by two ancient white-gloved retain-ers. A really good bouillon with custard cubes, trout from the nearby Wendel stream — *arrosée de* Bollinger '37 — a salubrious *volaille au riz* accompanied by the best Burgundy I have had in a long time.

"What is it?" I asked the Comtesse.

"Oh, vous savez, moi, les vins —" She shrugged. *"Sans doute un Bordeaux quelconque."*

"You find it good?" Mademoiselle de Wendel asked.

"Better than good. What is it?"

"Guess." A dirty trick.

"A Corton — 1923 perhaps?"

"Not *too* far off," she said. "Hospice de Beaune, *Cuvée* Charlotte Dumay, 1915."

Despite her oenological shortcomings, the Comtesse is quite nice, and almost pretty in a blond *bien-élevée* kind of way. "It is not possi-ble that those young ladies are your daughters," I said, meaning it for once.

"Not only are they my daughters," she said, "but from where they came from — at home, I mean — there are seven more, nine in all."

"Incredible." Then, by way of making conversation, "Do you happen to know Madame Paul-Cavallier of Nancy, mother of six?"

"Madeleine and Michel? Naturally. *Ils sont de la maison.*"

The French iron and steel business evidently believes in self-perpetuation. An exception may be Mademoiselle Ségolène de Wendel, who at any rate does not lend herself to ready classification. Not really good-looking, yet not without charm. Prisoner in Germany for almost a year. Questioned by the Gestapo for twelve hours a day for a solid week. Rather vague as to how she got out. Wish there were more time to look into this.

During the drive home the General turned to Colonel Campanole.

"What do you think of our magnate friends?" he asked.

"Fine, substantial people," Campy said earnestly. "Nothing cheap about *them*."

The General loved it.

Back in my room to find the best of nightcaps — a letter from you. How strange that you should have received a letter from Marin la Meslée* the same day his death was announced. I know how you feel about it, and am terribly sorry. Have written to Louis de Fouquières for further particulars but so far have received no answer. All I know is that on a dive-bombing mission he was shot down by flak.

March 21, 1945. What a month this turned out to be! The start of the attack had something of the feel of our breakout from the Cotentin, though, of course, the terrain could hardly be more dissimilar. By March 12, Third Army had closed in on the Moselle from Trier to its confluence with the Rhine just south of Koblenz. Within twenty-four hours the attack, which may prove to be one of the most spectacular of the entire war, was on. By March 21, two German armies had been annihilated, the entire Palatinate had fallen, and we were on the Rhine.

* Commander Marin la Meslée, who shot down twenty German planes in six weeks in 1940, was killed in action on the Alsace front at the age of thirty-two.

The General, as you can imagine, has been busy. On the fourteenth we took a fast run up to Trier to visit 10th Armored. The city is badly beaten up. From there we headed for General Maloney's 94th Division, which is now doing a good job, and from there to 80th and 26th Divisions. The following day, visit to General Middleton, who outlined his plan for taking Koblenz.

On the morning of the sixteenth, telephone call from General Bradley to say that General Eisenhower and Beetle had been prevented by weather from landing at his headquarters and were probably hovering over ours. We rushed out to the airstrip to find that they had, in fact, just landed. General Eisenhower spent the night, and as usual, when he and General Patton actually get together, everything was hunky-dory. At our briefing the next morning, the Supreme Commander astounded us all by rising to his feet and making a speech. "The trouble with you people in Third Army," he said, "is that you do not appreciate your own greatness; you are not cocky enough. Let the world know what you are doing, otherwise the American soldier will not be appreciated at his full value."

After the briefing we proceeded to the airstrip, where the General's C-47 had been set up to fly the party to Seventh Army Headquarters at Lunéville for a conference with Generals Devers and Patch. Five minutes out, we were met by our Air cover. It gave one an unusual feeling of security to watch our nimble P-51's weaving and swooping by the windows on either side.

General Eisenhower, who had just approved assignment to Third Army of another Armored division, the 12th, continued in expansive vein. "George," he said, "you are not only a good General, you are a *lucky* General, and, as you will remember, in a General, Napoleon prized luck above skill."

"Well," the General laughed, "that is the first compliment you have paid me since we served together."

General Devers and General Patch were at their airstrip to meet us. The conference, whose purpose was to correlate the attack, fix boundaries, etc., had for once all the earmarks of love-fest. Everyone most cooperative. Well pleased with his visit, General Eisenhower left in his own plane for Rheims. As the doors were closing he called out to General Patton, "Tell Morris," he said, "that if Tenth Armored takes Saint-Wendel before nightfall, I will give him a medal."

After some further discussion of details with General Patch, we took off for our own headquarters.

Cutting across the eastern suburbs of Nancy, we passed directly over the French airdrome atop the Plateau de Malzéville. Many of the installations were new to me, but the woodland about the plateau's edge quite recognizable. The copilot came back to say he had radioed our E.T.A. to the airstrip at Luxembourg.

Above and ahead, the wings of our P-51's glinted in the afternoon sun. I could not help thinking that aviation had come a long way since that other afternoon almost exactly thirty years ago when from the field below us a French pilot in an open Voisin bomber treated me to my first ride in an airplane.

At dinner the General was relaxed, gay. "I think Ike had a good time," he said. "They ought to let him out oftener."

"What I can't get over," General Gay said, "was his statement to the effect that Third Army isn't cocky enough. How do you explain it?"

"That's easy," the General said, stirring his soup. "Before long Ike will be running for President. Third Army represents a lot of votes." Sensing the half-incredulous smiles, he looked up sharply. "You think I'm joking? I'm not. Just wait and see."

It looks as though the Palatinate campaign, which the General considers unique, is pretty nearly all over but the shouting — and the exchange of the kind of telegrams Generals love to send one another, e.g. Gerow to Patton: "Congratulations on your brilliant surrounding and capture of three Armies, one of them American."

Patch to Patton: "Congratulations on your being the last to reach the Rhine."

Patton to Patch: "Thanks and congratulations to you for being the first to be kicked off the Rhine."

Gerow's message was, of course, a dig at Seventh Army. The Patton to Patch report referred to the withdrawal of a corps soon after Seventh Army's early arrival on the Rhine.

This morning at breakfast, the General announced we would fly to General Eddy's XII Corps Headquarters, now somewhere near Simmern.

"Have two Cubs set up," he said. "We'll leave at ten."

Between here and there, a lot of fluid territory and a certain amount of reported German Air. Unfortunately, the General takes a dim view of Air cover. "It's all right for Ike, if he wants it," the General says, "but I'll be goddamned if I'm going to waste gas and fighter-pilot hours protecting a couple of Cubs."

Nevertheless, at the briefing I tipped off General Weyland.

"Only please don't quote me, sir," I said.

"O.K.," he laughed. "It will be just a coincidence."

At ten o'clock, strapped in the oversnug confines of our diminutive crates, we took off over the hills. The sun was warm, and for the first quarter hour the heat columns tossed us about like corks. At three thousand feet, the air smoothed out and we settled down to a nice even gait over the slowly unrolling spring countryside under a blue empty sky. Correction: SWOOSH — a fighter plane diving out of the sun roared over us. SWOOSH — another one, across and under. The Cubs careened madly as the pilots, taken unaware, now watched the two wide semicircles described by the returning fighters. Close on our left, the first one eased up in a virtual stall. The cowling was slipped back. A wave. A grin. Colonel Brown, Chief of Staff of XIX TAC. Second fighter on the right. Same maneuver. Wings almost touching those of the General's Cub. Open cowl. Wave. Grin, a wider grin. General Opie Weyland. Seconds later, each shirred off in skimming turns ending in two spectacular zooms. For the next half hour they cavorted all over the heavens. Quite a show. Then, with a final waggle of wings as our airstrip became discernible, they disappeared into the blue.

"You don't fool me, Codman," the General said, easing himself out of his greenhouse. "I saw you talking to Opie at the briefing. However"

— he pursed his lips — "when the Air cover is *that* high class, I guess I can't complain."

Next day, a kind of return match. "Opie," the General said at the briefing, "I'm going to run up and visit the Eightieth and the Tenth Armored and also take a look around in the direction of Ludwigshafen and Mannheim. Want to come along and see how the other half lives?"

"Yes, sir," General Weyland said with alacrity. At nine o'clock we pulled out of the headquarters yard in the General's peep. General Weyland sat behind with me. Due east to Saarburg, then southeast to Saint-Wendel, which the 10th Armored had finally taken without benefit of a medal from General Eisenhower.

General Weyland really got an eyeful. The smashed-up towns and villages, from whose remaining window frames hung sheets, pillow-cases, anything white betokening surrender, à la Sicilian. The stunned, silent inhabitants going sullenly about their business amidst the rubble. Higher headquarters kept issuing warnings of Werewolves and last-ditch stands, but so far the German populace had given little trouble. Now and then a village completely intact, bypassed, presumably, by our headlong advance.

"Of course, we may have to come back here and create another Third Army memorial," the General said, "but for the moment they seem to get the point."

In Kaiserslautern, General Weyland had an opportunity to view with satisfaction and in detail the handiwork of his own outfit. They had done a nice job.

Most of the road signs had been removed or reversed by the departing *Wehrmacht,* and in the next town I distinguished myself by getting the party hopelessly lost. After finding ourselves for the third time in the same square, we stopped. A crowd of civilians with a sprinkling of tattered uniforms clustered slowly, deliberately around the peep. Even discounting the Werewolves, it was not entirely pleasant. My German, as you know, is negligible and I was getting nowhere fast when a tall gangling figure with a red beard and green corduroy pants pushed his way to the front.

"Puis-je vous être utile?" he said.

"Vous êtes français?" I was much relieved.

"Enfin" — he shrugged — *"je parle français."*

It seems we were in Frankenstein, hardly reassuring under the circumstances, and that to gain Neustadt, our next objective, it would be necessary to turn back and take a detour. Having cleared matters up, he saluted, murmured *Bon voyage,* and melted backwards into the staring, impassive crowd.

"Practically Old Home Week," the General said, as Mims let in the clutch and the crowd parted. "Wonder what the hell that Frog is doing here."

"I don't think he wanted to be asked," I said.

The road to Neustadt runs through dense woodland bordering a ravine. The day before, one of our tank companies, together with a company of armored infantry on the way north, had run head on into a German supply column coming south. Ten miles from Frankenstein we came upon what remained of it. It was all there, but no longer on the road. Cannoned, machine-gunned, or simply pushed over the edge, hundreds of splintered vehicles, dead horses, and Germans literally filled the deep gully below. For a time we viewed it in silence. Finally the General spoke up.

"That," he said with awe, "is the greatest scene of carnage I have ever witnessed. Let's go home."

March 23, a red-letter day, or, more accurately, the dawn following a red-letter night, for just before midnight of the twenty-second, the advance elements of the 5th Infantry Division, following out the General's careful and very secret plan, stole silently through the little vineyard town of Oppenheim, embarked upon waiting boats and rafts, and paddled across the River Rhine. For obvious reasons, I could not write you that Al Stiller had pleaded to be allowed to accompany the expedition and that the General had acquiesced. Accordingly, Al took part in the first assault landing across the Rhine. The Germans, who had been encouraged by us to expect a crossing attempt near Mainz, were so surprised that the early resistance was almost nil and our casualties hardly exceeded a total of thirty.

Bright and early in the morning the General was on the telephone to Twelfth Army Group in Namur. "Brad," he shouted, "we're across."

A muffled exclamation. "Across what, George?"

"The Rhine. And you can tell the world Third Army made it before Monty."

Next day we flew to Bad Kreuznach to meet General Eddy and Stiller, who had returned to corps headquarters over the newly installed pontoon bridge. From there we proceeded to Oppenheim, through the town, down to the barge harbor, from which the Oppenheimer vineyards are plainly visible. The General's manner was casual as he led the little procession across the low-lying bridge. Halfway across he stopped.

"Time out for a short halt," he said. Walking to the bridge's edge, he surveyed the slow-moving surface of the great river. Then without further comment, suited action to the words, or a paraphrase thereof, of the old Rip refrain from "Plus ça change" — *Je fais pipi dans le Rhin pour embêter la flotte allemande.*

"I have been looking forward to this for a long time," the General said, buttoning his trousers.

Where the bridge met the further shore the grassy bank had been churned into sand and loam. As he stepped off the last pontoon the General stumbled, sank to one knee, steadied himself against the bank with both hands. Rising, he extended his fingers, allowing two handfuls of earth to sift groundward.

"Thus, William the Conqueror," the General said.*

March 25, 1945. This morning, a letter from you. The right way to start a new day. No, the yarn about the General swimming the Moselle in full regalia to rush dripping into the fierce battle raging on the further shore is apocryphal. Unfortunately, the story has gained considera-

---

* "William landed, as the tale goes, and fell flat on his face as he stepped out of the boat. 'See,' he said, turning the omen into a favorable channel, 'I have taken England with both hands.'" *The Birth of Britain,* Winston S. Churchill, Dodd, Mead, 1956.

ble currency and I only hope that it will not give the General ideas.

Actually, he spent most of the day packing, as tomorrow or the next day we shall move our C.P. into Germany. Prince Felix called to say good-by.

"My wife has a shooting lodge in Bavaria not far from Bad Tölz where we occasionally go in the autumn," he said. "If you should happen to pass near there we would both appreciate it if you could let us know whether the house and our old caretaker are still extant."

Another caller was Margaret Bourke-White, who came to the house and took a lot of pictures of the General and also of General Weyland, who had her in tow.

Photos were also taken, but not by Bourke-White, of the three hundred thousandth German prisoner to be captured by Third Army. He was processed today and seemed to enjoy it thoroughly.

March 26, 1945. Accompanied the General on a flight across the Rhine, an impressive sight from the air. First stop, General Eddy's headquarters, where the General ordered an expedition sent to Hammelburg to liberate nine hundred American prisoners reported to be in a P.O.W. camp there. Al Stiller, who now really has blood in his eye, is going with them.

Next we flew to Bad Kreuznach on what proved to be a very sad mission. Colonel John L. Hines, Jr., the son of General Patton's old friend, General Hines, was terribly wounded leading a tank attack near Frankfurt. While standing in the open turret he received a direct hit from a German 88. In spite of the loss of his upper jaw, nose, and both eyes, as well as several fingers of his left hand, he managed to retain consciousness long enough to radio General Gerow and report the situation. When we arrived at the hospital, Colonel Hines was on the operating table. His chances of survival appeared slight.

"At least, I can tell his father that I saw him and that he was not in pain," the General said.*

Thoughts jotted down during the flight back: It is strange how imperfectly and incompletely the hard, bright light of modern publicity

* Colonel Hines did survive the operation and was awarded the D.S.C.

reveals the character of those on whom it is directed. Take General Patton. What impression of him as a man has the public received from the press? Primarily, I should think, a kind of two-dimensional colored cartoon of a swashbuckling, sulfur-breathing, pearl-handled "superman" packaged in tinsel and labeled Old Blood-and-Guts. It is fair to say the General has done little to discourage this type of portraiture, and on occasion has even played up to it. Skill in public relations as such has never been his forte. His whole being is concentrated on the job in hand; his standards, values, and preoccupations antedate the technique of present-day publicity. For what seems to have escaped most contemporary journalists is the fact that General Patton is not a contemporary figure.

To be sure, he has contributed to the science of warfare professional proficiency of the highest modern order. More significantly, however, and it is this that sets him apart, he brings to the art of command in this day and age the norms and antique virtues of the classic warrior. To him the concepts of duty, patriotism, fame, honor, glory are not mere abstractions, nor the shopworn ingredients of Memorial Day speeches. They are basic realities — self-evident, controlling. Bravery is the highest virtue, cowardice the deadliest sin. For him, seeking the bubble reputation even in the cannon's mouth holds no hint of irony, and death upon the battlefield is a consummation devoutly to be wished. In the time of Roger the Norman or in ancient Rome, General Patton would have felt completely at home — with one important qualification having to do with an overriding characteristic of the General himself.

I am sure you are aware of the quality I have in mind. To those close to him it is obvious. To his commands in the field it is a quality sensed rather than perceived. To the public at large it has been overshadowed by the publicized version. And yet the voltage of that quality was potent enough to galvanize hundreds of mothers, fathers, grandparents, wives, sisters into pouring their hearts out on paper. I refer, of course, to the voluminous mail which flooded our headquarters at Palermo after the two soldier-slapping incidents, and which it fell to me to classify. It was not a difficult job. There was no middle ground. Every letter was either for the General or against him. The letters of protest, in many cases both obscene and anonymous, confined themselves to ringing the changes on "You are a cowardly so-and-so for striking a defenseless enlisted man." The pro-General letters, mostly from relatives of servicemen, also bore a close resemblance one to another. "I want you to know we are proud our son is serving in your Army," a typical letter ran. "From the newspaper accounts we are not clear as to exactly what you did and why, but we want you to know *we are for you.* Keep going and God bless you."

In the first tabulation, all communications from personal friends of the General were eliminated. The results: letters of protest, 11%; letters in support, 89%.

It seemed to me at the time — and still does — that even more striking than the decisive percentages was the fact that not one of those who expressed their good will had the opportunity or the possibility of knowing at firsthand that side of the General's nature which remains thoroughly unpublicized: the side of his nature which on countless occasions in Africa, Sicily, France, Luxembourg, and now Germany impelled him to visit, unheralded and unsung, the wounded of our field and base hospitals. Not one of his correspondents had seen him standing, or sitting, or kneeling by a bedside or cot, the hand of a desperately wounded soldier in his — the murmured words of encouragement and the pain in his own eyes, the measure of this man's innate humanity and kindliness. Yet, surely, if mysteriously, these correspondents must have sensed the quality which seemingly eluded the commentators and the politicians — the quality of compassion. The simple truth of the matter is that all his life General Patton has been obsessed with an almost neurotic aversion to suffering and cruelty in any and every form. It is this quality — so difficult, nay, impossible to square with the business of war making — which sheds light upon some of the contradictions and anomalies of the General's character.

The tough vocabulary, the emphasis on frightfulness, the simulated rages, so many symptoms of the conflict between his inner nature and the demands of his chosen medium. The disparity sometimes, though not often, leads him astray. After bawling out a delinquent in his own inimitable manner it is not unusual for the General to remark, "A good

cussing-out is the only way. I've got to make them more scared of me
than they are of the Germans."

Well, on such matters one doesn't argue with the General, but when
you come right down to it who, other than the enemy, *is* scared of
him? Not his staff, nor his household, nor his drivers and orderlies.
Not his dog, at whom in public he thunders and in private croons a
kind of baby talk. Not the exhausted division commander whom the
General has brought back to his own quarters, patted on the back, put
to bed, and, a day or two later, sent off refreshed, rejuvenated, re-
charged — confident in the knowledge that whatever is in store, he will
be backed to the hilt. Certainly not the tanker or the rifleman up front
to whom the name of Patton means the captain of the winning team, a
captain who demands much, but nothing that he himself has not done
or is not prepared to do. No, other than the congenital shirker, the
phony, and the misfit, I can think of no one under his command who
has reason to be unduly scared of the General. His gift for leadership is
based not on fear but rather upon a dynamism of total dedication and
communicable humanity.

There are signs that already the old gory legend of the profane, hard-
drinking, hard-living primitive is beginning to wear thin, and since,
upon inspection, even its superficial aspects fail to pass muster, future
biographers and historians should have little difficulty in piercing its
speciousness. The General's language — picturesque; when addressing
troops, freely sprinkled — mostly for laughs — with goddams, S.O.B.'s,
a few four-letter words, and those scatalogical rather than porno-
graphic, as our old friend, *le professeur* Louis Allard, used to say of
Rabelais. In more than two years under the same roof, tent, or sky, I
have never heard the General tell a really sacrilegious or dirty story or
encourage the telling of one. Alcoholic intake? Except on very rare occasions, an average of one whiskey-and-water before the evening meal,
and possibly (when and if available) a glass of wine with it. The fair
sex? Any serious interest on the General's part in any women other
than the members of his own family would be news to me. Tobacco?
Here we are on thin ice, for, to the General, cigars could indeed be a
dissipation. His nicotine tolerance is low and tobacco irritates his

throat. However, a household conspiracy organized by Charley Odom in which humidors and cigar boxes are mysteriously emptied or just disappear has proved reasonably successful in holding him down to three or less stogies a day.

What does that leave? Gluttony perhaps? Well, the General's breakfast consists of cereal, two eggs, tea, and toast. Lunch, one course usually, cold meat or hash, and a dessert. Dinner, soup, an entree or roast, vegetables when available, dessert, coffee. Since the beginning of the French campaign, he has on trips to the front eliminated lunch entirely, as a waste of time. This means that Al and I are reduced to concealing dry rations in our pockets with the hope of nibbling them unnoticed. To this end a division latrine often serves a useful and double purpose.

Only once since North Africa do I remember the General taking any particular interest in food, other than that it be simple, wholesome, and not too hot. It was upon our return to the royal palace at Palermo after that rugged alfresco session up in the mountains and olive groves of Sicily. It was our first sit-down dinner with knives and forks and a tablecloth in weeks. The meat was overcooked and one of the vegetables burned.

"What we need is a good caterer," the General said. "I wish I could remember the name of the man who used to produce those chicken croquette lunches around Myopia before the war."

"Creed?" I hazarded.

"That's the man," the General said. "Find out where he is and get him over here by air right away."

It took thirteen months and as many top-priority cables for the General's requisition to catch up with Captain Edward Creed on duty at the Quartermaster School, Fort Lee. Since joining us at Étain, he has reorganized not only the General's mess but the entire system of food supply and service to all Third Army hospitals. In terms of morale dividends, the Captain has already proved a blue-chip investment.

And now I see the airstrip ahead so will close this rather rambling letter with an incident having perhaps a certain bearing on the foregoing. It was early morning in our first Normandy apple orchard and

I had knocked on the door of the General's trailer. He had finished shaving and was standing before the glass pensively stroking his jaw.

"Codman," he said without turning round, "I wish to hell I had a real fighting face."

"I should have thought it was a reasonable facsimile," I began.

"No, no, no," he said impatiently. "You are either born with a fighting face or you are not. There are a lot of them in Third Army, Paddy Flynn, Stiller, and many others. Having practiced for hours in front of the mirror, I can work up a fairly ferocious expression, but I have not got, and never will have, a natural-born fighting face."

And there for the moment let us leave the General's unresolved problem — the reconciliation of the fighting soldier and the gentle man.

CHAPTER XV

Germany
(March–May, 1945)

The Rhine was crossed on the twenty-second day of March by the 5th Division of the XII Corps. Orders from higher headquarters stated not more than ten divisions could be pushed across the Rhine; the others must be held in reserve. The VIII Corps, under General Middleton, was crossing the Rhine at Boppard, the scene of the mythical Lorelei. General Patton remarked, "I wonder if we will find gold." Just a few days later, the salt mine and its billions of gold — a strange coincidence.

Soon the Third Army was moved rapidly to the northeast through Frankfurt on the Autobahn to Kassel. A strange sight to see the 4th Armored Division on one side of the Autobahn and the 6th Armored on the other — racing each other. The spirit was "On to Berlin." The 6th Armored was pulled back, and a great tragedy had its beginning. The Third Army was turned southeast toward the Redoubt, and the Russian armies came on through Berlin. The war ended with the Third Army moving rapidly into Austria and Czechoslovakia. At that time it consisted of four corps, HO's-Corps troops, and eighteen divisions, namely, the III, V, XII, and XX Corps; the 1st, 2d, 4th, 5th, 26th, 65th, 70th, 71st, 80th, 90th, 97th, and 99 Infantry Divisions; the 4th, 9th, 11th, 13th, 14th, and 16th Armored Divisions.

It probably was the strongest army in the history of the

*world up to that time, numbering well over six hundred
thousand fighting men.*

March 28, 1945. As of yesterday, our headquarters are finally in Germany at a place called Idar-Oberstein. The offices are in the former barracks of a German Infantry regiment and the General's mess and living quarters in a modern building atop a nearby hill which housed the erstwhile Officers' Club. It is still replete with monogrammed regimental silverware, china, and champagne buckets heavily embossed with swastikas.

Things are moving swiftly and reasonably well, although so far no news has been received from the Hammelburg Task Force. I doubt if we are here long.

April 4, 1945. Yesterday we moved again. This time to Frankfurt. On the long drive we passed through Mainz, the first sizable German city we have visited to date. It is well destroyed. Frankfurt, too, is badly smashed up. Again our headquarters are in some large German barracks in the northern suburbs of the city.

Early to the office this morning to see that the General's desk, flags, etc., are properly placed. On a table in the otherwise bare room an unopened, unstamped letter addressed to "General Patton or his Aide." No one knew how it had got there. I opened it. It was from Gertie Legendre.*

For the last few days, if the German radio is to be believed, things have looked bad for the Hammelburg Task Force, which numbers less than three hundred men. This afternoon two lieutenants, escapees from the camp itself, arrived here at our headquarters. They reported that on the afternoon of March 27 our tanks had broken into the camp and the German Commandant had surrendered. Of the twelve hundred American inmates, as many as possible, two hundred or more, were placed in the tanks and other vehicles, and the rest advised to follow the column on foot. The two lieutenants decided to cut across country. During the first day they heard heavy firing but do not know what

* Mrs. Gertrude Sanford Legendre, who was captured by the Germans and later released.

became of the task force. They themselves made our lines this morning.

Later in the afternoon General Patch called up to say that several escapees from the camp had arrived at his headquarters and reported that on its return trip the task force had been ambushed and overwhelmed by superior German forces. Many of them were now prisoners. From General Patch, General Patton learned that among the inmates of the camp was his own son-in-law, Colonel John K. Waters, who had been a prisoner since the Tunisian campaign, and that in leaving the enclosure Colonel Waters had been severely wounded. Of Al Stiller, no news.

April 7, 1945. Johnny Waters is here, safe and sound — that is, he will be sound. Here is the story relayed by Seventh Army: As our task force, consisting of a company of tanks and a company of armored infantry approached the P.O.W. camp, the German Commandant sent a German captain and Johnny Waters and two other American officers out under a white flag to meet the leading column and arrange for a cease-fire. They had left the camp through the main entrance and proceeded a certain distance, when, from behind a fence, a German, disregarding the white flag, fired at Johnny at short range, inflicting a bad groin and hip wound. He was taken back to the camp hospital, where he received treatment — apparently fairly good treatment — from the Serbian doctor in charge. Meantime the camp surrendered and the prisoners were released. About two hundred and fifty of them were able to ride the tanks and the remainder, except for the hospitalized, were directed to set off on foot and head due west.

On the way back both columns of the task force were attacked by superior enemy forces from three different German divisions. Surrounded, they fought until their ammunition was exhausted, and then surrendered. Al Stiller was reported to have put up a great fight — he would — and was last seen being marched off with the others in the direction of Nuremburg.

Yesterday, Seventh Army's 14th Armored Division overran Hammelburg and took charge of the hospitalized, including Johnny. Charley Odom flew there and arranged for him to be brought by plane to Frankfurt. The General saw him this morning (April 7) and has just written a full account to his daughter (Johnny's wife), "Little B." Johnny is awfully thin, but his morale is good and he is going to pull through.

April 10, 1945. The last few days have produced a stream of visitors and sight-seers, a phenomenon which invariably takes place whenever our headquarters are located in a large city.

First, Elmer Davis, whom I went to fetch at the airstrip in the middle of the night. Despite a rather rough trip, he was most agreeable. His first words to the General were, "Since arriving in Germany the thing that has surprised and touched me the most was to be asked by your aide here about the health of my cat."

You remember his article in *Harper's* on the famous cat who completely took over his household and existence. On the way from the airstrip in a heavily armored car it seemed like a good idea to pick a subject likely to keep his mind — and my own — off the Werewolves. The latter have not, so far, materialized, but enemy resistance has stiffened considerably and everyone has been warned to remain on the *qui vive*. Anyhow, I did ask him about his cat and was glad to learn, as I know you will be, that he has reached the ripe and at the same time green old age of thirteen, and is well and happy except that he has recently developed a marked dislike for New York, in fact, for all cities.

"What are you doing about that?" I asked.

"We are giving up our apartment in town and building a house in the country," Elmer Davis said. "It will be ready this summer and we shall move there permanently. That is," he added, "unless the cat changes his mind."

Other visitors: Elliott Cutler, who is flying Johnny Waters to a base hospital; Mr. John McCloy, who gave the General a decided lift by repeating substantially what he had once before said to him in Sicily. "One advantage you have over other Generals" — he grinned — "is that you *look* like a General." Barney Baruch, who gives the impression that even without his double-thick lenses and his hearing aid he would see more, hear more, and certainly talk more than most men half his age. We all got a big kick out of him.

Last but not least, General Giraud's two sisters-in-law and the Princess Ruspoli, whom the 4th Armored had rescued from an internment camp at Friedrichroda.

Tomorrow we leave Frankfurt — hurray — and move the C.P. north to Hersfeld.

I greatly miss Al Stiller. However, barring accidents, we should be overrunning him before long. Another serious loss is that of Bob Allen[*] — Colonel Robert S. Allen, Assistant G-2. A couple of days ago, he and three other officers, while making a forward reconnaissance up near Gotha, were ambushed with most unfortunate consequences. One officer was killed and the rest, including Bob Allen, captured. Ever since joining us in England, Bob has done an extraordinarily able job and the General thinks the world of him. To get conked at this late date is a hell of a note.

The General has appointed Lieutenant Francis Graves, Jr., his junior aide. He is a nice kid and has a fine combat record. Otherwise, our household remains the same except for the welcome homecoming of Ed Creed, who rejoined us at Idar-Oberstein.

P.S. (April 11). We have arrived at Hersfeld, a small and not particularly attractive town, after a long drive which included a stop at Wiesbaden to lunch with General Bradley. In the afternoon we passed an impressive number of German demolitions and a depressing number of empty gas cans which the supply people had failed to salvage. The General was already fairly exercised about this and making a mental note to have the responsible colonel personally gather them up, when we came upon an interesting and idyllic roadside group composed of two G.I.'s breathing down the necks of two not undecorative young ladies.

"Stop," the General roared.

Screeching of hot rubber as we slewed to the grassy side of the *Autobahn*.

[*] Formerly a Washington correspondent of the team of Drew Pearson and Bob Allen, authors of "Washington Merry-Go-Round."

"What the so-and-so do you mean by fraternizing with those so-and-so German so-and-sos?"

The more self-possessed of the G.I.'s unwound himself from his partner.

"Sir," he said, "these are two Russian ladies who have lost their way. We are trying to learn their language so as to direct them properly."

For a moment the General glared in silence.

"O.K.," he said, turning away. "You win."

Then to Mims, "Go ahead."

Out of earshot he relaxed.

"That," he murmured, and there was admiration in his tone, "is really a new one."

April 13, 1945. Yesterday was a full day, and a grueling one. General Eisenhower and General Bradley arrived in the morning to inspect the industrial salt mine at Merkers in which, General Eddy had reported, was stashed away the entire German gold reserve. We were met at the mine head by Generals Eddy and Weyland, also a Colonel Bernstein from the Finance Section of SHAEF. The party was ushered into a primitive freight hoist operated by an unprepossessing German civilian. The General began counting the stars on the shoulders of those about him as the jittery elevator rattled with ever-accelerating speed down the two thousand feet of pitch-black shaft. He glanced up at the single cable now barely visible against the diminishing patch of sky.

"If that clothesline should part," he observed thoughtfully, "promotions in the United States Army would be considerably stimulated."

A voice from the darkness, that of General Eisenhower.

"O.K., George, that's enough. No more cracks until we are above ground again."

At the bottom of the shaft we stepped out into a dimly lit tunnel leading to a high-vaulted area not unlike the champagne cellars of Reims. Boxes, cases, crates, stacks of paper currency, gold coin and bullion, jewels, paintings, dental bridgework and fillings. More than one hundred million dollars' worth, Colonel Bernstein estimated. In a corner by itself a dozen sizable bales of reichsmarks.

"What are those?" General Eisenhower asked.

"They are earmarked to meet future German Army payrolls," the interpreter explained.

"I doubt if they will be needed," General Eisenhower said.

If the morning visit to the salt mines seemed to have about it a quality of unreality, the afternoon was stark and terrible. After lunching at XII Corps we flew to XX Corps at Gotha, and from there proceeded to the recently overrun German concentration camp at Ohrdruf. In the midst of this lovely spring countryside, a festering wound. Rows of hideous wooden barracks surrounded by a double enclosure of barbed wire. Even before reaching the entrance, the smell of death and corruption was almost overpowering. An officer from XX Corps, still pale and shaken, received us. "They tried to eliminate the evidence before we arrived," he said, "but as you see, they were not very successful."

Lying individually and in piles throughout the area, the bodies of recently murdered inmates, in most cases shot at close range through the base of the skull. An ex-guard acted as guide. We were spared nothing. The building piled to the roof with emaciated naked bodies. The gallows — contrived to effect death as slowly and painfully as possible. The whipping racks, the butcher's block for the cleaving of jaws and smashing out of gold fillings. The half-filled and still-smoking ovens in the crematories.

The General officers present all are men who have seen much of life in the raw, yet never on any human faces have I witnessed such horror and disgust. At one point General Patton frankly disappeared behind the corner of a building and was violently sick to his stomach.

As we stood by the entrance waiting for our transportation to draw up, one of our enlisted men accidentally bumped into the Nazi ex-guard, and from sheer nerves began to giggle.

General Eisenhower fixed him with a cold eye and when he spoke, each word was like the drop off an icicle.

"Still having trouble hating them?" he said.

Before leaving, General Eisenhower addressed the others.

"I want every American unit not actually in the front lines to see this place," he said. "We are told that the American soldier does not know what he is fighting for. Now, at least, he will know what he is fighting *against.*"

April 14, 1945. This morning at breakfast, the General told us of how, on going to bed last night, he had turned on the radio in order to get the correct time by which to set his watch. At that moment the program was interrupted for a special bulletin: the announcement of the death of President Roosevelt. The General hurried to General Bradley's room and together they brought the news to General Eisenhower. All three sat up for some time discussing the possible repercussions on the conduct of the war.

Later in the morning the General drove up to Erfurt to visit Bob Allen, whom we had overrun in a German military hospital during the Weimar push. Bob's morale is remarkable considering that his right forearm was shot away, necessitating amputation near the elbow. Luckily the Austrian doctor who performed the operation not only did a good job, but deliberately delayed his removal to higher headquarters for questioning by the Gestapo. Bob's one idea is to see it through with Third Army and avoid being evacuated. A very courageous guy.

April 15, 1945. Ohrdruf was the first, and all of us prayed the last, concentration camp any of us would ever see. No such luck. Within forty-eight hours XX Corps had overrun a far bigger one north of Weimar, the notorious Buchenwald. It was after the morning briefing and the General was in his office when Colonel Réthoré, our senior French liaison officer, came into the outer office where my desk is. Colonel Réthoré is an experienced officer with a long and distinguished career in both the regular French Army and the underground, in which he assumed the pseudonym of Bilbane. Serene, composed by nature, I had never before seen him other than complete master of himself and of the often demanding situations inseparable from his job. This morning, standing before my desk, he was white as a sheet, and trembling with what I at first took to be anger. He was angry, all right, but his eyes conveyed an even stronger emotion — that of undiluted horror. For a minute or two he seemed unable to speak at all. Then in a low monotone he began. "I have just now come from something so terrible, so incredible, that it cannot possibly be believed unless seen at first hand." He had by chance been with XX Corps when before dawn they had overrun the camp. Ohrdruf all over again, only here the inmates numbered from twenty to thirty thousand.

"In spite of medical teams supplied by Twentieth Corps they at this very moment are dying like flies. Will you ask the General to send help?"

"I will."

It did not take the General long to react. "Get up there immediately and bring back a full report. Before you go, tell Odom to collect the necessary hospital teams. Have Muller send up food and transportation. Tell Air Transport to stand by. My own plane is available if you want it."

Three telephone calls, and a fourth to arrange for photographers.

"Shall we go up there in your car?" I asked Colonel Réthoré.

"Yes," he said.

Once on the *Autobahn* headed north, he pressed the accelerator to the floor boards.

"How many of your compatriots are there?" I asked.

"Twenty-four hundred and sixty, as of early this morning," he said.

Thereafter, except for the hum of the engine and the rush of wind, the miles ticked off in silence.

Weimar must have been a rather attractive city — physically, I mean. Some of it still is. Northward the road winds through wooded country for three or four miles to burst abruptly upon an open sunlit area covered, until recently, with the buildings of a thriving German armament establishment, now a mass of rubble. The "heavies" do a good job. A quarter of a mile further on, the road — symbolically enough — comes to an end before a reddish-brown wooden pavilion from both of whose extremities stretch miles of wire fence encompassing long, low barracks of the same color. If you didn't know what it was, you might take it for the entrance to a third-rate amusement park. In a sense it was that

— to the SS. From the short pole on the wartlike cupola a flag hangs listlessly. A black flag at half-mast for the President.

Inside the gate is a spacious yard of rough flagstones. By prearrangement, our Military Government officer and a number of the French prisoners were waiting for us — Colonel Marhes, formerly head of the resistance movement in northern France, and Marcel Paul, member of the Paris Municipal Council; General Audebert of the Cavalry, and General Challe, Aviation. All of them in for "resistance activities," for it must be understood that Buchenwald, while its inmates include many former officers and soldiers, is not a compound for military prisoners of war, but for those who have committed, or are suspected of having committed, "crimes against the Reich."

"You might as well see the end product first," the Military Government officer said, "and then work backwards."

While not large, the crematory is, as I remember it, the only solidly constructed building in the camp. In a smaller yard, enclosed by a wooden fence, a large wagon like a farmer's cart had just been brought in. Over it the flies buzzed lazily. Its contents, the Military Government officer explained, were part of the day's toll — thirty or forty bodies, naked, crisscrossed like matches, and about as substantial. The crematory itself is not unlike the standard variety, with certain additional features. It seems that the routine was as follows: Prisoners who died from "natural causes" were simply carted into the ground floor of the crematory proper and tossed into six coke ovens, in which are still to be seen the charred remains of the last overhasty and incomplete job that the arrival of our troops interrupted.

The unusual feature is the basement. Here, according to eye witnesses whom I have no reason to disbelieve, were brought prisoners condemned of capital crimes — for example, attempting to escape, insubordination, stealing a potato, smiling in ranks — usually in groups of twenty or so at a time. They were lined up against the walls, each one under a hook fixed at a height of about eight feet from the floor. (The hooks are no longer there. They were hastily removed the day we came in, but the emplacements are clearly visible.) A short slip-noose was placed about the neck of the condemned, who was then raised by the guards the distance necessary to affix the end of the noose to the hook.

If the ensuing strangulation took too long a time to suit the mood of the guards, they beat out the brains of the condemned with a long-handled club resembling a potato masher. (Specimens of the nooses and "potato mashers" are on view in the basement.) The remains were then placed on an elevator which lifted them directly to the crematory proper, the final run being made on a miniature railway of metal litters leading from the elevator platform to the furnace doors. Efficient.

Having seen and photographed the end products, we proceeded to the place whence they came — the infamous Barrack 61. Exteriorly, Barrack 61 is like the other barracks, roughly 150 feet long by 30 feet wide. Inside, four tiers of wooden shelves incline slightly towards the central corridor. In the rush season this single barrack housed twenty-three hundred prisoners jammed together on those shelves, twenty-three hundred "nonworkers" that tuberculosis, dysentery, pneumonia, and plain starvation had rendered incapable of the daily twelve-hour stretch at the armament factory or nearby quarries. There were fewer when I was there. I did not count them, but the shelves were still well filled. Some of them were living human beings, but the majority were almost indistinguishable from the corpses we saw in the death cart.

On one shelf barer than the rest, three shadowy figures huddled together for warmth. Cold comfort for the outside two, since the middle one had been dead for several hours. Under the old regime he would eventually have been stripped and thrown out onto the flagstones to await the next tour of the wagon. Farther on, an emaciated specter of a man who had managed to get to the latrine and back was attempting to crawl up onto the first shelf. It was only three feet from the floor, but he could not make it. As he collapsed, his shirt — he had no other clothing on — fell open. A living — barely living — skeleton, with a long prison serial number tattooed on the inside of the thigh. Two of the inmates who accompanied us picked him up by the shoulders and ankles and placed him on the shelf.

So much for Barrack 61. Barrack 47 was like it, but frankly, I hadn't the stomach.

Any redeeming features? Yes. A number of individuals who

through sheer will power and incredible fortitude managed to preserve their sanity and their self-respect, such as Professor Richet of the Académie de Médecine. An inmate of the camp for over a year, he had been allowed to organize his own clinic within the prison. With means so slender as to be negligible from the German point of view, he nevertheless brought some relief to those who could find room in the meager space allotted him — meantime amassing a wealth of informative data. From Barrack 61 we went there.

"What seems so pointless," I said, "is the elaboration of horror. If extermination is the object, why haven't they just wiped you all out once and for all?"

"Ah, my friend, there are certain considerations to be taken into account," he said.

"Such as?"

"Applied slave labor, turnover, example, and even public opinion."

"What public opinion?"

"German public opinion."

"The system is not pointless," he continued. "It is carefully thought out. In this camp are twenty-five thousand Russians, Poles, Czechs, French, Belgians, and others who are in disagreement with the tenets of the Reich. True, they must disappear, but before they go they must contribute their bit. On arriving here they are put to work, twelve hours a day at the factory or in the quarries or elsewhere. A workingman requires a diet of two thousand or twenty-five hundred calories per day. Here he is put on a diet of eight hundred calories per day — a diet calculated to produce death by starvation in a certain period of time. That period may be lengthened or shortened in accordance with available replacements. If the replacements are ample, the quotas of nonworkers sent to what are frankly known as extermination camps, such as Ohrdruf, are increased. There the principle is the same, but the tempo is accelerated."

"Why not exterminate them here?"

"They do. During the months of January, February, and March of this year there were fourteen thousand deaths. With the milder weather the rate has dropped slightly. Around three thousand a month."

"From what cause?"

"Overcrowding, disease, beating, hanging, starvation — chiefly starvation."

"Then why bother with extermination camps?"

"A certain amount of distribution spreads the number of 'deaths from natural causes' over a wider area. Public opinion, you see. Also, among the workers the threat of being sent to an extermination camp has its uses.

"I have managed," he went on, "to retain a good many of my written observations of the system. Several volumes. I should like to get them to Paris."

"I think that can be arranged."

On the way out one of the Frenchmen said, "Did you know that Colonel Heurtaux is here?"

Good God, Heurtaux! Twenty to thirty German planes to his credit during the last war — perhaps more. I only saw him once, in 1916, when we were alongside the Cigognes at Bar-le-Duc. It was out at the field. He was talking to one of his pilots, a quiet, unassuming young lieutenant with very clear eyes — Lieutenant Guynemer.

Well, here was Heurtaux again. We sat in the office of the former superintendent of Buchenwald and smoked cigarette after cigarette. He looked fine — that is, he looked like a fine man who has been through hell and still remains a fine man.

"Yes, I remember you," he said, "and Norman Prince, and Cowdin, and Thaw."

I gave him news of his old squadron, of Accart, of Murtin, and of the death of Marin la Meslée.

"A great leader," he said.

"What were you accused of?" I asked.

"Organizing resistance, sabotage, spying, and hostility to the Reich."

"An honorable indictment."

"And true, thank God. But they had no proof. My interrogation ran to one hundred seventy-five typewritten pages. I saw it. But all they had was accusations and they don't like to shoot an Army officer without some 'semblance of proof.' "

"Who accused you?"

He was silent for a moment and then smiled — the saddest smile I have ever seen.

"A compatriot," he said. "I believe he thought he was doing his duty."

We talked some more — of other things.

"Are you also of the opinion that the whole system here is carefully worked out?"

"Does anyone doubt it?"

"Well, *who* works it out? Are there general directives, with the details left to the individual camp commanders, or what?"

"Listen, my friend," he said, "make no mistake. Down to the last detail it comes from the top, with many willing hands to carry out both the policies and the details. Coming across France you must have learned of their interrogation methods — burning matches under the fingernails, pulling out tongues, eye-gouging, crushing the testicles with nutcrackers. Standard procedure. Occasional improvisations, as in the case of one of my comrades, who was seated naked on a dining-room table that was pulled apart sufficiently to contain his private parts and slowly pushed together from either end by a couple of SS men.

"Or the case of the four girls at Lyon suspected of knowledge of resistance activities. Stripping and beating them was merely standard procedure. An SS noticed, however, that one of the girls was having her monthly period. Being a man of fantasy, he removed her sanitary pad, dipped it in gasoline, replaced it, and struck a match. The other girls received treatment in terms of gasoline-soaked wads of cotton. It was four days before the last one died. One can go on endlessly. But to what good? Those who cannot or will not believe — and I don't blame them — say 'propaganda.'

"But I say to you that the obscene violence, the sadism of the interrogation chambers, is merciful compared to the prolonged inferno of the concentration camp. You yourself have seen the physical effects. What you have not seen at work is their diabolical ingenuity in breaking down morale. Do you think, for example, that when a contingent of prisoners is destined for the extermination camp at Ohrdruf the names are simply announced by the German officials? Certainly not. They make us do it. The head or heads of the prisoners' committee are summoned. They are told, 'You will this evening submit a list of a hundred prisoners to be ready to leave for Ohrdruf at five o'clock tomorrow morning. When it has been approved, you will call the roll and announce the names to your section and have them ready at the appointed time.'

"In the same way prisoners are put on the cremation detail, the burial detail, the flogging detail. Anything and everything that is calculated to engender internal distrust, bitterness, hatred is applied, often with considerable effect. That these people are individually and collectively mad there is no possible doubt. But there is method in their madness and a kind of genius for evil. The important thing is that this evil should be fully understood."

I have taken a bath, changed my clothes, smoked two packs of cigarettes, but the overpowering moral and physical stench of Barrack 61 remains in my nostrils — the sour-sweet stench of death, dysentery, and despair. Perhaps it is meant to.

April 17, 1945. In the General's C-47 on our way to Paris for twenty-four hours. At the moment we are making a slight detour up the gorge of the Rhine to take a look at the rock of the Lorelei where the 80th Division made their crossing. From the air the great river winding between steep terraced banks is a spectacular sight, but I am heartily sick of Germany and all its works.

This is more like it, for now we are skimming over the undulating woods and symmetrical fields of eastern France. How peaceful they look.

Orly. General Hughes has sent a car to meet us. Porte d'Italie, across the river, Place de la Concorde, the Champs Élysées, "April in Paris, chestnuts in blossom," but very few holiday tables under the trees.

At the George V, the General looked at his watch. "It is now six o'clock (P.M.). I am going to visit Johnny Waters and then dine with General Hughes. We take off at two tomorrow afternoon. Between now and then your time is your own."

Travelers' Club to meet Bunny, to whom I had radioed from the plane. Message there to the effect that I was expected to dine with him *chez* Monsieur et Madame Percherons, two of the many agreeable French friends of Bunny whom we saw during that first hectic trip to Paris.

Very pleasant evening during which I briefed them on Germany and they, in turn, brought me up to date on Gertie Legendre's capture and escape, the latter effected just before our arrival in Frankfurt. Her letter to the General and/or me was to recommend understanding treatment for a German family who had been kind to her and helped in her getaway.

A long, sound sleep in an enormous bed. Breakfast in same. First breakfast in bed since England. Always extreme contrasts. Either palaces, private planes, breakfast in bed, or wet sleeping bags, ice, mud, tropical heat, insects, and K rations. If variety is the spice of life, I expect to end up this war as a bottle of Colonel Gray's Chutney.

With my tray they even sent up a copy of the *Stars and Stripes*. Lucky they did. The announcement was in a box on Page One. General Patton, promoted to full General. From then on, a busy morning. The PX, Ordnance, Chief Quartermaster. The last set of Four-Star collar insignia in the E.T.O.

Orly. By the time the General got there we had the plane really fixed up. Four-Star pennants outside, huge Four-Star flag inside, on a table-shelf by his seat Four-Star auto plates, and a bottle of Four-Star Hennessy. Upon his arrival, we formed squads of four and stood at rigid attention. He got quite a laugh out of it. As a matter of fact, he was very much pleased. So are we all.

April 21, 1945. Logically, this war should be on its last legs, yet the immediate outlook is by no means clear. The Russians have overrun Vienna and are rolling westward. Ahead of them, swarming hordes of displaced persons. From the air they cover the landscape, crawling like ants along the roads, overflowing into the fields, camping hopelessly in the suburbs of rubbled cities, creating a problem to which no one has found a solution.

A dreary chapter. The initial satisfaction of bringing the war home to Germany is wearing off. The Germans themselves are beaten, but their leaders refuse to throw in the sponge and there is still talk of a bitter-end stand in the so-called Redoubt, located somewhere in the Bavarian mountains of the south. Meantime, perfectly good Americans and their Allies are being killed and wounded.

G-2 keeps warning of impending glider raids of German commandos with plans for the assassination of high-ranking officers, beginning with the Army Commander. The General takes little stock in this — "like the cries of Werewolf," he says — but he does keep a carbine next to his bed. During the daytime we keep a close watch on him. Such are the fortunes and ironies of war, however, that yesterday marked the General's closest call since Italy.

It happened this way: In the morning we flew in two Cubs to XII Corps, to say good-by to General Eddy, who, to the General's and everyone else's deep regret, is going back to the U.S.A. for treatment of a serious high-blood-pressure condition. Thence to XX Corps and General Walker's recently requisitioned headquarters, the imposing if preposterously ornate Schloss Weissenstein. On leaving, the General gave his own Three-Star collar insignia to General Walker.

"I have certainly been lucky in having such corps commanders," he said as the Cubs were warming up. "Eddy, Walker, Middleton, Van Fleet — all great soldiers."

Our last stop for the day was to be III Corps Headquarters at Reidfeld. The afternoon was fine, sunny and cloudless. The flight from III Corps uneventful until within a mile or two of the Reidfeld airstrip. We were letting down for our approach, the General ahead, when from out of the sun a fighter plane screamed over and past the General's Cub with a clatter of machine-gun fire. Near the ground the fighter leveled, then zoomed up and out of sight into the sun, presumably for another try. The puzzling feature was that it looked like a Spitfire. The only evasive action an unarmed Cub can take is to get down low and hedge-hop in the hope that the fighter's excess speed will cause him to overshoot. In the course of the Sicilian campaign, one of our Cub pilots chalked up three enemy kills by luring as many German fighters into a like number of narrow ravines where each in his overeagerness crashed against the mountainside. Here, unfortunately, no ravines — just fields, a few fences, and some wooded area. Here he comes again. My Cub is behind the General's and high. The fighter makes a pass. He misses. Now he has the General's Cub lined up. The General is pointing something at him. His pistol? No, his camera. What a man. Rat, tat, tat, tat. Over and past, another miss, another zoom. Both Cubs are down low now, contouring the fences, the hollows, and the treetops. A terrific whining scream, guns chattering. Another miss? Yes, thank God. Pull-up? No, too fast, too low. The fighter hits a knoll in the field ahead, ricochets like a flat stone on the surface of a still pond. Hits again, slews, disintegrates. Finis.

Tragic, in a way. It *was* a Spitfire, manned by a Polish volunteer flying for the R.A.F. He was out of his sector, and doubtless had never seen a Cub before and presumably mistook us for a couple of German liaison planes.

April 22, 1945. Today the C.P. moved from Hersfeld to Erlangen. It was a long, cold, wet drive over the Harz Mountains and we were glad to find that our quarters, in a sizable house on high ground overlooking this old university town, were both warm and comfortable. Even more heart-warming was to find your letter about Gus. Ted Curtis has evidently followed through on the matter and expects Gus to arrive at his headquarters in the near future. General Spaatz is due here within the next few days and I shall probably be able to get further information from him.

As you doubtless now realize, Third Army is driving south to isolate the Redoubt. General Van Fleet is doing wonders with III Corps and should be on the Danube within a matter of days, or even hours.

April 28, 1945. Yesterday we flew to XX Corps and the General pinned three stars on General Walker. We all then proceeded to a point opposite the fabled city of Regensburg, or Ratisbon, and on the recently installed treadway bridge crossed the Danube, a river less evocative of the *Blue Danube* than of a scherzo in muddy brown.

" 'You know, we French stormed Ratisbon: a mile or so away' " — the General intoned — " 'on a little mound, Napoleon stood on our storming-day.' "

"Which only goes to show" — he resumed his normal speaking voice — "that in those days Supreme Commanders were even less anxious to get up near the front than they are today."

On the way back from XX Corps we flew over Nuremberg, which is the most completely pulverized city I have ever seen.

Today Generals Doolittle, Spaatz, and Vandenberg came to lunch. A great trio. To celebrate their recent promotions, the General had a guard of honor for General Spaatz and General Vandenberg. Flourishes, ruffles, the works. They got a big kick out of it. General Spaatz has promised to let me know when Gus arrives and General Patton says I can pay him a visit.

Open season again for sight-seers and rumors. Of the former, the pleasantest have been Lewis Douglas, Marlene Dietrich, and Emil Ludwig. Of the rumors, the least credible are the German threats of poison gas and a last-minute ultimate bomb which reduces everything to nothing.

May 1, 1945. Good news. We have overrun Al Stiller. With about ten dead Boches to his credit and the loss of an equivalent number of pounds around his waistline, Al seems none the worse for his P.O.W. experience.

This morning the General visited the big prison camp at Moosburg and was given an ovation by the thirty-odd thousand Allied prisoners there. As we arrived, a contingent of Russian prisoners were being assembled near the main gate. With their stained tattered uniforms and scraggly beards they looked a motley and dejected crew. Then a remarkable thing happened. The senior Russian officer blew his whistle, barked a sharp command, and through the now open gateway, the Russian column marched out at a fast rhythmic clip. Bearing, precision, staying power, discipline. Somehow the beards were no longer unkempt. They bristled with stored energy, and the faded tunics took on the lines of dress uniform.

Fascinated, the General had stepped up onto a box to watch the endless column of ex-prisoners now magically reconverted into seasoned troops, veterans of a hundred battles, combat soldiers on their way HOME.

"That's it," he said, "the Russian Infantry. Hard to beat." His eyes gleamed. "But it can be done and that is undoubtedly just what we shall have to do."

We were scheduled to return after lunch to our headquarters. Change of plans.

"Codman," the General said, "before going back, we'll have a look at the Ninety-ninth Division." He glanced at his watch. "By now they should be crossing the Isar. The town they are taking on the other side should be of interest to you."

It was stupid of me, but I had missed the morning briefing, and the General's words did not at the moment ring a bell. Even when we arrived at the treadway bridges I was slow in tumbling to it. Smoke was rising from the town on the opposite shore into which the division was pouring, and from half the dormers and casements the usual array of sheets and pillowcases flapped their surrender signal. Finally I got it. The smoke had cleared and there, perched on the top of the hill whose craggy sides rise sheer from the town's center, a storybook castle, aloof, severe, impersonal, yet very, very familiar. Schloss Landshut. Talk about things coming full circle. I turned around. The General had his camera out. He was smiling.

"Go on," he motioned, "keep looking at it. I'm going to take a picture."

If it comes out well, you should have no difficulty in spotting the barred windows of our World War I prison and the drawbridge and the walled courtyard through whose postern gate Norman Hall and Browning and Lewis and myself made our getaway one dark night some twenty-six years ago.

May 9, 1945. On getting the green light to enter Czechoslovakia, the General pushed right on, not only to Pilsen, designated as our stop line, but into the very suburbs of Prague — from which, however, higher headquarters ordered us to withdraw. Meantime XII Corps has captured Linz, and thus we end up further east than any other Army of the Western Allies.

Since Kesselring's surrender in Italy and the meeting between First Army patrols and those of Marshal Konev, it has been merely a question of time when and where the whistle would blow. On May 2 the German radio announced the demise of Hitler. On May 3 General Patton himself came close to death. His jeep was bowling along at high speed when from a blind side lane an ox-drawn cart lumbered out into the highway. Mims avoided a crash by inches, but even so the heavy wagon pole which protruded ahead of the ox team grazed the General's head.

"After all I've been through," he later remarked, "think of being killed on the road by a team of oxen."

Our headquarters here in Regensburg are located in the German barracks on the outskirts of town. We live, if you can call it that, in the palace of the Prince of Thurn and Taxis, which occupies an entire block in the center of the city and includes three chapels, a theater, an armory, innumerable salons, dining halls, and bedrooms — all in execrable taste, more horrific if possible than the Weissenstein monstrosity.

Last week the General had a pleasant surprise when one of our divisions in overrunning a Tyrolean prison camp liberated an old World War I friend of his, le général Houdemon. He spent a night here in the palace with us and is really a wonderful old boy. He must be the oldest pilot in the French Army and was actually flying a Morane right up to the 1940 armistice. After that he retired to his home in Pont-à-Mousson, but his activities there displeased the Germans and he was hustled off as a hostage just before our own arrival. He is the father-in-law of our Colonel Réthoré, who thus has some very good news to communicate to his wife, who herself has a remarkable record with the resistance. The evening he dined here also marked the visit of three Mexican Generals who seem to be making a late tour of the front.

There was much three-way toasting and speechmaking. The climax came when, glass in hand, the senior Mexican General in a crescendo of eloquence and good will proclaimed, "Never, never will Mexico attack the great United States of America." And as the "Hear! Hear's" died down, he added, "We Mexicans are too intelligent to attempt to spit upwards."

Next morning I accompanied General Houdemon to the airstrip, where the General's plane was readied to fly him back to France. It was arranged with the pilot that on reaching the border, General Houdemon would be invited to take over the controls and have the fun of flying himself home. We later learned that this had made his day.

General Patton was still asleep in his trailer in the palace garden when, early in the morning of May 7, the green telephone by his bunk rang insistently. General Bradley on the wire. "It's all over, George," he said. "Ike has just telephoned from Reims. The German Army has surrendered, effective midnight tomorrow, May 8. As of now, everyone is to stay put in line."

That evening we were expecting several more guests, including Judge Robert Patterson, Undersecretary of War. "See that everything is done to make the Secretary happy," the General said. "I want to obtain his promise that we shall all be sent immediately to the Far East."

For the gala event Ed Creed put in a busy day perfecting his preparations. That the latter were indeed perfect was shortly to receive spectacular confirmation and forever mark the evening as Captain Creed's Big Moment.

The Judge arrived in the late afternoon. By the time cocktails were over and we marched into the great banquet hall it was dark. The huge crystal chandeliers threw a brilliant, if merciless, glare on the uncomely portraits lining the brocaded walls, the floral decorations, and the Thurn and Taxis gold dinner service which the Captain had discovered and been saving for just such an occasion. The Judge's last spoonful of soup was in mid-air and the General's eye alight with eloquent argument when with a fizzle and a pop the lights short-circuited and the entire palace was plunged into total blackness. Silence, complete, ominous.

We got set for the expected explosion. It never came. Within a matter of seconds, the doors at the end of the dining hall opened to reveal what appeared to be a slow-motion flight of fireflies. On approaching the table, the now brightly burning points of light were seen to emanate from half a dozen four-branched candlesticks borne aloft by the smartly uniformed kitchen crew closely followed by waiters bearing the next course. With ecclesiastical gravity and precision the candelabra were placed upon the table and the viands served.

"Beautiful," the Judge said. "A great improvement. Nothing like real candlelight."

"At least," the General said, "we are spared the sight of those goddam portraits."

Despite less than definite assurance that we should soon be heading for the Orient — as far as I'm concerned, the less definite the better — the evening was a great success and Captain Creed a hero.

P.S. 3 A.M. Awakened from a deep sleep by the tramp of feet and blinding light. My first thought, fire. Wrong. By my bedside under the brilliantly lit chandelier, an M.P. sergeant at attention. In the doorway, a platoon of M.P.'s.

"Sir," the Sergeant said, "the blackout regulations are not being observed in this room."

As you have probably gathered, the lights had come on again.

May 9, 1945 (continued). The morning of May 7 we flew Judge Patterson to XX Corps.

General Walker had again distinguished himself by liberating still another château — this time of special interest because it was found to house the entire Imperial Spanish Riding Academy of Vienna, the pride and joy of every Emperor since Charles V.

In their flight from the Russians they had been hiding out here for some time and were only too delighted to put on a show for us. In a rather dilapidated outbuilding, to the strains of a cracked disk played on an old horned phonograph of the vintage of "His Master's Voice," the *Hofreitschulemeister* — if that is the proper name — and his team of green-coated buckskin-panted assistants put their elegant mounts through a remarkable series of courbettes, croupades, caracols, and other intricacies of the *haute école*. Impressive but somehow a little pathetic. A faint, if touching, echo from the vast and brilliant equine ball-room of Imperial Hofburg and the Old Vienna of wine, women, and waltzing horses.

However, the Judge seemed to enjoy it. So did the General, that is, until he came to ask himself, as well as those about him, why the hell a score or two of able-bodied men, obviously capable of carrying rifles, should spend the war years teaching a bunch of horses to wiggle their behinds. To this somewhat pointed question, neither the *Spanische Hofreitschulemeister* nor anyone else seemed to have a satisfactory answer.

On the morning of May 8, at the usual time, the staff assembled in the German barracks for the regular briefing. The General, followed by Willie, Al, and myself, entered the room, walked briskly to his seat, sat down. G-3, G-2, Air, and the PRO officer presented our own and the enemy picture. It was a short briefing. At its termination General Gay would normally have risen to make the announcements for the day and adjourn the meeting. Instead, General Patton himself arose, took three steps to the situation map, studied it for a moment, then turned and faced us. For a space of time difficult to measure, there was silence as the General and his staff looked at one another. When he spoke, his words were short and to the point.

"This is the last of our operational briefings in Europe," he said. "I trust we shall have the privilege of renewing them in another and more distant theater of war. One thing I can promise you: if I go, you go."

He thanked the staff for their performance over the last two and a half years. "Probably no Army Commander in history ever did less work," he said. "You did it all."

The General snapped his fingers. Willie uncurled himself from the chair under which he was gently snoring. The staff members sprang to their feet. With Willie trotting behind him, the General marched to the door and down the steps.

Back in his trailer, the General went over the General Order he had prepared for release the following day thanking the personnel of the six corps and thirty-nine divisions which, since August, 1944, have comprised Third Army. It follows:

DRIVE

During the 281 days of incessant and victorious combat, your penetrations have advanced farther in less time than any other army in history. You have fought your way across 24 major rivers and innumerable lesser streams. You have liberated or conquered more than 82,000 square miles of territory, including 1500 cities and towns, and some 12,000 inhabited places. Prior to the termination of active hostilities, you had captured in battle 956,000 enemy soldiers and killed or wounded at least 500,000 others. France, Belgium, Luxembourg, Germany, Austria, and Czechoslovakia bear witness to your exploits.

All men and women of the six corps and thirty-nine divisions that have at different times been members of this Army have done their duty. Each deserves credit. The enduring valor of the combat troops has been paralleled and made possible by the often unpublicized activities of the supply, administrative, and medical services of this Army and of the Communications Zone troops supporting it. Nor should we forget our comrades of the other armies and of the Air Force, particularly of the XIX Tactical Air Command, by whose side or under whose wings we have had the honor to fight.

In proudly contemplating our achievements, let us never forget our heroic dead whose graves mark the course of our victorious advances, nor our wounded whose sacrifices added so much to our success.

I should be both ungrateful and wanting in candor if I failed to acknowledge the debt we owe to our Chiefs of Staff, Generals Gaffey and Gay, and to the officers and men of the General and Special Staff Sections of Army Headquarters. Without their loyalty, intelligence, and unremitting labors, success would have been impossible.

The termination of fighting in Europe does not remove the opportunities for other outstanding and equally difficult achievements in the days which are to come. In some ways the immediate future will demand of you more fortitude than has the past because, without the inspiration of combat, you must maintain — by your dress, deportment, and efficiency — not only the prestige of the Third Army but also the honor of the United States. I have complete confidence that you will not fail.

During the course of this war I have received promotions and decorations far above and beyond my individual merit. You won them; I as your representative wear them. The one honor which is mine and mine alone is that of having commanded such an incomparable group of Americans, the record of whose fortitude, audacity, and valor will endure as long as history lasts.

G. S. Patton, Jr.
General

May 9, 1945

General Bradley and his Chief of Staff came to lunch to discuss future dispositions of the armies. They left about three o'clock.

And now we are alone. General Patton, General Gay, Paul Harkins, George Murnane, Charley Odom, Ed Creed, Al Stiller, Willie, and me. An Air Marshal and a Bishop having at the last minute been unavoidably detained, the General and his household, for the first time since our occupancy of this depressing pile, sat down to dinner in solitary grandeur.

Under the protruding eyes of the Teutonic family portraits and overweight marble cherubs, the evening meal progressed in complete silence save for the expensive clink of silver knives and forks on gold plates. No popping of corks, no paper caps, confetti, or tin horns. The silence of those who know one another too well for small talk. Disparate thoughts harking back over two and a half years of campaigning together — two and a half years of sharing ships' quarters — eight to a stateroom — the open skies of Africa, tents in the olive groves of Sicily, the apple orchards of Normandy, the forests of Lorraine, not to mention the odd assortment of shell-shocked palaces, villas, apartments, and dubious hotel rooms from Washington, D.C., to the Czechoslovakian border.

Dessert was being cleared away. The General folded his napkin and sighed deeply. "No more fighting until we get to China," he said. "I don't know how I am going to stand it."

We followed him across the tiled upper hall to the top of the great staircase leading down to the garden. Placing his hand on the marble banister, he turned to us. "Good night," he said. "I shall be in my trailer." He started down the broad treads, turned once again. "There is a species of whale," he remarked solemnly, "which is said to spend much of its time lying on the bottom of the deepest part of the ocean. I don't mind saying," he continued, unsmiling, "at the present moment I feel lower than that whale's arse."

CHAPTER XVI

The Russians

(May, 1945)

May 15, 1945. A few days ago we went to a party in Linz in honor of the Commanding General of the Fourth Russian Army and his staff. We had previously been advised by General Bradley to take along a suitable number of Legion of Merit medals since it had become standard procedure when American and Russian elements met to decorate one another in a big way. For foreigners, though not for us classless Americans, there are various grades of the Legion of Merit, as in the case of the *Légion d'honneur* and other European orders. Thus the Russian General became a "Commander," his Chief of Staff an "Officer," and the others simple "Legionnaires." The Russians were big, burly, and inclined to be friendly, but since we had no common language and only one interpreter — Major Popovsky, attached to our headquarters — the atmosphere for a time remained somewhat formal. At lunch, however, provided by the 65th Division at their Officers' Club, the Russians were introduced to American whiskey, neat. By the end of the afternoon several mixed quartets and choral groups were emitting barbershop chords and other evidences of Russo-American solidarity. A pleasant, if rugged, time was had by all.

Yesterday had been set by the Russians as the date of their return party for us. And what a party it turned out to be. They were mysterious about the arrangements, vouchsafing only that we would be met at the Linz airfield and from there escorted into the Russian Zone. At nine-thirty we assembled at the Regensburg airstrip. General Patton, General Gay, General Hughes, Maddox, Muller, Conklin, Harkins,

Koch, and Hammond. Major Popovsky and I were in charge of the two boxes containing individual phials of mineral oil prepared by Charley Odom. Pursuant to their bourbon baptism, we knew the Russians would be laying for us and that the ordeal by vodka would be severe.

"Swallow entire contents of the phial," Dr. Odom had prescribed, "but wait until the last possible moment."

The moment was at hand. On the apron of the Linz airfield we could see the guard of honor drawn up in front of the hangar. We glided in to a nice landing. As we turned to taxi up to the hangar, the Major and I issued the phials.

"Skoal," the General said. "Bottoms up."

We were greeted by our Russian General and his Chief of Staff, their Legion of Merit medals gleaming newly on their barrellike chests. General Patton was inspecting the guard. Another C-47 with U.S. markings circled the field and came in for a rather uncertain landing.

"Find out who that is," the General said.

Major Popovsky and a Russian officer went over to investigate.

"They are taking off again right away," the Major said on his return. "Journalistic mission, London to Rome. Head winds. Low on gas. Saw group on field. Will fill up and take off."

"What journalists?" the General asked.

"Only one," the Major said. "A lady journalist. The name is Doris Duke."

The cars provided by our hosts were large and expensive-looking. General Patton and the Russian General led off in an oversize Mercedes — a special custom job. The rest of us were assigned to models hardly less plush.

"There must be quite a few German and Austrian millionaires going about on foot around these parts," Harkins said as we climbed into a leather-upholstered convertible.

Crossing the bridge at Enns, a few miles southeast of Linz, we entered the Russian Zone. Guard of honor. Band. First sight of the *"Regulirowshitza"* — at least that is what the designation of the spectacular Russian girl traffic cops sounds like. Big, husky girls in smart black uniforms, equipped with colored signal paddles like mammoth ping-pong bats. On the approach of vehicles they go into violent calisthenics, ending in a dramatic Statue of Liberty pose, one paddle pointing straight up, the other horizontal across the chest — and I mean chest — indicating the direction to be taken. Really makes you feel you are going places. As a matter of fact, we were.

The Linz–Enns–Vienna road runs south of the Danube, roughly paralleling the river, through fields and partly wooded country. The day was fine and the sun shone brightly from a blue May sky. On either side of the road, at intervals of about a hundred yards, were stationed M.P.'s of the Fourth Russian Army who presented arms as the cortege swept by. At every intersection, down to the smallest country lane, a *Regulirowshitza,* sometimes two. At the end of fifteen or twenty miles we still found their semaphoric ritual exhilarating.

We roll into a small town. Left turn onto a narrow woods road leading in the direction of the river. Only then did it strike us that, despite the powdery white surface of the Linz highway, there had been no dust whatsoever. Later we learned that during the morning the entire stretch had been swept and watered — by hand.

A clearing in the woods. The column halts. Guard of honor. Band. A tall, rather pale figure in a Marshal's uniform advances to greet General Patton. Marshal Tolbukhin, Commander of the Third Ukrainian Front, conqueror of Vienna. In military rank, second only to Stalin. We proceed to a small reviewing stand and the decoration ceremonies. General Patton is awarded the Order of Kutuzov (First Class), about as high as they come and which can only be conferred by one, like Marshal Tolbukhin, who himself holds it. The rest of us receive appropriate tokens of lesser amperage. Mine, the Military Order of the National War (Second Class), complete with handsome red sunburst, entitles me, when in Moscow, to aisle seats for the ballet and free rides in the subway. No one seems to know whether wives are included.

The ceremonies end. The band strikes up only to be drowned out by the formidable roar of three squadrons of Russian fighters, diving, zooming, crisscrossing. Directly overhead, perfectly framed by the trees around the clearing, the red stars on their wings flashing in the sunlight, they provide as fine an exhibition of aerial acrobatics as any one of us has ever seen.

Marshal Tolbukhin signifies that it is time for lunch. With General Patton on his right he proceeds across the clearing, along a woodland path debouching suddenly onto high ground into a sort of outer court-yard. Directly before us the ramparts, the moat, the drawbridge of a fairy-story castle, former summer *plaisance,* we are told, of the Emperor Francis Joseph. Skyward the Russian fighters soaring, gliding; below, far below, the sparkling waters of the Danube. The guards present arms. We cross the bridge and enter a paneled hall large and cool. Uniformed attendants with shoe-shine equipment kneel down and polish our boots. Girls in Ukrainian costume usher us tactfully to the powder room, hand us towels and soap, and, as we emerge, envelop us with an aromatic mist from small but efficient atomizers.

At the end of the hall, two large doors are thrown open. The Marshal and the General advance into the vast banquet room. The long table, set for over a hundred places, is a riot of color. Bowls of fruit, garlands of flowers, clusters of bottles of all sizes and shapes. Standing stiffly be-hind the chairs, uniformed servitors and a new flock of prettily cos-tumed girls. From the paneled walls the Hapsburg portraits coolly sur-vey a scene which might well surprise their originals.

The whole thing is beautifully organized. For each visiting fireman an interpreter. Mine, who is on my right, is a tall young man with glasses. He introduces me to the Russian colonel on my left — thick-set; bull neck; frank, open face; easy smile; hard, cold eyes. We ex-change politenesses. They ply me with hors d'oeuvres, smoked salmon and herring, cheese, smoked goose, mountains of fresh gray caviar.

"Kummel or vodka?" the Colonel questions, picking up a bottle of each.

"How about that interesting-looking wine?" I asked, trying to play safe.

"Ah, yes." The Colonel shrugged. "Our white wine of the Crimea is refreshing. We drink it instead of water. Doubtless you are thirsty after your journey."

Not bad. Like and yet unlike a Rhine wine. Perhaps a Russian variety of the Riesling grape. The interpreter did not know.

"What is your name?" I asked.

"Serge" (followed by something long and unpronounceable), he said.

"Let's just say Serge," I said. "Where did you learn English?"

"We have a special school for interpreters," he said.

"With your people's great gift for languages, I suppose many of your officers here speak several."

"No," Serge said. "These officers have been taught a certain amount of German. For the invasion of Austria and Germany, that is sufficient."

The little waitresses clear away the dishes and begin serving an excellent greenish soup with sour cream. At the head of the table the General and the Marshal seem to be getting along nicely, and as the wine takes hold, our staff members and their Russian neighbors converse with increasing animation. Course after course. Sturgeon, veal cutlets, whole suckling piglets, game, including a delectable snipe. Bottle after bottle emptied and replaced. From a general survey of the hall, my own colonel neighbor appears to be a fairly typical representative of this very high-level Russian staff. Of the earth, earthy, enormous vigor and vitality, efficiency and forcefulness. Surface affability and good humor. Underneath, hard as nails. Young in grade. Each a striking example of selective promotion based on ability. No duds.

Our little waitress is passing him a platter of cold ham in jelly. He makes a jocose remark. She smiles, but only slightly. In withdrawing the platter she tips it a bit. A piece of jelly slides off and down the front of the Colonel's uniform. He barks at her like an overheated machine gun. Turning a sickly green, she rights the platter and leaves with it, on the run. Back in no time with water and a napkin. The Colonel is now talking to his other neighbor. He pays no attention as she mops him off and bows out.

"It is now time for the toasts," Serge says, filling my glass with vodka.

The Marshal is on his feet, glass in hand. "Premier Stalin," he intones. Everyone rises. Everyone drinks. Bottoms up. More toasts. The President of the United States. The Russian Army. The U. S. Army.

The Fourth Russian Army. The Third U. S. Army. Marshal Tolbu-khin. General Patton. General Eisenhower. Premier Stalin. What, again? Hope Charley Odom's mineral oil has a high flash point.

We are seated again and the Colonel is filling the glasses. Through the haze of smoke a squad of soldiers is mounting a platform, which I had not noted, at the end of the room. Another squad, and another. They form a group. A noncom raises his hand. The swell of a Gregorian chant. Volume, tone, phrasing, unity — perfection.

"For God's sake, Serge, who are they?" I whispered.

"Just a few of the boys in our Headquarters Company who sing together in their spare time."

"Who are you kidding?" I said. "Never mind, let's listen."

There followed two hours of singing, dancing, and sketches which, if transported intact to New York, would insure S.R.O. signs at the Metropolitan and the old Hippodrome simultaneously for the entire season. That the artists had, in fact, been flown in from Moscow for the occasion, Serge finally broke down and admitted.

It was at the end of a devastating sketch on Hitler, the latter played by a nameless genius embodying the combined talents of Katchaloff and Bert Lahr, that I noticed the Marshal seemed to be questioning General Patton and pointing down the table. Leaning forward to follow the direction of his finger, I was surprised to see, at the far end on the same side, a feminine figure in a uniform resembling that of our WACs. Seated between two Russians, she appeared to be doing nicely.

A handsome soprano who had earlier rendered a number of arias again mounted the stage. While her accompanyist was readying the music, General Patton removed from about his shoulders and waist the wide sash and huge sunburst of the Order of Kutuzov, which he doubtless began to find cumbersome, and handed them to an interpreter with directions to bring them to me for safe keeping. I placed the whole collection, which must have weighed several pounds, on the table directly in front of me where we could all admire the colors, texture, and workmanship of its myriad jewels.

Now the soprano is giving tongue. The Marshal beckons to one of his officers. Whispered orders. The officer hurries down the length of the room and escorts the mysterious WAC to the head of the table, where a chair is drawn up for her between the Marshal and the General. Something familiar about her appearance. The diva hits her terminal high note and takes several bows. The Marshal rises and makes a speech. He seems to be putting quite a lot into it. The interpreter translates. At this auspicious meeting of soldiers of our two great democracies, etc., etc., it gives me particular pleasure to pay special honor to a worthy representative of the proletariat, one who has spent her life combating the forces of reaction and corruption. I ask you to rise and with me drink to the health and happiness of this noble exponent of the laboring classes, this brave and stalwart American working girl, Comrade Doris Duke.

General Patton, not to be outdone, leaps to his feet. Casting swiftly about him, he spies the diva descending from the platform. He seizes her hand, leads her to the table.

"It gives *me* particular pleasure," he said, "to express our appreciation for the magnificent hospitality here extended to us, and especially to thank and commend this gracious lady who in bringing us the healing balm of lyric song in its most exalted form has inspired us to become even better soldiers and better men." With a flourish, the General rips a medal from his chest—I can't see from here whether it is his D.S.C. or D.S.M.—and pins it to one of the generous contours of the diva's surprised and heaving bosom.

"G-1 is going to have its hands full straightening out the paperwork on all these decorations." Harkins's voice from across the table.

"And now"—the Marshal is up again—"I ask you to drink to the long life of Marshal Stalin."

My colonel neighbor, deep in conversation with *his* neighbor, is slow in rising. Behind my back, Serge nudges him. "To Marshal Stalin," he says. The Colonel mutters a few sour words. Two of them are "Marshal Stalin"; the other three sound suspiciously like a Russian equivalent of "to hell with." Serge and Harkins's interpreter exchange glances. Would be interested in seeing the Colonel's next Efficiency Report.

We are seated again. Without warning, the General springs one of his sudden, unpredictable switches. Rising like a jack-in-the-box, he bows to right and left, shakes hands with the Marshal, and strides rapidly down the hall. We scramble up, murmur hasty good-bys and thanks, and hurry after him. In the courtyard the cars are drawn up ready to go. In and off. The band strikes up. The girl traffic cops wield their ping-pong bats. 5 P.M. The sun is still high in the heavens. The cool, moving air is refreshing.

In the General's plane the passengers slept peacefully and it was only on arriving back at Regensburg that I felt a slight gnawing sensation. Indigestion, or maybe a vague feeling of unfinished business. Can't think what. Must have eaten something. At supper—a very light supper—the General was describing the party to George Murnane and Ed Creed.

"You should see the jewelry they adorned me with," he said. "Show it to them, Codman."

No more gnawing of the stomach. That had just dropped like an elevator with a broken cable.

"I'm afraid I left it on the table," I heard myself saying.

An awful silence. Sometimes when the General has cause to be really angry, he isn't. This happened to be one of those times.

"But, Codman," he said, more in sorrow than in anger, "I'm flying to London tomorrow and I want to show it to my friends."

"General," I said, "I'll have it here the first thing tomorrow."

A busy evening. Set up L-5 for predawn take-off. Phone division headquarters at Linz. Exactly where was that party today? Sorry, we have no idea. They didn't tell us. Oh, fine. Engineers, map section.

The airstrip before dawn.

The darkest hour. Cold, too. Have seldom felt worse. Yes, I certainly must have eaten something. The L-5 is warming up. The exhaust crackles and glows in the darkness. Take-off over black treetops. As we gain altitude, pink streaks appear to the east. Now over the horizon the orange disk of the sun bobs up with almost the celerity of a *Regulirowshitza's* paddle. Going to be a hot day. Regensburg to Linz is

about an hour's flight for an L-5. The greenhouse is warming up. Why
did I have to leave that goddam regalia on the table? Who the hell is
Kutuzov anyway? Fields, forests, lakes. Pretty, I suppose. Ahead, a
dark splotch. A city. Linz.

Enns, and the frontier bridge. Wonder what the rules are about flying
unannounced over their zone? Oh, well, they are buddies, aren't they?
The waters of the Danube are still sparkling. No clouds or Russian
fighters in the sky. Below, quite a few castles. Let's take a look at that
one. No, doesn't look right. There's another one, out on that promon-
tory, with the river curving round it. Seems familiar somehow. Or
does it? That *must* be it!

O.K., so where do we land? Good question. Where do we? Nothing
but woods and vineyards. Ten or fifteen minutes of circling. A field.
Not big, but big enough, I hope. We come in brushing the treetops. As
we level off to put her down, a company of Russian infantrymen race
out from the woods, and before the wheels have stopped rolling, we are
closely surrounded by a ring of forbidding-looking boys with rifles at
the ready. I get out, point to myself, to the plane, smile broadly.

"American."

No answering smiles. No lowering of the rifles. Blank, noncommittal stares.

A noncom advances and begins speaking.

"Get an officer," I said, "and an interpreter." No impression. After a
couple more futile interchanges, the noncom detaches two of his riflemen and makes a peremptory gesture. The two riflemen close in. We
march across the field and into the woods.

A well-concealed shack. Presumably company headquarters. A bare
room with a single window.

After a while, a lieutenant comes in. He seems puzzled. I went into
the officer-interpreter routine. The lieutenant shrugged, nodded, departed. You could hear a field telephone ringing. When the lieutenant
reappeared he seemed relieved. On the other side of the shack, a narrow wood road, a battered old truck. Fifteen-, twenty-minute drive.
Village. Building on main square. Regimental headquarters. Another
bare room. Slightly larger. This time a lieutenant colonel. In broken

German I got through to him to the extent of explaining that I was on a mission for General Patton. A matter for higher headquarters, he felt. More telephoning. A car. A half-hour drive. A town. A fair-size building on the main stem. Divisional headquarters. At least, we're going up in the world.

Down a corridor to a railed enclosure. Through an open door I caught sight of a familiar face bending over a typewriter. Too good to be true.

"Serge," I shouted.

It was true. He peered over his spectacles. His first look of surprise was almost immediately replaced by one of wariness. Coming out into the hall, he first spoke for some minutes with the lieutenant colonel. An empty room across the way. At least it had a table and some chairs. We sat down.

"Listen, Serge," I said, "here is the story."

He listened carefully.

"Your statement," he said when I had finished, "is that the insignia of the Order of Kutuzov was left on the dining-room table and that General Patton himself sent you here to bring it back to him?"

"Yes. So highly does he prize it he cannot bear to leave for England without it."

Serge was silent. Plainly something was bothering him. "Please wait," he said. "I will return." He did, after a considerable while, accompanied by a colonel. The lieutenant colonel jumped up and saluted. The colonel said something. The lieutenant colonel saluted again and took his departure. The colonel drew up a chair.

Serge cleared his throat. "Please repeat your statement," he said, "so that I may translate it exactly to the Colonel." I did.

More silence. For what seemed like a long time the colonel remained sunk in thought. Finally he spoke a few rapid words to Serge and left.

"What now?" I said.

"After the Colonel has telephoned we shall take an automobile ride."

"To the castle?" I said hopefully. "I can show you exactly where the order was left."

"No, no." Serge shook his head impatiently. "The castle was requisi-

tioned for the day only. Last night it was completely dismantled and
closed."

"To corps headquarters then?"

"No, Army headquarters."

"Good, it's about time."

Army headquarters was in an impressive building on the main thor-
oughfare of a town to me unknown, since all the signs appeared to be
in Russian. A handsome paneled room with double doors at both
ends. Before them, two huge armed sentries.

"The General will be here shortly," Serge said. "Meantime I must
ask you a few questions."

His manner was impersonal, his questions less so. Place of birth,
parents, relatives, residence, occupation in civil life, virtues, hobbies,
vices, religious and economic beliefs, attitude towards the proletariat, towards Russia. My answers seemed to satisfy him. Then suddenly, "Do
you know William C. Bullitt?"

"Yes, saw him not long ago in Alsace."

"Oh, you did, did you?" Serge's eyes narrowed unpleasantly. "Well,
if you see him again you might ask him why on September 26, 1940,
he saw fit to publish in the *Philadelphia Inquirer* an article stating that
all Russians are Tartars under the skin, and most of them sleep in their
underclothes."

"I must have missed that one," I said.

"Why does your government say such things about us?" Serge was
getting quite worked up.

"Listen, Serge," I said, putting my hand on his shoulder, "if such an
article appeared, it certainly did not represent the views of the President, or the State Department, or any other official body. In our country, the individual can say or print practically anything he pleases.
You're a good guy and I like you. I hope you will soon come to visit
us in the U.S.A. and look around for yourself. Meantime, how long do
we have to keep up this game of Alice in Wonderland? I am here on a
simple mission for General Patton, who at this minute is waiting for
me to get back."

Serge seemed momentarily mollified but still genuinely puzzled. He was wiping his glasses when again the door opened and he sprang to attention. A General and a colonel, both strangers, in the sense that neither had been at yesterday's party. Polite but formal. I saluted. They saluted. We sat down.

"Would you mind repeating your statement for the benefit of the General and the Colonel?" Serge said.

Once again the record was turned on. At its termination, the General, who had a bland, round countenance and a penetrating eye which, during the recitation, never left my face, gazed for a moment at the ceiling. Then he got up, bowed, signaled for the others to follow, and marched out.

The sound of the General's voice filtered through the heavy closed doors. He was speaking loudly and clearly, evidently on the telephone, presumably long distance, and there was something in his tone which suggested that his interlocutor was of exalted station. The conversation ended abruptly with a click. Almost immediately the double doors at the other end of the room were thrown open by invisible hands. From what appeared to be a well-appointed dining room with a table set for half a dozen, the colonel entered, bowed, and rattled off a short speech.

"The General," Serge translated, "desires you to do him the honor of sharing his modest breakfast."

"Delighted."

The General. Another General. Three colonels. Good God, the table. Again *les fruits, les fleurs.* Smoked salmon. Radishes. Heaping bowls of caviar. Sour cream. Bottles. Lots of bottles. Breakfast?

Marshal Stalin. The President. Here we go again. The Fourth Russian Army. The Third Army. Marshal Tolbukhin. General Patton. And no mineral oil.

An hour. An hour and a half. Two hours. Past noon now. The room seems to be revolving slowly. The General and the colonels are a queer color.

"Look, Serge," I said, "come clean. What is the score?"

"Have patience," he began.

The swoosh of a fast plane directly overhead drowned out his next words. An interval — it might have been a few minutes or half an hour — and things began to happen. The doors through which we had entered flew open, the guards presented arms, and there marched into the dining room at a brisk, assured pace a very young lieutenant with rosy cheeks surmounted by a pair of bright, inquisitive eyes. Around one shoulder he wore a braided cord. Across the other, the strap of a shiny leather dispatch case. The assembled Generals and colonels scrambled to their feet, clicked heels, saluted with marked vim and conviction. The lieutenant acknowledged their greetings graciously, if a trifle cavalierly. A colonel hastily dusted off the empty chair between the two Generals — I had been wondering about that chair — and held it as the lieutenant nonchalantly seated himself. Making patently polite conversation, the Generals plied him with food and drink. Fresh hors d'oeuvres were hurried in, new bottles uncorked. Pretty soon the head General was on his feet again. To the health of Premier Stalin. Oh, no! Oh, yes — the works.

At length the lieutenant wiped his mouth. A discreet burp appeared to signify his immediate needs had been satisfied and that he was ready to get down to business. Pushing back his chair, he arose with poise and deliberation, addressed a few words to the General and his staff. Turning to me, he then made a short speech. The gist of it, as translated by Serge, was to the effect that Marshal Stalin, Marshal Tolbukhin, and the General Staff of the Russian Army all were deeply touched by the high esteem in which the modest token of their appreciation was evidently held by General Patton, and that it was an honor and a pleasure to furnish him with a set of the regalia to take to England. With a flourish he opened the brief case and from it withdrew the lustrous sash and sparkling sunburst of the Order of Kutuzov (First Class). I responded with a speech to the effect that I knew General Patton would feel that the honor and pleasure were all his, that he would be deeply touched by this additional expression of solidarity and good will between the great Red Army and its valorous soldiers and the Armies of the United States, and that I would like, on General Patton's behalf, to propose a toast to Premier Stalin, Marshal Tolbukhin, and the Red Army.

An hour and a half later, under the slanting rays of the late afternoon sun, the L-5 coasted in for a landing on the Regensburg airstrip.
Clutching the regalia tightly to my breast, I commandeered a peep. "To
the palace, and don't spare the horses."

As the quarter-ton bounced along over the road into town, it seemed
to pound out Browning's insistent rhythm:

> *You know, we French stormed Ratisbon:*
> *De da, de da, de da,*
> *Out 'twixt the battery-smokes there flew*
> *A rider, bound on bound*
> *Full-galloping; nor bridle drew*
> *Until he reached the mound.*

The door of the General's trailer was shut. I knocked.

"Come in." The General was shaving. "Hello, Codman," he said
pleasantly into the mirror. "Where have you been?"

"It took longer than I thought it would, General, but here it is."

> *"You're wounded!" "Nay," the soldier's pride*
> *Touched to the quick, he said:*
> *"I'm killed, Sire!" And his chief beside,*
> *Smiling the boy fell dead.*

The General drew the razor around the point of his chin. "Here is
what?" he said.

"Your regalia."

"Oh, good," he said. "That will make a spare set."

"A spare set?"

The General carefully rinsed the blade and with a sideway motion of
his head indicated his open traveling case on the bunk. Illumining the
top tray like a Turner sunset, the Order of Kutuzov (First Class).

"I forgot you did not know," the General said. "Five minutes after
your departure this morning, Major Popovsky reported that yesterday
afternoon, as we were leaving that high-powered castle on the Danube,
the order you left on the table was handed to him by someone called
Serge."

May 16, 1945. This morning General Patton, General Hughes, Ed Creed, Sergeant Meeks, Sergeant Mims, and Willie fly to London. I am to be dropped off in Paris to meet Gus, who has finally arrived. Will write fully in a day or two.

May 18, 1945. Have had two lovely days with Gus and can report that he is well, in good spirits, and that an interesting job for him is now assured. Ted Curtis came in to Paris and drove us out to his head-quarters at Saint-Germain. Very pleasant evening with him, Bruce Hopper, a young Symington, which one I don't know, and Senator Jim Wadsworth and *his* son.

The following day your brother Joe blew in from London. We all three lunched at the George V, where Gus and I are making good use of the General's hospitable suite. In the afternoon we browsed around Paris and drove out through the Bois to the lake on which you and I used to go rowing — an activity which came as a great surprise to both Joe and Gus.

In the evening Gus and I dined with Barbie Iselin and several of the younger O.S.S. set who all live at the Elysée Parc — am really happy, and am sure you will be too, about Gus. Tomorrow he reports officially to Ted Curtis at Saint-Germain and from there will be assigned to a technical job in Germany, having to do with airplane engines. His Pratt and Whitney training should come in handy. I do think he has himself well in hand and will do a good job. For me it has been a wonderful two days, particularly to have firsthand news from Gus that your morale is good and you yourself in fine form.

May 25, 1945. The General's leave was cut short. He was told to hasten back and be prepared, by his presence and that of half a dozen Armored divisions, to blanket the saber-rattling noises which Mr. Tito seems to be emitting at the upper end of the Adriatic. As of now, things have quieted down, so there is nothing particular for the General to do.

We have moved from Regensburg to Bad Tolz, south of Munich, where we, i.e. the General and his household, are occupying the elaborate and supermodern villa of Herr Max Amann, publisher of *Mein Kampf* — a book which, judging from the number and high plumbing standards of the bathrooms, must have done well financially.

Am writing this in the General's plane, which I have had to myself all day to do some errands. Said errands have been, so to speak, interstate, since I breakfasted in Munich, lunched at Liège, where I took delivery of the General's new shotgun and had tea with Prince Felix, the Grand Duchess Charlotte, and their son and daughter in Luxembourg. Early supper with the Paul-Cavalliers in Nancy.

The Grand Duchess is charming in a shy kind of way. It was a nice visit. Prince John and his sister, Elisabeth, are attractive, quiet, reserved, and the palace looks more lived in than it did the last time I saw it.

And now here is the big news which I have saved for the last. All day I have been making a complete failure of pretending to be calm about it. Last evening the General was notified that he is to make a quick trip to the U.S.A. and I am to go with him. It is very hush-hush and it may be another week before we know about dates and itinerary. However, it looks as though I would be seeing you before long. It seems too good to be true, but it *is* true. Think of it, my darling, I'll be *seeing* you.

Am now going up forward to do a little copiloting in the cool of the evening.

Epilogue

On the morning of June 8, 1945, the General's C-54, escorted by Flying Fortresses and fighter planes, circled the field and waiting crowds at Massachusetts's Bedford Airport. The plane taxied slowly up the wide cement apron, and, as it stopped before the reception committee, the door opened to frame the General resplendent in his best uniform. The morning sun glinted from polished boots, gold-buckled belt, the pistol thrust into it, the handle of his riding crop, the varnished helmet with its four stars and three insignia — I Armored, the Seventh and the Third Armies.

In the forefront of the roped-off area were the General's wife and children. Behind them, my own wife and immediate family. The mechanics rolled the steps to the entrance. A cheer went up, to be almost immediately drowned by the booming seventeen-gun salute.

The memories of that day and those immediately following are crowded, hectic, a little unreal. The triumphal procession into Boston and up Beacon Hill, the General standing erect in an open Fire Department car. The cheering crowds. The ballroom of the Copley Plaza. The General's speech, his emotion, his tears. The cross-country flight to California. His visit to the chapel outside Los Angeles where he was baptized and confirmed. The placing of a wreath in memory of Dick Jenson. The movie people — puzzling to the General. "Codman, who are those two strange women who seem to know me better than I know myself?" "Louella Parsons and Hedda Hopper." "Never heard of them." The evening spectacle at the jam-packed Hollywood Bowl.

Speeches by everyone from Bogart to child actress Margaret O'Brien. The simulated tank battle — complete with real tanks, land mines, and rockets. The live microphone, carelessly left open.

"Magnificent. Almost as good as the real thing. And God help me, I love it." The General's phrasing was clear, distinct, and coast to coast.

For the General and his family a few all-too-short weeks at Green Meadows, their lovely country place at Hamilton, Massachusetts. Later, Beatrice Patton told me that for long periods she and the General would simply sit on the sofa hand in hand and together look out over the rolling fields — silently, timelessly. When there is so much to go into, where does one begin?

At length the time came for his return to Germany. My last sight of him was at the airport. "Take care of yourself," he said.

"Same to you, General. And thanks — for everything."

On December 9, the newspapers of the world carried the story of the collision of his limousine with an Army truck near Mannheim. Like the close call with the ox cart — and so many others — the factors were unpredictable, fortuitous, freakish. No one but the General was injured. Hap Gay, who was sitting beside him, seeing the oncoming truck swerve across their path, thrust out his arm in an attempt to shield him. A split second later the impact threw the General forward. His head struck the upright between the front and rear seats — not violently, but at an angle and hard enough to cause spinal injury and paralysis. On December 21, 1945, General Patton, with his wife at his bedside, died peacefully in his sleep at Seventh Army Headquarters Hospital in Heidelberg.

"After all I've been through, think of being killed in an automobile accident." Do not be concerned, General. Bullet, shell, bomb, shipwreck, plane crash, car crash — all were your daily occupational hazards. In the hearts and minds of every man who served with you the record is crystal clear, and the final words of that record unequivocal:

George S. Patton, Jr., 02605
Killed in Action

A Tribute

by
Bernard S. Carter

ON a warm, sunny morning in October, 1942, I was walking down
Constitution Avenue in Washington headed in a bewildered way for
the Munitions Building, where I had been told to report. Suddenly and
to my joy I saw ahead of me my old roommate at Harvard, Charley
Codman, looking very smart and military in his summer uniform as
Major in the Air Corps. "This is good," exclaimed Charley. "I bet you
can't guess my assignment for today! To investigate the security qualifications of one Bernard S. Carter."

This was the first intimation I had had that Charley and I were to
serve on General Patton's staff and in the same G-2 Section.

I can never begin to describe what a comfort it was to me to have
Charley near at hand during those long months starting at 5 A.M. October 23, 1942, at Fort Myer, when we were loaded down with huge
unfamiliar Tommy guns, heading by convoy for our transports at
Hampton Roads, until I left Third Army Headquarters at Luxembourg on an icy morning on January 5, 1945, towards the end of the
Bastogne drive.

Charley and I couldn't help feeling distinctly "civilian" among our
very professional and hand-picked comrades on General Patton's staff
however friendly they were, and this they certainly were; and it was of
course immensely refreshing for the ex-banker and ex-real-estate-
wine connoisseur to be able to get together occasionally for a drink and

a laugh at the preposterous places where we happened to find ourselves.

I am deeply thankful that Charley, before he died, had time to write
as he did in the preceding pages about General Patton, for I consider
that he has succeeded in painting a portrait of that remarkable character which only he could have produced.

I must confess that when it was announced in Mostaganem that
Charley was to become General Patton's aide, I could not help but feel
certain misgivings as to whether Charley "could take it" — I mean
physically.

The job of aide is a grueling one — especially to a dynamo like General Patton. It means being available and on the alert at all hours with
little or no moments of privacy or relaxation, which I knew Charley
needed. It means always finding the right road in a jeep traveling at
full speed, and Charley was always weak on road maps.

The fact that Charley was able to achieve such a complete success for
his formidable, if sympathetic, chief is a tremendous tribute to his extraordinary tact and sense of balance.

There is no doubt that Charley was universally loved and respected
by his fellow officers; in fact, he became a truly legendary figure in the
Third Army. As he was known to be so close to the General, he was
often under pressure to approach him directly on matters "outside of
military channels." This he very rightly refused to do. There was one
occasion, however, when he did so intervene and at my request.

When our headquarters moved into Palermo, we took over the Sicilian Central Post Office for staff office space. In one large room in the
post office were kept all the postal savings accounts of Sicily — some
two hundred fifty thousand of them. Orders were given to "throw
them all out." Realizing what havoc this would mean in postwar Sicily,
I reported the matter to Charley, who immediately understood and
spoke to the General. As a result, these savings accounts were left intact.

As far as I am personally concerned, Charley was my oldest and
dearest friend. We first met at Groton over fifty years ago, and fate
threw us together in both world wars and, thank God, very often in

between them when he visited France on his wine-buying expeditions with his beloved Theo, who incidentally is reputed to have as delicate a palate as Charley's.

It was always a delight to see him. Even in May, 1956, the last time I saw him, when he was far from well, he had the same trenchant, yet always kindly, sense of humor about the life which he knew he was soon to leave.

One of Charley's favorite expressions when a story or situation appealed to him was "good." I am sure that all who knew him will agree that "good" is the perfect summary of Charley's character.

Appendix

Colonel Codman's Citations

FOR his services in the two world wars, Charles R. Codman received the following decorations and awards: Decorations: Silver Star; Legion of Merit; Bronze Star Medal; and Purple Heart. Service Medals: World War I Victory Medal with clasps for Defensive Sector and St. Mihiel European-African-Middle Eastern Campaign Medal with one silver service star and two bronze service stars for participation in the Algeria-French Morocco, Sicily, Normandy, Northern France, Rhineland, Ardennes-Alsace and Central Europe Campaigns; World War II Victory Medal; two overseas chevrons and five overseas service bars. Foreign Decorations: French: Legion of Honor, Grade of Officer; Croix de Guerre with Palm (WW II); Croix de Guerre with Palm (WW I); Fourragère of the 69th Régiment d'Artillerie d'Afrique with colors of the "Medaille Militaire"; Luxembourg: Order of Adolphe of Nassau, Grade of Officer; Croix de Guerre; Morocco: Grand Commander of the Order of Ouissam Alaouite Chérifien; and USSR: Order of the Fatherland, Second Class.

Citation for Legion of Merit

CHARLES R. CODMAN, 0448161, Lieutenant Colonel, Military Intelligence Service, Headquarters Western Task Force, for exceptionally meritorious conduct in the performance of outstanding services in North Africa from 25 November 1942 to 14 February 1954. Lieutenant Colonel Codman served with great distinction in a most important position as the Special Liaison Officer, G-2 Section, Western Task Force (later I Armored Corps), attached to the Direction des Affaires Politiques, French Protectorate, Rabat, Morocco. His intermediate handling of military, economic, and political negotiations with the French Protectorate and the native chieftains of Morocco, including the maintenance and strengthening of the security of the Spanish Moroccan border and his special work in connection with the French delegates at the Anfa Conference, Casablanca, was both successful and brilliant. Well equipped with the necessary background of intimate acquaintance with foreign countries and a thorough command of the French language, he contributed a superior degree of tact, energy, sound judgment, and devotion to duty in the accomplishment of this most difficult mission. By his understanding and thorough approach to the countless problems that arose in the relations with the French Protectorate Government, and by an unusual grasp of the subtleties of the complex interests of that government, he rendered invaluable service to the United States. Entered service from Massachusetts.

Citation for Silver Star

UNITED STATES ARMY

USA   AEF

CITATION

1st Lieut. Charles R. Codman, 96th Aero. Sq.,
FOR DISTINGUISHED AND EXCEPTIONAL GALLANTRY AT *Conflans, France*
ON *Sept. 16, 1918,* IN THE OPERATIONS OF THE
AMERICAN EXPEDITIONARY FORCES
IN TESTIMONY THEREOF, AND AS AN EXPRESSION OF APPRECIATION OF HIS
VALOR, I AWARD HIM THIS CITATION

AWARDED ON *May 13, 1919*   s/ John J. Pershing
COMMANDER-IN-CHIEF

Index

INDEX

INDEX

INDEX